THE BIG DISCONNECT

the story of technology and loneliness • Giles Slade

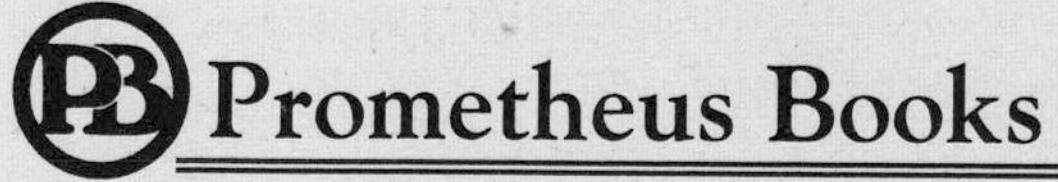

59 John Glenn Drive
Amherst, New York 14228–2119

Published 2012 by Prometheus Books

Cover design by Jacqueline Nasso Cooke

Inquiries should be addressed to
Prometheus Books
59 John Glenn Drive
Amherst, New York 14228–2119
VOICE: 716–691–0133
FAX: 716–691–0137
WWW.PROMETHEUSBOOKS.COM

16 15 14 13 12   5 4 3 2 1

Library of Congress Cataloging-in-Publication Data

Slade, Giles.
The big disconnect : the story of technology and loneliness / Giles Slade.
p. cm.
Includes bibliographical references and index.
ISBN 978-1-61614-595-8 (pbk.)
ISBN 978-1-61614-596-5 (ebook)
1. Technology—Psychological aspects. 2. Household electronics—Social aspects. 3. Human-machine systems. I. Title.

T14.5.S577 2012
303.48'3—dc23

2012013319

Printed in the United States of America

Man is the only being who knows he is alone, and the only one who seeks out another. His nature (*if that word can be used in reference to man who has "invented" himself by saying "No" to nature*) consists in his longing to realize himself in another. Man is nostalgia and a search for communion.

—Octavio Paz, *The Labyrinth of Solitude*, 1961

CONTENTS

INTRODUCTION

IMMORTALITY AND FREE WILL

> The laboring man has not the leisure for a true integrity day by day . . . his labor would be depreciated in the market. He has no time to be anything but a machine. . . . The finest qualities of our nature, like the bloom on fruits, can be preserved only by the most delicate handling. Yet we do not treat ourselves or one another this tenderly. . . .
>
> We are for the most part more lonely when we go abroad among men than when we stay in our chambers.
>
> —Henry David Thoreau,
> *Walden: A Fully Annotated Edition*, 2004

The first decade of the twenty-first century has ended. Machines still proliferate. Human relationships are still in decline. We no longer have the time to take time even with those closest to us. We look to machines to perform human functions: they provide communications, calculations, care, and company. Once, if a man was courageous and strong enough, he could hope to wrestle an angel to a draw. Although we recognized our own mortality, we believed the angels envied us our free will and stood slightly below us in the hierarchy of heaven. We were God's finest handiwork.

In those days, excellence and genius were very human qualities. Today, tragically, our planet is no longer the center of the universe, and we are no longer naïve. What it is to be human has diminished under pressures from technology and from the application of economic reasoning to every aspect of human life. Man has shrunk to an atomic unit orbiting, serving, and servicing the machinery of his city and his economy. Human longing persists, but it is no longer projected backward toward our divine, parental origins. Instead we project our longing into the technological future where we imagine—again—that we will soon be fulfilled and finally free.

The size of the average American workspace declined from the ninety square feet allotted to workers in 1994 to only seventy-five square feet in 2010. Although they are much more difficult to quantify, human relationships have also shrunk. Fewer and fewer people have a friend or single trusted confidante. More and more people live alone. Many have "friends" on Facebook® but go home to lonely dwellings where they divert themselves during the empty hours with technological distractions: the Internet, HD or 3D television, videos, electronic games, entertainment systems, exercise machines, sports programs, Jacuzzi® tubs, personal automatic baristas, and automatic sex toys that would have embarrassed sex-trade workers of an earlier generation. This is not good for people; but for manufacturers and marketers, human beings are best when they are alone since individuals are forced to buy one consumer item each, whereas family or community members share their cars, their washing machines, their televisions, their PCs. Technology's movement toward miniaturization serves this end by making personal electronics suitable for individual users. You carry your phone, your music device, your tablet with you. For today's carefully trained consumers, sharing is an intrusion on personal space.

Increasingly, the lack of human interaction breeds the lack of human interaction so interpersonal difficulties become easier and easier to avoid. Instead of visiting, we phone; instead of phoning, we text; instead of texting, we post "updates" for our "friends" on Facebook's wall, and when they don't like these updates, we "unfriend" them. In public, we catch up on our smartphones with people we no longer have time to visit, or we steal a few moments during our commute to listen to a playlist while reading an eBook on a Kindle®. The liminal spaces of our cities are full of people experiencing and practicing uncomfortable "elevator silences." Fifty years ago, Paul Simon described "people writing songs that voices never share."[1] Community fails in exactly this way. "No one dares / Disturb the sound of silence."[2]

As Thoreau observes, long ago we accepted an economic rather than a human role. When life was a bitter struggle, we agreed to technology's promise of abundance and safety and worked hard to achieve it. During the twentieth century as we became increasingly invested in technology, we became increasingly short of time, and for this reason, too, our humanity is distorted and deformed. We no longer have sufficient time, attention, or energy to devote to the one thing that makes life truly worth living: our relationships with others. Thoreau made his observations in 1854, so it should be clear that we are trapped in a technological dilemma with a considerable history. Modern technology, of course, has a solution for this historical dilemma: technology always has a solution. In fact, if the first thing we mean by *technology* is "abundance" or "cornucopia," the second thing we mean when we use the word is "solution."

Technology's ultimate solution for economic man's problematic and chronic shortage of time is immortality. It is not yet available, of course, but it is on the cards now. A group of technological visionaries headed by inventor and futurist Raymond Kurzweil believes that by 2020—within this decade—the power of computers as measured by the millions of instructions per second available (the MIPS rate) for US $1,000 will have increased to such an extent that we will be able to reverse-engineer the human brain and begin to replicate its entire processes *in a machine*.

Raymond Kurzweil is a recipient of the National Medal of

Technology and Innovation, the highest honor to recognize achievements related to technological progress. Previously, he has often predicted remarkable technologies—talking computers, for example—which have then come to pass.

If Kurzweil is right, we will be utterly transformed. In fact, we will become much like Shia LeBeouf's friend Bumblebee in the film *Transformers* (2007). Like Autobots or Decepticons, the simulacra that replace human beings will stamp through the organic world and be completely indifferent to it. If we understand technology not as a system of tools and skills but as an ideology that encourages the endless refinement of tools and skills in order to dominate and subjugate nature, Kurzweil's machine men will achieve technology's ultimate goal by becoming completely indifferent to nature. If and when Kurzweil's predictions fulfill themselves, people will become truly obsolescent, as Günther Anders predicted we would in 1956.[3] We will have, at last, conquered and overcome nature. We will then exist outside it, having no need for organic materials, for company, for sex, or even for time. History, in fact, will end.

Kurzweil's vision extends our unexamined assumptions about technology to their utmost costly end. Describing such "scientism" in its embryonic manifestation as a preparation for the industrial revolutions, Lewis Mumford wrote, "By renouncing a large part of his humanity, a man could achieve godhood: he dawned on this second chaos and created the machine in his own image: the image of power, but power ripped loose from his flesh and isolated from his humanity."[4]

This view—humans' indifference to nature; our attempt to challenge, overcome, and use nature—is fundamental to the technology enterprise and is also, therefore, fundamental to our technological society. This is why the purveyors and inventors of technology are indifferent to issues of pollution, waste, human intercourse, and satisfaction. It is why science can objectively inform us about climate change and global warming, and yet we deny climate change and global warming. Inherently, our faith in technology relies on a disdain for the natural world that is almost complete in our own time, a historical moment characterized by what Richard Louv describes as "nature deficit disorder" in his seminal book *Last Child in the Woods* (2005).

What you will read in the coming pages is a description of how we progressively sacrificed the quality of human life for our economic well-being. If, currently, your best friend is your iPhone® or iPad®, after reading this book you will understand why that is so, and also you will finally understand the real cost of numbing the pangs of human loneliness with human-mechanical neo-friendships. A neuroscientist we will meet again in later pages puts it best: "The pain of loneliness is a deeply disruptive hurt. The disruption, both psychological and behavioral, can turn an unmet need for connection into a chronic condition, and when it does . . . trying to make ourselves feel better with fatty foods and reruns of *Friends* will only make matters worse."[5]

Machines *can* dull the pangs of loneliness. One of the principal jobs of personal electronics is to distract us or to provide prosthetic substitutes for human company. In the near future, they will become much more adept at filling even the most intimate human needs. Still, even now, there are a few moments left to decide if this is what we really want or need. Will we become *isolates* consoling ourselves with any variety of electronic toys, fathers and mothers to the first generation of human-simulation machines, or will we limit the application of technology as we now limit the uses of weapons and dangerous drugs? These are the choices confronting us in the twenty-first century in the few moments we have left before the arrival of truly intelligent, autonomous machines, machines that will be able to fool us completely into believing that they are adequate, nourishing substitutes for human company.

CHAPTER 1

BREADCRUMBS

We have given our hearts to machines, and now we are turning into machines.

—William Deresiewicz, "Faux Friendship,"
Chronicle of Higher Education, April 20, 2012

INCUNABULA

Paper or plastic, gentle reader?

By which I mean, are you reading these words as print on a traditional wood-pulp page *or* are they reaching you (as is increasingly common, these days) through electronic images of letters whose configuration changes with each new screen?

There is a real difference involved in your choice of literary delivery system, although it's not a difference of good or bad, as bibliophiles often claim. You may already know that book lovers say electronic books do not have the "aura" of a physical object: they can't be hefted or smelled. These same people go on about a print book's texture and tactility, observing that eBooks prevent you from enjoying the guilty pleasure of writing in the margins or turning down the corner of a memorable page. An author's signature on the title page might also bring to mind some personal impression of the man or woman who wrote a favorite book (although publishers are now working hard to overcome this).[1]

eBooks don't provide the simple satisfaction of well-stocked bookshelves (some call this the books-as-furniture argument). eBooks also don't advertise your personal taste or sense of humor on the subway or at the beach in the same way that a physical copy of *The Brief Wondrous Life of Oscar Wao* might. Moreover, for some reason no one has yet figured out, electronic books take 10 percent more time to read; *and* accessing the footnotes on a Kindle® eBook is a tedious, time-wasting burden.[2] Lastly, you can't hide photos, documents, or money in eBooks, something that sounds silly, unless you're artist-poor and suddenly rediscover a twenty-dollar bill marking a memorable passage in a well-read book, or unless one day you find an old snap of a much younger, skinnier man doing a dip with a much younger woman—not yet his wife—while both of their faces quite clearly show the first flush of love.

Notwithstanding these minor advantages of paper books, the longing for a palpable book-object is a familiar kind of nostalgia that disguises people's discomfort with new things and devices. A similar discomfort may be the birthplace of racial prejudice, but such anxieties always accompany technological change. In fact, the prejudice against the new is so strong, so fundamentally human, that in order to make new technologies more familiar and acceptable, the physical appearance of an older technology is always repeated in the design of the first generation of replacements.[3] Our Neolithic ancestors may have experienced similar feelings when pottery replaced woven baskets. We know that the peculiar beauty of Anasazi pottery, for example, depends on its starkly linear geometric designs, an unavoidable structural necessity built into the warp and woof of the woven baskets that precede pottery.

And, in our own time, many eBooks have "pages" that need to be turned.

Okay. But there is a more significant difference between hard, paper copies and their electronic replacements, and this difference is at the heart of this book. The sale of any physical object once required a physical, interpersonal exchange. Until very recently, money was traded for goods *in person*. Things actually changed hands. In ancient times, such transactions took place in the agora or marketplace and the word *agoraphobia*—"fear of the marketplace"—still describes the unreasonable and inconvenient fear of other people.[4]

Like all marketable items, paper books used to require human interaction and distribution. They had to be warehoused, handled, shipped, unpacked, and sold. In fact, until 1995, the act of purchasing a book demanded that you enter a bookstore, make a selection from a shelf, then interact with a human cashier as you completed your purchase. When you handed over your money, the cashier might say, "Paper or plastic, sir?" This might be the only thing he or she said, but it was human, and since it required an answer, something social happened. According to Jane Jacobs, it is the repeated process of such trivial interactions that establishes, over the course of time, social familiarity and "trust," the intangible glue that holds our society together.

Amazon.com changed all that by introducing online shopping in 1995. They began with books. Book people no longer needed to travel to a bookstore for a full-fledged fix. This was partly a good thing since back in the day it was very hard to find a comprehensive brick-and-mortar bookstore that endured for any length of time. It's true that there were many in cities with very high levels of literacy like Berkeley, Chicago, DC, Manhattan, San Francisco, Seattle, and most college towns. But elsewhere it was a different story. In Los Angeles (my former home), bookstores were transitory things with eccentric and spotty selections that favored the film industry. You could always find copies of *Movie Maker* or *American Cinematographer*, but God help you if you wanted something by little-known local writers like John Fante or Chester Himes. In LA, whenever someone started a good bookstore (Papa Bach's, for example), it went bust in a very short space of time. In 1995, however, Amazon's innovative retail model made it easier to have a literary habit if you lived in la-la land or in any other place where the idea of books-as-furniture had not yet penetrated.

The best thing about Amazon was that it worked very well. Internet banking began in 1994, but, more tellingly, Pizza Hut began selling its pies online that same year. Amazon CEO Jeff Bezos, who must know something about pizzas, since he invented the "two-pizza management team," immediately recognized a good thing. "Why wouldn't that work for books?" he wondered. And it did.[5] So right from the very beginning, Amazon was successful. Bezos had nonetheless overlooked the single disadvantage of Pizza Hut's retail model, and no wonder, since it was a disadvantage that Pizza Hut never shared. For Amazon, even in the United States where the postal system worked very well, there is a substantial delay when books get shipped by mail or courier. This delay doesn't apply to national pizza chains, which have so many local outlets that pizzas are still (sometimes) enjoyed hot from the oven. But for books there was a problem of delivery lag time, and so, despite vigorous competition from Amazon's comprehensive selection and competitive pricing, face-to-face book selling continued to thrive at brick-and-mortar bookstores for the next decade.

Meanwhile, more and more people became accustomed to online shopping via eBay, which began its operations in 1996. Music lovers also began downloading free MP3 files the same year Pizza Hut went online. But portable MP3 players didn't arrive until 1998, and the file-sharing program Napster itself was also a late bloomer, arriving in 1999. After 1996, Steve Jobs had returned to Apple as a consultant, but he was preoccupied as iCEO (interim CEO) of NeXT, whose software became the basis of the operating system for the iMac®, which was released one year after Jobs took up the reins at Apple again in 1997. It took Jobs three more years to extend the company's brand by developing its portable music player. Jobs put the digital player together with an online store selling single, virus-free music downloads at affordable prices. By this time, the *i* in NeXT's iCEO had come to mean "indefinite." Jobs powerful iPod®/iTunes combination appeared in October 2001.

From the start, Jobs, a pianist and an audiophile, was entirely focused on digital recordings, and he had little interest in the book business. Despite his interest in music, he was aware that the iPod could expand into digital video, but to him, print was an antique media. This seems a noteworthy lacuna for such a man, gifted both with formidable technological foresight and—strangely—a profound love of both typography and calligraphy. Moreover, Jobs had already developed generations of electronic devices based on a scribal interface. Nonetheless, much as Edison overlooked the commercial opportunity of recording music after inventing the phonograph, Jobs lacked insight into ordinary people's fondness for reading. He had been involved early on (1978–1982) in the development of the Apple Lisa (1983), a costly and cumbersome failure. In addition, Jobs later returned to Apple in 1998 after CEO Gil Amelio was fired over the $100 million failure of the Newton, whose main mistake was really its prematurity since it anticipated both the personal digital assistant and iPad® tablet phenomena. Subsequently, Jobs was fundamentally unwilling to risk the company's resources on anything but mature product ideas like the iPod and, later, after long delays, the iPhone® and iPad. When the Kindle debuted in 2007, Jobs dismissed the market possibilities for eBooks out of hand. The market hole into which such a product might be successfully inserted was not yet visible to him. "The whole concept is flawed at the top," he said, "people don't read anymore."[6]

Oddly, Jobs's views about universal illiteracy appeared in a print interview. Since he was more aware of people's real reading habits, bookseller Jeff Bezos read them in the *New York Times* and immediately disagreed. Once again, Bezos recognized a very good thing in its earliest stages. In fact, Jobs had laid it all out for him. iTunes was, of course, an online store selling downloadable digital files that played only on Apple's proprietary device. You couldn't play iTunes' AAC-formatted songs on an ordinary MP3 machine. As Bezos turned this idea around in his mind, he realized the Apple model not only guaranteed repeat customers; it also simultaneously solved the dilemma posed by Amazon's shopping lag time. Bezos was probably not interested in the fact that, as it did these things, iTunes inadvertently had an additional profoundly sociological impact. The iPod acclimatized customers to a method of consumption that is even more impersonal than in-person, hand-over deliveries of CDs, books, or pizzas. (This happens, incidentally, through their involvement in the closed loop of online shopping and digital delivery.) By eliminating a tangible product, iTunes also eliminated the need for a delivery person. At the time, all Bezos was interested in was the possibility of customers' immediate gratification and the elimination of the costly and cumbersome delivery component from his retail model.

So in 2007, Amazon extended the range and appeal of the impersonal retail shopping experience by introducing their Kindle eBook reader. As Amazon extended its reach into more and more retail areas by selling music, movies, toys, games, what have you, *and* as more and more online stores copied them, many fewer social exchanges took place whenever anything got bought and sold: if the transaction was digital, nothing social happened at all.

When these events took place, eBook readers had been around for a decade (Rocket eBook and Softbooks first appeared in 1998). But Amazon's Kindle possessed a distinct retail advantage distinguishing it from its humble predecessors. Kindles allow instantaneous "impulse buying" at the touch of a button.

The download takes place over the cell phone network, so Kindle users don't even need an Internet connection to download music, as do users of the iPod, iPhone, or iPad. In addition, Kindles are fast. They're cheap (the Fire® model now retails for under $200). And, of course, initially they were fundamentally cool to receptive early adopters who quickly recognized when a new technology does an old job much more effectively.

Most of all, however, the Kindle is deeply impersonal, and for this reason it represents the culmination of a long line of self-serve automata—including writing and the book—that remove the "human factor" from the minute human exchanges and retail interactions that used to be essential to the life of the agora or business district, the active mercantile heart of every city. Most of the exchanges that take place in this neighborhood are, as Jane Jacobs writes, "utterly trivial, but the sum is not trivial at all. The sum of such casual public contact at a local level . . . is a feeling of public identity of people, a web of respect and trust and a resource in time of personal or neighborhood need. The absence of this trust is a disaster. . . . Its cultivation cannot be institutionalized."[7]

It is true that Kindles depersonalize retail exchanges unintentionally. Nonetheless, throughout the twentieth century, the process of dehumanizing retail exchanges accelerated. It is a central claim of this book that, throughout the twentieth century, human interactions declined rapidly. Even the loss of superficial ones like those involved in retail exchanges radically reduced our opportunity to acquire, hone, and maintain social skills. Not surprisingly, contemporary research indicates that a vast majority of Americans feel rudeness has overtaken most aspects of daily life in public.[8] In terms of America's social capital, the consequences are tragic. Without everyday practice in sociability, civility, and charm, these basic components of interpersonal relationships became replaced with reluctance, suspicion, and hostility. But more than this, with the erosion of casual interactions comes the erosion of familiarity, which sweetens and ferments the most essential ingredient of social capital: interpersonal trust. As Jacobs writes: "A continuity of people who have forged social networks . . . are a city's irreplaceable social capital. Whenever the capital is lost, from whatever cause, the income from it disappears, never to return."[9]

In this way, as technology slowly replaced intrapersonal interactions, agoraphobia and isolation wandered hand-in-hand into modern life like Hansel and Gretel innocently making their way into the depths of the forest toward the witch's house. Moreover, recent breakthroughs in neuroscience reveal that chronic loneliness is a powerful human force and is responsible for the increasingly prevalent tendency to imbue "non-human agents with humanlike characteristics, motivations, intentions and emotions. . . . These non-human agents may include anything that acts with apparent independence . . . nonhuman animals, natural forces, religious deities and mechanical or electronic devices."[10]

It is hard to judge to what extent contemporary behavior is shaped by such anthropomorphism. Animistic beliefs in anthropomorphic natural forces have declined steadily with the acceptance of scientific investigations, and there appears to be a more recent if slight decline in churchgoing religiosity among Americans (although only 13 percent of Americans claim they have no religion). Still, recent research suggests that it is the "social and participatory mechanisms" that contribute most to "religion's impact on life satisfaction."[11] Moreover, the population of the United States currently spends over $40 billion per year to maintain about a hundred million cats, dogs, fish, and other assorted pets that are universally described as family members and are often spoken to in the "motherese" dialect specific to utterances directed at human newborns. Moreover, there is a disturbing trend to anthropomorphize our personal technology (iPods, iPhones, and BlackBerries®). The tendency to feel connected to inanimate gadgets unsettles MIT psychologist Sherry Turkle, who wonders when "we feel together [with these devices], but really . . . are alone, where are we?"[12]

Developments in neuroscience may provide the answer to the puzzle of why and how contemporary Americans find substitutes for human company in their personal technological devices. Since the discovery of mirror neurons in the 1980s, neuroscience has repeatedly shown that individual human beings are transitive verbs always searching for direct connections with human objects. We are neurally programmed to complete ourselves *only* in genuine relationships with other human beings. But our programming is so powerful and so deeply embedded in the primate fabric of our brains that when the possibility of same-species relationships are absent from our lives, we compulsively invent substitutes out of whatever animate or inanimate material is at hand. In ages past, we invented gods and goddesses, but in our own time theological mythologies have been replaced by scientific ones, and we now fill the absence of human company with tiny personal machines. Psychologist Lisa Merlo observes that "there's a . . . quick progression from having a basic phone you don't talk about to people who love their iPhone, name their phone and buy their phones outfits."[13] This substitution—of machines for human company—began in earnest in the early decades of the twentieth century, long before our modern era when mobility and the digital revolution evaporated the need for national brick-and-mortar chain stores like Tower Records, Blockbuster Video, and, most recently, Borders. Still, our longing for human company and connection persists. If we rarely mourn the passing of a local chain outlet, we often feel a deep sense of personal loss when local retail institutions disappear; for this reason, the simple threat of closure to a place like Ray's Pizza (27 Prince Street in Little Italy) merits front-page coverage in the *New York Times*. Its ironic epitaph is already written: "The sad fact is that the 2011 version of *Little Italy* . . . is not designed in the interests of mom-and-pop pizza parlors that people come there expecting to see."[14]

SELF-SERVE

> A customer for cigarettes . . . goes into a store to obtain [them]. . . . The salesman . . . has only to deliver. Any additional motion or words waste time for both . . . salesman and customer . . . customers resent superfluous motions and words. They take a slice from the store's good-will and . . . the proprietor has to pay . . . for . . . wasted moments.
>
> —Peter O'Shea, "Mechanical Retailing," *Magazine of Business*, November 1928

The above epigraph encapsulates one of the ways in which self-service has made us lonelier and less sociable. In the Arab world (a former home), haggling over pennies is a sociable game that passes the time, enables people to get to know one another, and guarantees repeat custom. America's reluctance to savor such microscopic social exchanges is the phenomenon that led me to write *Made to Break* (2006) and this book. Both are attempts to explain how America lost the ability to enjoy human company. As soon as making money became our society's primary imperative, the casual interpersonal exchanges that fill our day but lack immediate monetary value became suspect, scrutinized, and ultimately expendable. We have come such a long way down this path that these days, social interaction is valid only if it is commoditized by a machine that mediates our exchanges and places a financial value on them: so much money for so many minutes or so many characters during each exchange.

No wonder, then, that people often complain that there are so few places to meet friends or eligible members of the opposite sex, and also that there's so little time to do it. Dating services like eHarmony.com proliferate in order to mediate and commoditize our most basic instinct: finding a partner. In fact, a majority of young people now meet their partners via online dating services. Unfortunately, these partnerships are increasingly short-lived. While 72 percent of Americans marry at some point in their lives, currently only half of adult America is married, a marked decrease from 72 percent in 1960. This is partly because the human affairs (no pun intended) of city dwellers have accelerated while human interactions (including opportunities to meet romantic or sexual partners) have been systematically devalued and factored out of daily life. It has become commonplace to observe that most Americans no longer have a single trusted confidante or friend and that—increasingly—people are marrying later, increasingly living alone, and also divorcing more without remarrying.[15] Moreover, science has long attributed increased rates of mood and anxiety disorders as well as radical increases in schizophrenia to those born and raised in cities. A recent (2009) article concludes: "Urbanization is modestly but consistently associated with the prevalence of psychopathology."[16] A slightly earlier study (2005) suggests pointedly that some city dwellers are especially at risk for specific disorders like schizophrenia: "Recent studies have focused on the developmental effects of . . . 'social capital' or 'the glue that holds society together' . . . [suggesting] that in particular cognitive social capital or aspects of the degree of mutual trust, bonding and safety in neighborhoods, exerts a developmental impact on the mental health of children growing up in these environments."[17]

The most recent neurological research provides a handy explanation for the heightened mental illness and solitude of city dwellers. An elegant study published in *Nature* during the summer of 2011 shows "that urban upbringing and city living have dissociable impacts on social evaluative stress procession in humans . . . [linking] . . . the urban environment for the first time to social stress processing."[18]

The connected problems of urban stress and unsociability are on the increase since 82 percent of Americans now live in cities, and by 2050 about 70 percent of the global population (about 9 billion, by that time) will also live in cities, expanding the world's urban population to 7.2 billion people or about 200 million more human beings than are currently alive on the earth. All together these facts present a bleak interpersonal picture for the near future. We have not only lost the opportunity to make friends and lovers, but we have also lost the time it takes to sustain friendship and the skills required to do so. Initially, as we became oriented to the goals of competition and personal advancement, we came to believe that the casual encounters were time wasters that lowered our productivity. Today, however, we view such activities as labor-intensive and fraught with interpersonal risks that promise very low rewards. In our predominantly urban lives, we are surrounded with opportunities to interact, but instead we choose to isolate ourselves, and we deploy increasingly sophisticated technologies to help us do exactly that. Increasingly, as the "singularity" or "robotic moment" arrives, we turn toward better and better electronic diversions that promise the ability to "friend" or "unfriend" strangers at the touch of a button. Of course, such serial friendships are always mediated by a machine. In our increasing isolation, these "user-friendly" devices gradually modify our ideas of friendship and become—as Lisa Merlo points out—our prosthetic friends (but more of that later). Moreover, "friendships" like those on Facebook, are so superficial and of such short duration that they are very poor substitutes for the satisfactions and genuine annoyances of real friendship and real love. Recently, in *Going Solo*, sociologist Eric Klinenberg observed that our transition to a singular modern lifestyle is increasing with no end in sight. It may now be old-fashioned to observe that this is a very sad and lonely state of affairs. Nonetheless, the full extent and history of technology's role in our transition to post-postmodern urban isolation and "humanity-lite" should be very informative. The interrelationship between technology and loneliness appears often in works about America in the twentieth century. In one of the best known of these, written in 1970, sociologist Philip Slater observed that "one of the major goals of technology in America is to 'free' us from the necessity of relating to, submitting to, depending upon, or controlling other people."[19] I would like to know what we learn—what places we visit—when we retrace the trail of the breadcrumbs that marked our passage to this technological isolation.

The trend toward eliminating human interactions for reasons of speed, efficiency, cost, or stress reduction began during the wave of urbanization that followed the Civil War. It was facilitated and encouraged by technology, and it continues today in the utility of time-saving killer apps for our smartphones and in online downloads and shopping. These days, as you enter a big-box store, you notice unusual black-and-white pixilated design posters on the walls. These are Quick Response (QR) Codes, replacements for the now-old-fashioned bar codes. They were designed by Toyota in 1994 to facilitate decoding: in computer terms, they can be recognized much more quickly than linear bar codes. Marketers have been quick to exploit them. The latest marketing gimmick requires you to take a picture of the design with your smartphone and then allow a recognition app to take you to a website where a coupon awaits you. At the checkout you scan your smartphone into the automated teller and receive the discount promised on the website. In all of this, there is no interaction with another human being.[20]

Our attitudes toward machines and other humans began to change radically when life accelerated with the assistance of reliable clocks, hourly wages, dependable railroad schedules, national methods of communication, and the intensification of the attitude of interpersonal competition that became a way of life in our most industrialized cities during and after the Civil War. Unfortunately, what we lose by relying on technological time-savers that eliminate seemingly meaningless micro-exchanges from the urban environment is the most essential ingredient of social capital. Jane Jacobs describes it eloquently:

> In speaking of city sidewalk safety, I mentioned how necessary it is that there should be . . . an almost unconscious assumption of general support when the chips are down—when a citizen has to choose . . . whether he will take responsibility or abdicate it in combating barbarism or protecting strangers. There is a short word for this assumption of support: trust. The trust of a city street is formed over time from many, many little public sidewalk contacts. It grows out of people stopping by at the bar for a beer, getting advice from the grocer and giving advice to the newsstand man, comparing opinions with other customers at the bakery and nodding hello to the two boys drinking pop on the stoop, eying the girls while waiting to be called for dinner, admonishing the children, hearing about a job from the hardware man and borrowing a dollar from the druggist, admiring the new babies and sympathizing over the way a coat faded. Customs vary: in some neighborhoods people compare notes on their dogs; in others they compare notes on their landlords. Most of it is ostensibly utterly trivial but the sum is not trivial at all. The sum of . . . casual, public contact at a local level . . . is a feeling for the public identity of people, a web or public respect and trust, and a resource in time of personal or neighborhood need. This absence of this trust is a disaster to a city street. Its cultivation cannot be institutionalized. And above all, it implies no private commitments.[21]

Today, the social web of unspoken trust created by tiny, repeated interactions is gradually being erased by the pervasiveness of increasingly sophisticated technologies. The process of eliminating social trust began slowly. In 1880, the first vending machines appeared on English train platforms. Not surprisingly, they sold a new invention—postcards—a development that reflects the origins of our accelerated age because they reduce the time needed to write a letter while also shortening the time required for a retail transaction—a very important concern in the rush and bustle of railway stations. In addition, vending machines provided a brief, consumable distraction by providing a way to spend some of the disposable moments that occurred (and still occur) in transit. In 1927, the year slot machines changed from being small-change start-ups run by private operators into a big-chain corporate business, the *New York Times* observed, "Veterans in the vending machine game 'fish' for the public penny or nickel in still waters . . . they ignore fast running streams since no strikes are made there. On subway and elevated platforms . . . the machines are placed some distance from the entrance . . . where people have come to a stop and are waiting. . . . These machines . . . capitalize an inability of the American temperament to sit down and wait without having something to do."[22]

While waiting for a train, you could find a coin in your purse or pocket, make a selection from the displayed goods, "wait for the penny to drop," complete your purchase, and even scribble a brief, informal note.[23] In 1903, in an influential essay called "The Metropolis and Mental Life," sociologist Georg Simmel observed, "Self-preservation in the face of the great city requires . . . a . . . negative type of social conduct. The mental attitude of the people of the metropolis to one another may be designated formally as one of reserve . . . if I am not mistaken, the inner side of this reserve is not only indifference but more frequently . . . a slight aversion, a mutual strangeness and repulsion."[24]

Similarly today, when we are bored or when a stranger enters our elevator or subway car, we suddenly remember our portable "shield"—BlackBerry or iPhone—and consult it immediately, grateful for a small mechanical excuse to avoid time spent enduring uncomfortable self-reflection or eye contact.[25] Despite the social necessity of developing trust, it is an awkward, time-consuming process, like forming friendships. Eventually, urbanites developed behaviors like "civil inattention" to limit the amount of energy required to render safe their brief interactions with strangers "who require only civil inattention and involve themselves in [our] affairs only to the extent of according the same courtesy."[26] Sociologist Erving Goffman describes this ritualized use of the gaze as a display of "unfurtiveness . . . [a] show of properly going about one's own separate business."[27] This was a necessary development since, as Jane Jacobs observed, "Cities are full of people . . . you do not want . . . in your hair."[28]

Conversation with strangers invariably brings awkward moments and slight but annoying interpersonal risks. Moving through the metropolis, we are overwhelmed by the number of strangers passing close to us. Sociologist Robin Dunbar has suggested that we are really only comfortable with 150 (or so) human contacts, but in the modern metropolis we encounter five times that number while leaving our office buildings to visit the local roach coach. At home we are husbands and wives, moms and dads. At the office we are colleagues, experts, working stiffs, bosses, or lackeys. But in between these geographically separate roles, there is little to provide the interpersonal context on which the modern personality depends. With nothing to shape ourselves against, introversion is the most familiar and prudent course to safeguard psychic energy. We wrap invisible technological shells around us like hamster balls and become "i-Pods" as we move from site to site in our native urban landscape. The sense of dissatisfaction we sometimes experience in our urban environment is often inexplicable since we don't really have a clear picture of the kind of life we were designed for or why we are missing it. Meanwhile, technological distractions have become our most accessible means of providing interpersonal security as we hurry through public spaces where we are least defined and most vulnerable.

It should surprise no one that in the decades since coin-slot vending machines first appeared, our distraction dispensers have become more portable and convenient. The development of affordable pocket-sized transistor radios (1954–1957) marks a watershed in our relationship to an assortment of machines that would become known as "personal" electronics. Of course, we now have much more sophisticated, smaller, and more useful devices. The distractions they purvey are no longer tangible but marginally useful products like postcards or gum. Where we once carried with us flint-and-steel kits, pocketknives, pocket watches, harmonicas, and sometimes small "Derringer" pistols, we now carry portable vending machines that dispense songs, videos, and information, or that simply engage us in addictive games like Angry Birds®. Since they are digital, these products are easy to transport and transfer; no physical exchange of goods is required. Nonetheless, we still refer to these weightless digital items as the "content" of our devices, using a metaphor perhaps inspired by vending machines to describe these post-postmodern time wasters.[29] Like vending machines, these devices completely eliminate the costly and inconvenient human factor.

The social value of time-filling diversions among late Victorians was not lost on Thomas Adams, the inventor of chewing gum. The first purveyor of vending machines in America, Adams installed them in train stations to market Tutti Frutti, his new brand of gum. Soon after that early beginning, one-armed bandits (devices without any content at all) were invented. The nature of games had already become much less sociable with the popularity of Patience and Solitaire in the 1890s. Machine games actually preceded this trend: Chimney Sweep, the first penny-in-the-slot "game," appeared in 1871 and required only a solitary player. Later machines took up the trend of providing diversion to solitary consumers and moved from single-player gambling slot machines (one-armed bandits) to similarly solitary games like Bagatelle, and then to games featuring more "pins," like Whoopie, Baffle-Ball, and Bally-Hoo. Electric lights and bells were finally added by Harry Williams in 1933.[30]

These early arcade games are clear precursors to Pac-Man®, Space Invaders®, Tetris®, and all the interactive video games that have become part of our lives. The addictive nature of such solitary machine games became obvious as early as 1934, when Mayor Fiorello LaGuardia shut down gangster Frank Costello's extensive one-armed-bandit operation throughout New York City. Costello's True Mint Novelty Company had distributed over twenty-five thousand nickel slot machines throughout the region. At the height of the Depression, the "King of Slot's" daily profits were about $500,000. Costello's books at this time reveal an annual profit in excess of $37 million.[31]

Automatic games and self-service strategies developed simultaneously but sometimes took separate tracks. The pay phone appeared in Philadelphia in 1889, while the first fully automated telephone system debuted in Laporte, Indiana, in 1892. As America's mania for coin slots and vending machines developed, the machines were installed in storefronts devoted to wildly different purposes. There were penny arcades, of course. But there were also phonograph parlors at major transit points, like ferry and railway terminals.

These simple businesses consisted mainly of an unobstructed open room with slot-machine phonographs installed on the surrounding walls. They provided commonplace if unsociable diversions. It was one of the marvels of the modern age that you could be among a crowd but separate from it. Travelers deposited their nickels and blocked one of their ears with a finger before listening to a short song through a monophonic listening tube placed in the other ear. In an age when epidemics of influenza and tuberculosis were common, the surviving photos of the era show small towels attached to each machine with which customers might clean the ear tubes before inserting them. The ability to cater to and encourage solitude progressed rapidly in America. In 1982, the French philosopher Jean Baudrillard would write "Sadder than the beggar is the man who eats alone in public."[32] But by 1902, eating alone had become a common American custom after Joseph Horn and Frank Hardart opened the first of their famous Automat℠ restaurants, which fed solitary city dwellers in Philadelphia. By 1907, nickelodeon movie parlors like the famous Orpheum in New York City proliferated in all American cities.[33] A solitary worker could sit among a crowd and yet remain completely separate while watching the flickering lights in the comforting darkness of a motion-picture hall.

Self-service businesses and automata that eliminated attendants, clerks, waiters, and the social exchanges they required spread like wildfire during a period in which civility was already in decline. As urbanization took hold, stress increased, and the interpersonal silences that characterized brief, one-time encounters between citizens expanded throughout the liminal spaces of the city. Victorian strangers tipped their hats, nodded, smiled, and traded innocent, formulaic greetings requiring a response ("Nice day, isn't it?" or "How are you today?"). But the moderns increasingly deployed solitary self-service distractions and avoided eye contact. In 1939, German sociologist Norbert Elias observed that the long process of self-isolation and privacy that characterizes Western civilization began in the early modern era as domestic spaces were enlarged and sleeping arrangements became more and more private.

Modern man's sense of privacy, self-differentiation, individuation, and eventual isolation, in other words, had been on the rise for a very long time. Elias theorized that as the crude conditions and cramped sleeping arrangements of the Middle Ages progressively gave way to more and more personal space, the threshold of personal shame rose, and people repressed their childlike and natural impulses to a greater degree becoming, in the process, more interior and isolated.[34] Civil War historian Bertram Wyatt-Brown suggests this process was repeated as colonial and later rural America shifted to urban locations. As Americans left rural farms where tiny farmhouses had to accommodate entire families and moved singly into the urban centers of the northeastern United States, people became more autonomous, interior, and alone.[35]

Cities had grown enormously since the Civil War. *Rudeness and Civility*, John Kasson's wonderfully readable account of the decline in American politesse, captures this growth succinctly: "As of 1880, seventy-seven cities could boast a population of over 25,000, and twenty of more than 100,000. By 1910, New York, now with five consolidated boroughs, claimed almost five million residents, Chicago had swelled . . . to over two million, and Philadelphia had tripled its 1860 population to reach over one and a half million people."[36]

Significantly, by 1905, city dwellers were able to shut themselves off from unwanted social interactions and distractions in their immediate surroundings when phone booths, originally called "silence boxes" appeared in major Eastern cities, and at this time, locked single-stall pay toilets were unknown.[37] The idea of isolating a single user may have come from the first voting machines (1892–1898), activated when citizens drew a privacy curtain around themselves. But in 1866, long before such machines appeared, Mark Twain described a growing interpersonal decline in America's cities: "A man walks through his tedious miles through the same interminable streets every day, elbowing his way through a buzzing multitude of men, yet never seeing a familiar face, and never seeing a strange one the second time . . . there is little sociability . . . and little cordiality."[38]

Exactly one hundred years later, the decline in sociability had become a commonplace topic in folk songs. In 1966, at age seventeen, Paul Williams—publisher of rock music magazine *Crawdaddy!*—identified what is sometimes called the decline of social capital in an essay about Paul Simon's popular song "The Sound of Silence." Williams described "today's city . . . where people . . . are pushed together more and more into their own worlds, [and] wrap themselves in . . . silence, [and] in the protection of 'not getting involved.'"[39]

The century that intervened between Twain and Williams saw the development of Piggly Wiggly self-serve groceries that eliminated most interactions with grocery clerks after 1916. Affordable domestic refrigerators like the Monitor-Top Frigidaire of 1927 eliminated daily milk and ice deliveries and their deliverymen, while a wide array of affordable domestic machinery simultaneously eliminated much of the family's need for domestic help like cooks, maids, and cleaning and laundry women. People without families had an even more solitary existence. A French factory worker who visited America during the 1920s describes the lonely conditions of an ordinary worker's living arrangement in the American city: "For a person of modest means . . . particularly for a worker living alone it [was] the common practice to take a furnished room or room and board in a private house."[40] By 1937, a small sample of Bostonians reported that solitary pursuits took up one-third of all their waking hours.[41]

So, in the years running up to Williams's "Sounds of Silence" review, new technologies and new businesses were continually introduced that limited, eliminated, or attempted to replace human interactions. These included drive-in restaurants, banks, and theaters (1920s and 1930s); talking vending machines (1928); pinball (1933); automatic answering machines (1935); round-the-clock self-serve washaterias (1935); and direct distance dialing (1951), which rendered conversations with human telephone operators obsolete. One year after Williams's article, Barclays bank in London, England, introduced the most publicized, if not the first, automated teller machine (ATM), which made ordinary personal interactions with bank clerks unnecessary. Around this time, in a bestseller called *The Pursuit of Loneliness* (1970), sociologist Philip Slater observed

> Americans attempt to minimize, circumvent or deny the interdependence upon which all human societies are based. We seek a private house, a private means of transportation, a private garden, a private laundry, self-service stores and do-it-yourself skills of every kind. An enormous technology seems to have set itself the task of making it unnecessary for one human being ever to ask anything of another in the course of going about his daily business . . . within the family Americans are unique in their feeling that each member should have a separate room, a telephone, television and car. . . . We seek more and more privacy and feel more and more lonely and alienated when we get it.[42]

It was my own father, however, who expressed the connection between technology and alienation that same year in what I believe is its pithiest, most epigrammatic form. Around the time that rumors of the Beatles' breakup were flying across continents, my dad told me: "The guy who figures out how to eliminate human cashiers will make a fortune." He was right, of course. Automated cashiers were introduced in the mid-1990s and have become increasingly common ever since. Yet, although my father clearly understood the commercial trend to eliminate human interactions, he did not comprehend its proportions. We now live in a society in which prerecorded marketing "robocalls" are routinely received by billions of people daily. In 1994, one year after robocalls replaced the "cold calls" of real human salespeople, a husband-and-wife team of immigration lawyers, Laurence Canter and Martha Siegel, gave the world "spam" in the form of a mass-mailing promotion to market legal services. Soon after, they wrote a book about Internet marketing that changed our world.[43] There is no end in sight for the removal of human agents and human interactions. As I write, robots are being deployed by major news agencies to write credible and substantially cheaper-to-produce sports stories, thus eliminating the need for human sports reporters. In the foreseeable future, a machine writer could do this job for me using algorithms and key-word searches to find all the information relevant to the history of technological isolation scanned into the online Google archive. I wonder who would buy a history book about the changes to human consciousness if it were written by a machine. Will we ever reach a point when artificial intelligences buy electronic books from robotic, online publishers?

Only Sherry Turkle knows.

SELLING ROBOTS

> People disappoint; robots will not.
>
> —Sherry Turkle, *Alone Together*, 2010

Widely held attitudes and expectations change over time either from training or exposure—this is the main idea of my book in a nutshell. Gradually, we came to accept machines as viable alternatives to human company. This may be a sad state of affairs, but it didn't happen overnight.

In 1890, a simple phonograph was added to a "silent salesman" vending machine in New York City. The new device was called the "talking scale." After inserting a penny, the customer waiting for his weight to appear was treated to an operatic selection played on a crude phonograph inside the machine.[44] Perhaps overweight New Yorkers who needed to weigh themselves were reluctant to invite comparisons between their physiques and the operatic build of the recorded singer; for whatever reason, this machine—a precursor to talking robots—quickly disappeared.

Today, if you dial 1-800-USA-RAIL, a powerful and sophisticated program called "AMTRAK-Julie" will talk to you with a conversational suppleness that consistently delivers better satisfaction than most humans. Not even Joe Biden has done as much to bring train travel back to acceptability. Julie is what is known as a "virtual robot," meaning she lacks a corporeal presence and is manifested only through sounds, images, or both. Julie has very solid American ancestors, and over the course of the last century, our increasing contact with robots encouraged their gradual acceptance and encouraged the idea that machinery might provide alternatives to human interactions.

Despite the failure of the penny scale, phonographs were successfully added to self-serve vending machines in the Jazz Age, at which time they became known as "selling robots." Machines that talk became big business in 1928 when Automated Vending Machines, United Cigar Stores, Remington Arms, and Sanitary (a postage stamp–vending machine company) raised $25 million in start-up capital and formed CAMCO, the first vending-machine consortium. Soon the press appropriated the word *robot* to describe an emerging generation of talking vending machines. As self-service devices, of course, they eliminated human interaction with a clerk. But talking vending machines are also a milestone in the development of technological isolation since they offered a substitute for human-to-human interaction with prerecorded messages of limited variety but with an appealing novelty.

Machines called "talkers" replaced "silent salesmen," uttering "Thank you," then repeating the slogan of your cigarette brand in deep and loud intonations as you completed your purchase. These appeared in the first United Cigar Store, located on Broadway in New York City, in 1928.[45] If you chose Lucky Strikes, the machine would say: "Thank you. They're toasted!" If you chose Chesterfields, the machine said, "Thank you. They satisfy!"[46] The best feature was that customers who inserted slugs were chastened with loud, prerecorded voices that said "Please use good coins only!"[47] In the first eight months, eighteen of these machines served nearly two hundred thousand customers, averaging 773 transactions daily.[48] Although Al Jolson did not record for CAMCO, some of the machine voices were appropriated from celebrities of the day. In the contemporary American imagination, this facility for speech made vending machines much more than simple "dispensers" of goods. This single human quality was enough to make them "robotic," a very popular buzzword in the late '20s.[49] In our own time, "sociable robots" deliberately "offer the illusion of companionship without the demands of friendship,"[50] but the humanization of machines was a trend that began in 1928 at Thirty-Third and Broadway with the purchase of packaged cigarettes from coin-operated talking machines.

Like several other phenomena of the era, the power of robots derives from anthropomorphic projections onto them. Recently, neuroscientists have determined that mirror neurons are likely responsible for the ache of human loneliness: the survival imperative of such painful loneliness, neuroscientists speculate, is that it drives people together to form social bonds. The same group of scientists has also speculated that mirror neurons may be the force that causes human beings to anthropomorphize when human interactions are scarce or nonexistent.[51] So if Tom Hanks's invention of "Wilson" in *Cast Away* (2000) can be seen as an emblem of the extreme loneliness of modern, single, friendless America, robots might well be a similarly topical emblem of the Jazz Age.

During the waves of migration to American cities, many Americans became friendless, time-poor, and cut off from familial ties. Time and distance prevented people from visiting their families, aging parents, or friends, and the increase in personal competition among city dwellers discouraged superficial relationships. Photography provided an essential and popular consumer service during this period of increased solitude: "At a time of great mobility with new separations of families . . . [through] . . . internal and external migrations [photography] became more centrally necessary as a form of maintaining, over distance and through time, certain personal connections."[52]

In addition, a plethora of rule books were published at this time (the 1890s), enumerating a variety of solitaire- or patience-type games simply because time was hanging heavily on many peoples' hands. During this period too, subcutaneous and intravenous use of two nineteenth-century inventions (morphine and heroin) achieved modern proportions through the widespread availability (after 1854) of hypodermic syringes, as did the use of opium and morphine during the Civil War as a treatment for pervasive ailments like diarrhea.[53] By the 1890s, refined opiates and cocaine were thought to cure an illness once called "neurasthenia" but since labeled "Americanitis." For those unwilling to use drugs, the nature of games changed. For city dwellers, games became consumable events played by professional athletic proxies that tired workers could enjoy simply by attending. At this same time, children's games became solitary activities played alone, and the intense competition of the city left parents with less time to spend with their children. For these reasons, the manufactured-toy industry came into being between the 1890s and 1920s. Among the first memorable toys were Edison's Talking Doll (1890) and the "B" Teddy Bear (1903). Brian Sutton-Smith is probably the first historian to observe the changes that took place in children's play at this time. As shared games became less common, manufactured toys encouraging solitary play replaced them; they were thought to train children for the isolation and self-sufficiency required of modern workers.[54]

Also at this time, the commercial pet industry came into being.[55] Increasingly, Americans projected human qualities onto animals and inanimate things that were ready-made company in an algid urban landscape. As robots rode their first wave of popularity in the 1920s, America's commercial pet industry (which had grown up with urbanization and industrialization following the Civil War) reached full maturity. The first industry journal, *Pet Dealer*, appeared in 1928.

Americans had always kept animals, of course. Horses were America's national beast of burden before cars, but dogs, birds, rabbits, and cats are seen in paintings and drawings of many founding families. Still, the commercialization of pet breeding, pet sales, and pet care was an urban phenomenon that arose after the Civil War. In large Eastern cities, whole districts (like Ninth Street in Philadelphia) became devoted to specialized pet shops where citizens could buy goldfish, trendy breeds of dogs (Scotch collies, Boston terriers), or birds often hand-painted by unscrupulous dealers to resemble more exotic and expensive species. In *Our Home Pets* (1894), Olive Thorne Miller makes the explicit connection between pet ownership and turn-of-the-century loneliness: "The companionship of cats and birds in solitary lives has unquestionably kept more people than we suspect out of the insane asylum; . . . if friendless men took kindly to them, there would be fewer misers, drunkards, and criminals. . . . It seems to be the divinely appointed mission of our furred and feathered friends . . . to inspire us with hope and hence health."[56]

In addition to pets and toys, another object that received America's anthropomorphic projections was the robot, which proliferated in the stories and images of the era.

The earliest appearance of an unquestionably robotic robot is the beautiful mechanical doll that becomes the romantic focus of the story's main character in E. T. A. Hoffmann's *The Sand-Man* (1817). There is also a robot creature in a Herman Melville short story, "The Bell Tower," from 1855. A few more appear before the end of the century, but then, in 1907, L. Frank Baum's character Tik-Tok appears in the novel *Ozma of Oz*.[57] Although his predecessor, the Tin Man, began life as a human being, Tik-Tok is presented as a "patent Double-Action, Extra-Responsive, Thought-Creating, Perfect-Talking, MECHANICAL MAN." Tik-Tok's unusual nature puzzles Dorothy sufficiently that she observes "This copper man . . . is not alive at all and I wonder what he was made for."[58]

Following Tik-Tok, robots took up their position as standard imaginative entertainments of the new century; no doubt they encapsulated the emotional forces of the new technological age. Visualizing them was a popular theme of silent films; a dozen or so of these early one-reelers still survive, providing us with fascinating contemporary images of the first mechanical men (some of which are now available on YouTube®).[59]

Robert H. Goddard launched the first liquid-fuel rocket from Auburn, Massachusetts, in 1926. Charles Lindbergh flew to Europe in May of 1927. His reception in Washington upon his return to America was broadcast nationally over the fledgling NBC network. It was a new—and miraculous—technological era. Planes suddenly and completely replaced trains as the emblem of America's technological might, and technological challenges which had previously seemed formidable were now openly entertained.

The year 1927 also saw the premiere of Fritz Lang's *Metropolis*. Lang's wife, Thea von Harbou, dramatized the vision of Georg Simmel's essay "The Metropolis and Mental Life" (1903) in a screenplay depicting "the loneliness of individuals in close proximity to others . . . oblivious to their existence."[60] The film struck a chord globally and propelled robots into a prominent and permanent position in the modern imagination. Since the only other appropriate English word, *android* (1847), was still very obscure, journalists relied on Karel Čapek's recent (1920) neologism—*robot*—to describe what Harbou and Lang called a *Machinenmensch*. The newspapers soon applied *robot* to any and all mechanical beings, and the name stuck.[61] That same year, historian David O. Woodbury complained that the robot had been "overdramatized" and that he was simply a useful tool, like the automobile or telephone. "Robots and men have differing duties in the world. Their functions do not conflict. Occasionally they overlap and then the human is emancipated and the machine takes up his burden. . . . Machines have been taking on labor after another off men's shoulders for years, but . . . have never remotely possessed the attributes of the men that made them."[62]

By 1928, walking, gesturing, and talking robots had been developed by engineers in America (where Televox controlled a power plant), and in England (where humanoid robot Eric addressed a scientific conference). Moreover, an increasing number of newspapers and magazines picked up the motif of mechanical men and ran factual and fictional accounts of robotic beings. The public couldn't get enough of them.

Robots brought into focus the threats and promises of contemporary technology at the same moment that inventor Lee de Forest's radio tubes reached inside American homes and the theory of management known as Taylorism tightened control of assembly-line workers.[63] With their anthropomorphic form, robots encouraged humanity's projections. The entire nation participated in Lucky Lindy's remarkable act of technological heroism, but at the same time, for the reasons Simmel gave in 1903, ordinary people felt they were being replaced by robots—that modern urban life was turning them into robots: "[the] money economy . . . has filled . . . daily life . . . with weighing calculating, enumerating and the reduction of qualitative values to quantitative terms."[64] Through it all, robots participated in the salty-sweet combination of fascination and fear that underlies fad and fashion. Writing in 1929, Hyacinthe Dubreuil, a solitary and highly literate French factory worker who traveled alone to America to experience life in the fountainhead of modernism, described the ambiguity of America's fascination with robots in the dying moments of the twenties: "The American . . . has as yet but shown to the world one great achievement—the machine . . . he has developed its magic power to such a point that he is beginning to become alarmed at it himself. His admiration is waning and beginning to become mingled with fear . . . [caused by] the growing shadow of unemployment. In the imagination troubled by fear of hunger, the myth again takes human form and the machine, formerly admired, is becoming a malevolent Robot."[65]

In the coming years, there would be many good and bad depictions of robots, but, except for genuine engineering developments, there would never be any morally neutral robots. Their appearance is simply too human for them to escape the judgments we automatically apply to real people.

The Japanese loved them first and still love them best. The first known tintype robot toy, the "Lilliput Robot," was manufactured in prewar Japan sometime between 1937 and 1941.[66] Because of the strategic scarcity of tin after 1938, Japanese manufacturers were forced to delay a successor to this yellow-colored robot until 1949, when the tin cans used by the American forces of occupation were retrieved and recycled for industrial purposes. The appearance of toy robots actually brackets the first generation of military computers among the Allies of World War II, since metal became a strategic material at the same time that computers became essential strategic weapons, necessary for decoding enemy messages or calculating accurate ballistic trajectories. The year 1949 saw the appearance of the last of the Allied war computers with

Australia's CSIRAC. That same year, the Mojinmi company received a patent for a second robot toy, a 5-inch khaki-gray figure called Atomic Robot Man, which retailed for eighty-five cents in postwar America.[67]

These boxy, stamped pieces of clockwork tin conceal a far-reaching cultural significance. The success of robot toys in Japan owes a great deal to the popularity of Bunraku, sometimes called "the most refined form of puppetry in the world."[68] From its origins in the eighteenth century, Bunraku was strongly influenced by the popularity of mechanized anthropomorphic automata called *karakuri*—mechanical tea servers—which were common items in well-to-do households.[69] In 1924, Karel Čapek's *R.U.R.* was first performed to an enthusiastic Tokyo audience at the Tsukiji Little Theatre. After 1926, popular performances of traditional Bunraku puppetry appeared at the same theater and throughout Japan after a fire destroyed the nation's preeminent puppet theater in Osaka, threatening the destruction of puppet plays as a living genre. Around this time, wooden Bunraku puppet toys enjoyed a surge in popularity, especially in Osaka where, in 1928, biologist Makoto Nishimura created Gakutensoku, a robot that moved its face and hands by means of an air pressure system that anticipated animatronics.[70] The next year (1929), a new Bunraku theater was opened in Tokyo, and by 1933, Bunraku was declared a traditional national art, the first to be protected and funded by the government. Sometime before the Pearl Harbor attack, as interest in both Bunraku and Gakutensoku increased, Japanese tin manufacturer K. T. Japan responded to the interest in Jinzo Ningen (artificial humans) by creating the first mass-produced robot toy (the Lilliput Robot, mentioned previously), claimed to be better than a handheld wooden puppet because—like Gakutensoku and the *karakuri* figures—it was self-propelled.

It seems self-evident today that Japanese people admire and accept robots more than any other nation. Their acceptance derives from a historic predisposition toward automata and puppetry. Twentieth-century robotic playmates were a natural development of Bunraku and *karakuri*; because of this, Japan was the first nation to have robotic playmates.

In America, robot toys had a similarly powerful cultural impact, but it was considerably delayed. If distance absorbed or absolved the Oedipal threats posed by robots for the Japanese, American robots had a much more complicated lineage. In their first consumer application as talking vending machines, they worked cheaply and unobtrusively. Because they radically reduced personnel overheads for retail sales of small consumer items, they made good business sense. In January 1929, nine months before the stock-market crash, *Scientific American* voiced this benefit succinctly: "Why [should you] have a high-priced human salesman perform the mere mechanical task of handing out a pack of cigarettes, receiving a quarter, dropping your money in a cash drawer and passing back to the customer ten cents in change? . . . Why not have automatic equipment do this automatic work . . . ?"[71]

Unfortunately, lurking behind the benign and compliant serfdom of these machines was the continuing threat of technological unemployment. Long before the Depression, vending machines began replacing people because they were cheap to own and operate. Of course, as people interacted more frequently with these machines, street vendors, smoke shop clerks, newsstand operators, lunchroom ladies, and snack-cart owners disappeared. As a result of selling robots, there were many fewer human interactions on the urban streets and in the urban workplace. Still, in the rush and bustle of the American workday, few noticed.

Then, in 1927, movies with prerecorded soundtracks ended the need for live orchestras, for musical ensembles, and for piano-playing "professors" following *The Jazz Singer*. A few years before the crash, technological unemployment became a prominent issue because—unlike street vendors, smoke shop clerks, newsstand operators, lunchroom ladies, and snack-cart owners—the musicians whose jobs were taken by talking movies had a powerful union.

The American Federation of Musicians (AFM) understood very quickly what the success of talkies meant to the working hours and paychecks of its membership. Joseph Weber, president of AFM, authorized a national advertising campaign to expose the sound movie as an "anti-cultural development," aiming to stop theaters from converting to "all-sound houses" capable of showing talking pictures.[72] H. L. Mencken borrowed from these striking ads when he wrote about robot musicians in 1930: "Observe the vogue of Robot, the musician! Stripped of his ballyhoo, this robot is a distorted echo of real music, but it has powerful support as an economy measure for the theatre—not, mind you, for the theatre patron."[73]

The following year, the journal *Outlook and Independent* used the same image to make an explicit connection between canned music and technological unemployment, describing "the hurdy-gurdy man's baffling problem. Why should his rival, the Robot of canned music, perform for money in a theatre while he and his monkey receive only adjurations to move off of the block?"[74]

Following the crash, America had become sensitized to the injustice of technological unemployment.[75] In the years before World War II, the number of unemployed AFM members reached fifty thousand. Tragically, during a decade of Depression, droves of Americans from other walks of life joined these musicians in fruitless, unending job searches.[76] Before any of this happened, the AFM authorized its ad campaign. Between 1929 and 1931, AFM members coughed up about half a million dollars to fund a series of print ads featuring "robot musicians" stealing their lifeblood.[77] These ads used the phrase "living music" to distinguish it from the robotic origins of "canned" music: "When a four star picture fails to bring them in . . . something is wrong . . . blame it all on the business depression or . . . do something about it . . . in troublous times men and women stand most in need of . . . bright lights, soft carpets, *living music* . . . a place to forget cares. . . . The all-sound house cannot fill the bill . . . such a theatre remains a dark and cheerless spot—likely to become a sick house. The salutary effect of *living music* is . . . indispensible."[78]

"Sick" movie houses were impersonal places without the charm, excitement, and interaction of live human entertainment. Nonetheless, their replacements, the all-sound houses, were considerably cheaper to operate, and so by 1932 the transition was nearly complete: "robot musicians" took over in America's theaters. Of course, the phonograph had long since initiated what was to become an irresistible trend against live music and live performance in the home. (This tendency would culminate in the practice of adding prerecorded audience reactions like canned applause or laughter to carefully taped and edited radio performances, beginning with *Philco Radio Time* show in 1947.[79])

Since much of Depression-era America was unemployed, robots and technology acquired a general taint that was difficult to shake. For this reason, favorable depictions of robots were uncommon during this time, despite the fact that robotic technologies advanced considerably during the Depression and again during the war that followed. Robots quickly became a toxic subject during the Depression. One of the rare examples of non-pornographic censorship in the United States involved a pamphlet bearing a cover illustration of robots glaring down at a solitary worker. William Ogburn's *You and Machines* was written as a textbook for Franklin D. Roosevelt's Blue Eagle employment programs, but after the booklet was printed, the Civilian Conservation Corps decided it was incendiary because it raised the issue of technological unemployment at a time when most workers had lost their jobs in the crash.[80] Another robotic image from the 1930s confirms robots' negative social value throughout the Depression. Appearing in 1936, true to the spirit of the time, an evil robot army bent on social destruction appears in a comic book by the same picture-and-story team who would later develop the character of Superman. On a secret "Mechanical Island," a group of felons plan to enslave America with superior technology, but FBI agent Steve Carson commandeers one of the giant robots and uses it to defeat the evil robot army before parachuting to safety.[81]

After America entered the war, science-fiction writer Isaac Asimov began reversing America's negative opinion of robots by sketching the Three Laws of Robotics in a story called "Runaround" in 1942. Asimov's first law stipulated that a robot could not harm a human. By 1951, good robots, like Gort in the 1951 film *The Day the Earth Stood Still*, had returned, as had children's robotic toys. Today, Americans draw on developmental experiences with four successive generations of toy robots. These have had a profound influence on our ideas of humanity and on the very acceptability of "sociable robots" as prosthetic caregivers, friends, and lovers.

It is well documented that in the late 1970s, children began to puzzle about the "aliveness" and "knowingness" of computer programs. The pivotal year seems to be 1978, when Space Invaders became available for Atari's one-year-old 2600 game system (the first to have plug-in cartridges).[82] That same year, children's interactions with Merlin (Milton Bradley, 1978), Simon (Milton Bradley, 1978), and the frequently redesigned Speak and Spell (Texas Instruments, 1978) prompted new ideas about aliveness in seemingly aware and knowing being-things. After marrying MIT's Seymour Pappert, graduate student Sherry Turkle began to notice these changes in the early 1980s, and has since built a career detailing stages in the rapid change characteristic of American children's interactions with our increasingly intelligent technologies.[83]

In Turkle's thoughtful books, one absence is glaring. A year before the first electronic educational games appeared, Hollywood expressed many of the issues raised in *The Second Self*, *Life on the Screen*, and *Alone Together* in the single most popular robot film of all time. *Star Wars* premiered in 1977. Simultaneously, action figures of the mute but competent R2-D2 and talkative but annoying C-3PO became globally available to an entire generation of enthusiastic children. The availability of these toy robots thirty years later attests to their enduring cultural force and popularity. Following the lead of Asimov's robot stories (collected in 1950 as *I, Robot*) and Martin Caidin's *Cyborg* novels (1972–1975), the *Star Wars* films explore the nature of human interaction with machine consciousness, as well as the potential to exploit and disenfranchise intelligent devices. Throughout these movies, droids are second-class citizens, but only short-sighted or unsympathetic characters disrespect them: a cantina manager excludes R2-D2 and C-3PO, saying: "We don't serve their kind here"; similarly, Luke's uncle refers to R2-D2 as "it," while Luke and C-3PO both call the R2-unit "he."

The qualities of disenfranchisement, exclusion, and shortness of stature are probably sources of the *Star Wars* droids' enormous popularity with children. But *Star Wars* offers a theological explanation for humanity's contempt for droids. Like all machines, they don't have souls. They cannot possess "the Force," an energy that emerges from microorganisms grown only in the living cells of biota. Since robots exist outside of this force, they are second-class beings in a biologically controlled universe. In the world of *Star Wars*, droids "lack an essential spiritual ingredient that all humans have in greater or lesser degrees."[84] As C-3PO reflects, "We seem to be made to suffer. It's our lot in life. . . ." But like Asimov before him, Lucas held a worldview bound to the twentieth century.

In the thirty-odd years since George Lucas began his

interstellar epic, the smug assurance that biological beings are inherently superior to machines has gradually eroded as socially disenfranchised humans, including children, seniors, and the infirm, are increasingly tended by robots. If, in the 1970s, people unquestionably had "souls" and machines did not, in the new century, there is much less metaphysical speculation and much more focus on practicalities. The late nineties were especially eventful in this transition: electronic "pet" Tamagotchis™ appeared in 1996, followed by robotic Furbys™ two years later. Several books by Sherry Turkle document the changes that took place in children's ideas about what constituted "living" and "knowing" beings in the years following the appearance of these virtual pets. This change is especially striking if we measure it against the belief systems of Jazz Age children who commonly imagined "little people" living and making music inside their parents' radios.[85]

The key to the increasing diversity and use of robots is our increasing familiarity with these devices. This alone makes them more and more acceptable to us. The upshot for modern consciousness is the erosion of the human soul as an interesting or productive topic in children's robot conversations. Religion is still a potent force in the world, but we should begin to wonder if it will always remain so; metaphysics seems to be disappearing through our familiarity with increasingly lifelike devices. Part of these changes, of course, is the decline of our investment in "heaven" as a productive image of hope and reward. Modern people are much more focused on immediate gratification and luxury than on spiritual promises of deferred, intangible comforts. We have come a very long way since 1928. In the intervening years, as sociable robots gradually became human simulations intended to facilitate and encourage anthropomorphic projections, so our uncritical acceptance of sociable robots increased. As this happened, humanity's fascination with metaphysical issues (like soul and spirit) simultaneously declined. I believe we are completing the long curve of an intellectual movement that Lewis Mumford offers as the impetus behind the rise of machines:

> The physical scientist . . . substituted for the body and blood of reality a skeleton of effective abstractions which he could manipulate with wires and pulleys. What was left was the bare, depopulated, world of matter and motion: a wasteland. In order to thrive . . . it was necessary for the inheritors of the seventeenth century . . . to fill up the world again with new organisms, devised to represent the new realities of physical science. Machines—and machines alone—completely met the requirements of the new scientific method . . . by renouncing a large part of his humanity, a man could achieve godhood: he dawned on this second chaos and created the machine in his own image: the image of power, but power ripped loose from his flesh and isolated from his humanity.[86]

More than any other nation, Japan has given itself to these ideas. Many Japanese now see emerging robotic technology as an economic force able to salvage their economy.[87] But while it is true that a radically aging population and declining birthrate make robots an attractive alternative for a homogeneous and subtly xenophobic society like Japan, it is also quite true that the Japanese are much more historically predisposed toward accepting robots than are Europeans or Americans, many of whom have profound misgivings about anthropomorphic machines.[88] Although it was a Japanese scientist who first formulated the "uncanny valley" hypothesis describing human revulsion at the false humanity of imperfect robots, the Japanese were the first to surpass this valley in their robotic designs.[89]

In the West, the strongest statement I've found concerning the changes in our attitudes toward machines, human versus nonhuman company, and the future of sociable robotics comes from former chess champion and IT consultant David Levy, author of some fifty-eight books. Levy is convinced that robots will become widely accepted as substitute lovers and friends before the end of this century. At the age of sixty-one, David Levy completed a PhD thesis and published it in book form. *Love and Sex with Robots* (2007) documents many of the changes that have already taken place in human-machine interactions, and it predicts some very disturbing directions in the near future:

> The mere concept of an artificial partner, husband, wife, friend or lover is one that for most people at the start of the twenty-first century challenges their notion of relationships. Previously the relationship between robot and human has always been considered in terms of master to slave, of human to machine. But with the addition of artificial intelligence to the machine-slaves conceived in the twentieth century, we have now made them into something much more . . . by building robots with the capability of communicating with us . . . and by building robots that have at least some appearance of humanlike features, we are rapidly moving toward an era when robots interact with us not only in a functional sense but in a very personal sense.[90]

CLOSED CARS

> There is only one man in most of those cars!
>
> —Nikita Khrushchev,
> "New Mass Transit vs. More Highways," *Life*, 1967,
> while viewing rush hour on the Golden Gate Bridge

Dr. Levy is very modern. I am not (although a shiny, brushed-steel iPod Nano Touch® is my favorite gym partner). For me, the company of humans is infinitely preferable to that of machines (even though there are many people I don't like very much).

But my preference for human company is not universal. In California, during the 1990s, a former neighbor lost her full-time job and savings. My wife and I offered up our spare bedroom, but she ended up sleeping behind the wraparound curtains of her prized vintage Mercedes® 300 SD sedan on our secluded hilltop in Silverlake. She preferred isolation, saying she needed her own space.

Daytimes, she showered in my bathroom, used the building's laundry facilities, and cooked sparingly on our kitchen stove. Sometimes she left coins on the counter to cover the price of an egg, a grapefruit, a bowl of muesli. There were many others in similar straits, but most were reluctant to surrender their cars even after their insurance expired and they could no longer legally drive. Automobile historian James Flink has a simple and elegant explanation of how the car first acquired its significance as a personal talisman for Americans, "[It] was an ideal symbol of status in our migrant society because, like cash in the pocket, it could be taken with the individual wherever he went as an immediately recognizable sign of his worth."[91]

In our small circle, the Los Angeleños who kept their jobs often had three-hour commutes. All felt their automobiles were *to some degree* alternative—albeit mechanical—homes. Their cars sheltered them and provided material comfort during their transitions to and from the workplace. They were also places to be alone while pleasantly distracted by the low-level task of driving. Americans developed a powerful taste for driving alone early in the history of the car. By 1909, many journalists noted a growing urge to drive solo, "The whole family has become so accustomed to auto-riding that some members generally prefer to ride alone."[92]

A variety of inventions contributed to America's view that the automobile was a useful public buffer offering shelter during one's solitary passage over the urban and rural road network. These developments included closed-car bodies

(1903), travel trailers (1913), fifth wheels (1915), drive-in restaurants (1921), electric garage-door openers (1926), professionally installed car radios (c. 1929–1932), and remote-control garage-door openers (1931).

Long before portable devices like the transistor radio (1954) or the Walkman® (1979) began insulating us in public simply by shutting out unwelcome noise and making us socially inaccessible, there was the comfort, isolation, and safety of the car. And for the same reasons, the closed car also played a central role in the ongoing sexual revolution that changed America completely during the twentieth century. In more ways than one, you could expose your true self in a closed car. The car was a safe and private venue for all the appetites—eating, drinking, and sex—in any combination.

What remained constant during this period was an escalating anxiety about unwanted interpersonal contact with total strangers that provided the designers and manufacturers of technology with a mandate to deliver increasingly ingenious ways to achieve social distance and inaccessibility. Of course, initially, much of this anxiety had to do with race. Into the urban crucible came African Americans from the southern states, as well as Irish (my grandmother), Italian, and Jewish immigrants from Europe. In America's cities, the "other" lived next to you, shopped at your market and passed you in the street. The difficulty of maintaining privacy and distance, as Jane Jacobs writes, had disastrous social consequences: "The common outcome in cities where people are faced with the choice of sharing much or nothing, is nothing. . . . If mere contact with your neighbors threatens to entangle you in their private lives, or entangle them in yours, and if you cannot be so careful who your neighbors are as self-selected upper middle class people can be, the logical solution is absolutely to avoid friendliness or casual offers of help. Better to stay thoroughly distant."[93]

To escape the other, Americans increasingly used cars to

take them out of the city to suburban safe zones. Of course, during their commutes, Americans traveled alone. An unusual legacy of the habitual solitude of the daily automotive commute survives in the etiquette of "slugging," the practice of commuter hitchhiking in large gridlocked cities like Washington, Houston, and San Francisco. The first slug line appeared in the parking lot of Bob's Big Boy in Springfield, Virginia, and served the country's largest single employer, the Pentagon.

To use the least-congested high-occupancy vehicle (HOV) lanes legally—and, later, to pay a lower bridge toll in the Bay Area—drivers began picking up slugs, or extra passengers, by offering them a free commute. Slug lines form in commonly known locations near public transportation depots and are city-bound in the morning and suburb-bound in the afternoon. This practice has been going on since shortly after the first HOV lane opened in DC in 1975. Along the city's main arteries—I-95 and 395, commuters can shave twenty to thirty minutes out of a thirty-mile commute by filling a car with strangers and becoming an HOV.[94] Significantly, one of the cardinal rules of slugging is "slugs do not talk." According to this rule, any conversation is initiated by the driver, but usually most commuters simply wanted a quiet ride home and a relaxing chance to think, sleep, or read.[95] The injunction against speaking is reinforced by another rule of slug etiquette that, under no circumstances, will any conversation turn to politics, religion, or sex. Clearly all participants agree that informal contact in and out of the American city is potentially highly charged.

While it's very hard to document the emergence of such an attitude, it's less difficult to find proof of its existence. An account by an Englishman transplanted to America in 1920 recounts the general lack of sociability in America:

> City life and customs [*in Chicago*] are less sociable than in England. If I spent an evening at a London hotel . . . I

> wouldn't long be without company. I would "chum up" with some fellow traveler from somewhere, and probably we would dine and spend the evening together. I have spent evenings in Chicago hotels and been as lonely as if I had been staying in the middle of the Arizona desert. Nobody seemed to want to speak to a stranger—whether it is in a hotel, restaurant, or Pullman club car. . . .
>
> My [American] friend smiled, and said it was largely true . . . the reason was that people in big cities were suspicious of each other to a greater extent than in England. There you know more or less who the other fellow is; here you don't. . . . Your purpose in the city is to get from the point you are at to the point you have marked out; you are not there to idle or to enjoy leisure, but to get on with the business.[96]

Today, we think little of weaving through the urban landscape in upholstered metal cocoons with our favorite music blaring. But this would have been a strange and disorienting experience for a city dweller of the early twentieth century. At that time, most people traversed American cities by walking; riding bicycles; sitting in horse-drawn carriages; or riding on buses, on electric trams and subways, or on local trains. Before World War II, city dwellers—with little more protection than their wits—were embedded in and exposed to the public texture of urban geography. Technology to shut out the city was sparse because the city was new and the practice of shutting yourself out was considered snobbish, and in America, which, unlike Canada, is the home of universal liberty, snobbism is an even more extreme antisocial attitude than is racism. For these reasons, as personal technologies to qualify and ameliorate urban stress gradually emerged, the advantages of privacy and solitude were not marketed in direct ways, even though they were increasingly sought after.

If vending machines reduced the number of urban interactions, and if robots encouraged our gradual acceptance that machinery offered a viable alternative to human company, the closed car added to the increasing isolation of city dwellers in the early decades of the twentieth century. Hours spent alone in a closed car during a commute were hours spent away from contact with other humans. This was one of the most important cultural phenomena during the great transition to our consumer society. In the 1920s, registration of vehicle ownership went from 9.3 million in 1921 (about 9 percent of the total population) to over 23 million (nearly 20 percent) in 1929. Today there are about 250 million cars on America's roads; most of these are "closed."

Sinclair Lewis's comic novel *Babbitt* explored the attractions of closed cars in 1922:

> Verona the older daughter cried, "Oh, Dad . . . why don't you get a sedan? That would be perfectly slick! A closed car is so much more comfy than an open one."
>
> "Oh, shoot . . . you never tried a sedan. Let's get one. It's got a lot more class," said Ted.
>
> "A closed car does keep the clothes nicer," from Mrs. Babbitt; "You don't get your hair blown all to pieces," from Verona. "It's a lot sportier," from Ted; and from Tinka, the youngest, "Oh, let's have a sedan! Mary Ellen's father has got one." Ted wound up, ". . . everybody's got a closed car now, except us."
>
> Babbitt faced them: ". . . you got nothing very terrible to complain about! I don't keep a car just to enable you children to look like millionaires! And I like an open car, so you can put the top down on summer evening and go out for a drive and get some good fresh air. Besides—a closed car costs more money."[97]

By the end of the decade, Babbitt's love of cheap cars and fresh air become a standard joke. When radio/television characters Amos 'n' Andy first arrived in Chicago in 1929, they scrounged to buy a car but could only afford one without a roof. Acting boldly, these new urbanites initiated the soon-to-be-famous Fresh Air Taxi Company. Today, of course, no one specifies whether their car is open or closed. We call some cars convertibles (sometimes rag-tops), but this is a special linguistic usage (a "marked" vocabulary item) that departs from *car*, the general, all-purpose word for a motor vehicle. The normal kind of automobile, we now assume, always has reinforced metal walls and a hard roof. In the twenty-first century, we don't have a specific name for such things. *Sedan*, which used to designate this type of car, now carries the vague meaning of a larger car with four doors intended to accommodate a family or many passengers. If a modern rental agent were to ask if a client wanted a "closed car," it might well provoke a sarcastic response like "Du-uh!" unless, of course, it were an especially sunny day in a beach state like California or Florida where a convertible might be quite desirable.

In the 1920s, "open" cars were the rule, so the linguistic situation was reversed. *Automobile* was still the normal word for car, and *closed car* was its only alternative. As the closed car became more common, it replaced *automobile* and was eventually shortened. *Closed car* became *car*, much as *cellular phone* became *cell phone* and then either *cell* or *phone.*[98] This linguistic change accelerated after 1926, the first year that the production of closed cars eclipsed that of open cars. In 1921, the year of the first drive-in restaurant, only 335,000 closed cars were manufactured, compared with 1,179,000 open ones, so customers at the first drive-through restaurant, J. G. Kirby's Pig Stand on the Dallas–Fort Worth Highway, ordered their ribs, po'boys, or pulled-pork sandwiches from open cars (although many of these had cloth roofs).

Over the next five years, the distribution of open to closed cars changed quickly as body engineers brought down the cost of closed-car bodies by firing skilled carriage workers and introducing rectilinear, mass-produced designs that were easy to manufacture. Priced at $1,495, Hudson's closed-body Essex County model invaded the midrange automobile market in 1922, followed by the 1923 Dodge®, which sported an all-steel machine-pressed body.[99] In 1926, for the first time, America produced more closed cars (2,900,000) than open ones (1,000,000).[100] *Automotive Industries* magazine described this shift as a "tidal wave of closed car sales."[101] This is not an exaggeration. The year 1926 is the watershed year for America's acceptance of the closed car; that year saw innovations in cheap interior heaters for automobiles, the first do-it-yourself car radios, and the *invention* of electric garage-door openers. (Radio-controlled garage-door openers were developed five years later, after it became clear that driveway push-button keypads were collisions waiting to happen.)[102]

In the early twenties, closed cars were luxury items. This change was the result of three manufacturing issues: the weight of the body, the relatively meager horsepower of early engines, and the expense of the skilled craftsmen—carriage makers—who produced car bodies.[103] At first, most people could not afford a closed vehicle, despite the fact that there was enormous demand for them in the affluent, urbanized Northeast, where most car buyers and most Americans lived. The closed vehicles of the time reflect these economic issues in odd ways. Contemporary limousines had enclosed "tonneau" seating for their gentrified passengers, but weight considerations forced manufacturers to leave the forward cab open, exposing the chauffeur to the elements.

In the years before effective, lightweight car heaters became available, a variety of car fashions, including rugs (blankets), mufflers, hats, goggles, and coats emerged to protect Northern motorists from wind, speed, and cold winter air they experienced in their open cars. Early issues of *Automotive Industries* refer to these fashions as "automobile toggery," and the most popular automobile tog was the male drivers' ankle-length raccoon coat. Its use spanned the first three decades of the century because it provided genuine insulation for winter driving.[104] Photographer James Van Der Zee immortalized the raccoon coat in a photo emblematic of the social changes reshaping America. His *Couple in Raccoon Coats* (1932) depicts a man and woman standing by a new open car, a Cadillac® coupe whose retractable roof is deployed as first-line-of-defense protection against the chill of a late fall on 127th Street in Harlem. The couple's luxurious furs attest to their comfort and success in the third full year of the Depression.

Not everyone could afford a fur coat. In 1921, one of the most popular mystery writers of the period, Octavus Roy Cohen, described the ordeal of a metropolitan taxi driver waiting for late-night fares outside a train station in *Midnight*:

> The city was in the grip of the first cold wave of the year. . . . On the seat of his yellow taxicab, Spike Walters drew a heavy lap-robe more closely about his husky figure and shivered miserably. . . . [He] . . . blew on his numb fingers in a futile effort to restore warmth, slipped his hands back into a pair of heavy— . . . entirely inadequate—driving-gloves and gave himself over to a mental rebellion against the career of a professional taxi-driver. . . . Ten minutes passed—fifteen. The cold bit through Spike's overcoat, battled to the skin, and chewed to the bone. It was well nigh unbearable. . . . He looked around. A streetcar, bound for a suburb, passed noisily. . . . Impressed in Spike's mind was a mental picture of the . . . conductor huddled over the electric heater within the car. Spike felt a personal resentment against that conductor. Comfort seemed unfair on a night like this; heat a luxury more to be desired than fine gold.[105]

Effective automobile heaters were an important issue in the development and acceptance of closed cars. Thomas Ahearn, a Canadian engineer from my hometown of Ottawa, invented the first one in 1890. By 1917, there was a radiant-style interior car heater that circulated exhaust fumes through pipes in the car's interior. Some heaters worked like small radiators passing supplies of heated water through a pipe system in the cab. There were also portable electric heaters that were most effective in the front seat. In 1929, Ford's Model A circulated hot air from the engine through the car, then, in 1933, Ford® introduced the first directional dashboard heating duct. Each of these devices was more effective than the last, but until the late 1940s, enormous room for improvement remained. The optional heater-defroster for the first postwar pickup truck (Chevy®) was the most popular automobile accessory of 1947. Every former GI who had suffered in an unheated truck during the long winters of the war in Europe wanted one. Air-conditioning was not introduced into cars until 1953.

Heaters and other gradual improvements in the closed environments of automobiles made the car an extension of America's living space, a private sanctuary on the public thoroughfare. Usually this was a tacit assumption, but in 1926, the *Automotive Manufacturer* wondered if "the closed car really measures up to good living . . . or drawing room standards?"[106] Since the car played a central role in dating, providing your car with a comfortable level of interior heat was an important challenge for the sexually active driver. But another major challenge was the car's operating noise, and—ironically—another pressing concern was excessive silence. Filtering out unpleasant noise was a problem of the period, but if you were successful, what followed was an uncomfortable silence. The same period that saw the development of the car radio also introduced an odd precursor of the Walkman or iPod in an invention called the "Isolator," or thinking cap of 1925. This was an air-fed helmet device that enabled workers to concentrate but left them alone in an uncomfortably still bubble. It never caught on.

Meanwhile, driving alone had become a distinctly American pastime, but being alone and in silence for prolonged periods was difficult for city dwellers who wanted shelter from the cacophonous and distracting soundscape of heavily metallic modernity.[107] Evan Eisenberg, a historian of recorded music, points out that, whereas "in the country music is the fulfillment of silence," in the city "music becomes a substitute for silence."[108] Besides providing welcome company to solitary drivers stuck in commuter traffic, suitable music was another very attractive feature in a "dating car." So, by 1926, inventors had turned their attention to the problem of developing workable mobile radios. From 1924 to 1926, magazines like *Popular Mechanics* frequently ran articles with detailed instructions for outfitting your car with an "auto radio."[109]

In 1928, RCA's radio manufacturing arm introduced its lowest-priced model to date, the Radiola 51 AC. For only $195, radio enthusiasts could now buy a cabinet radio whose loudspeaker—the new Radiola 100-A—had excellent fidelity.[110] RCA had been advertising, selling, and improving Radiola receivers since 1922, so, by 1928, Radiola was the most widely known American radio brand.

At that same time, brothers Paul and Joseph Galvin owned Galvin Manufacturing, a small Chicago firm that marketed "battery eliminators," which enabled you to switch your radio's power source over to your home current. As built-in radio loudspeakers became smaller and more efficient, the Galvins realized that the hobbyist trend of installing radios in cars would produce the next market surge: they correctly anticipated an enormous demand for manufactured, ready-to-install auto radios.

With the help of radio engineers from a firm headed by William Lear (who later developed the Learjet®), Galvin set his technical staff to work designing a complete after-market auto radio in 1929. Playing to the popularity of RCA's brand, this new line was called "Motorola." One year later, with the working model installed in his Studebaker, Galvin drove to Atlantic City and parked in front of the Radio Manufacturer's Association convention with the radio blaring, just before the participants broke for lunch. Advanced orders for this first Motorola—the 57T1—priced at $110 poured in. Galvin's Motorolas made putting a radio in America's cars a relatively simple process of attaching a few wires although the most difficult part of the installation was not a wiring issue at all. Decades before plastic grommets were developed, people who purchased their all-in units from the Galvins had to remove and then replace (re-stitch) their car's ceiling upholstery since the first automobile radio antennas were mesh nets of copper wire that lay directly under the metal roof.

Despite the Depression, the demand for car radios was enormous and remained steady for several years. At a time when $700 would buy a new car, Galvin's car radio cost a hefty $110, but it was still much cheaper than a cabinet model. Philco followed Motorola's lead into this lucrative market and began manufacturing car radios in 1930. Then car manufacturers began offering factory-installed versions as an option in 1932.[111]

It was the first wireless age. Movie attendance fell. Magazine and newspaper subscriptions suffered. Record sales dropped to devastating lows. But once you bought a radio, the free content that flowed over America's airwaves provided a welcome respite from the country's hard times. Gas was ten cents a gallon. In the first years of the Depression, leaving trouble behind was still as easy as driving away from it with the radio blaring "Happy Days Are Here Again." By 1946, 40 percent of American passenger vehicles (about nine million cars) had radios, "but . . . by 1963, 50 million cars—60 percent—were radio equipped."[112] By that time, a vast majority of Americans listened to radio only in their cars. As American cities grew, suburbs expanded, and the neighborhoods of the inner city were broken into islands to accommodate increased car traffic by modern commuters. Jane Jacobs summarizes the processes by which city planners broke apart the sociable neighborhoods of America's cities to facilitate access by closed automobiles:

> The erosion proceeds as a kind of nibbling, small nibbles at first, but eventually hefty bites. Because of vehicular congestion, a street is widened here, another is straightened there, a wide avenue is converted to one-way flow, staggered-signal systems are installed for faster movement, a bridge is double-decked as its capacity is reached, an expressway is cut through yonder and finally whole webs of expressways. More and more land goes into parking to accommodate the ever increasing numbers of vehicles while they are idle . . . cumulatively the effect is enormous. Erosion of cities by automobiles is . . . an example of what is known as "positive feedback" . . . an action produces a reaction which in turn intensifies the condition responsible for the first action. This intensifies the need for repeating the first action, which in turn intensifies the reaction and so on. . . . It is something like the grip of a habit forming addiction.[113]

In her brilliant description of American city life, Jacobs continues illustrating the discovery of the positive-feedback traffic process by Victor Gruen, who described Fort Worth's traffic dilemma in 1955. But the concept of positive feedback can also be applied to our increasing reliance on personal technology and on the technological isolation that results from it. Jacobs was careful to point out that "the destructive effects of automobiles are much less of a cause than a symptom."[114] Urban "improvements" designed to provide convenience and comfort increasingly led to isolation, just as car privacy and security led to increasing car use and a modern city designed more for machines than for human beings because the "needs of automobiles are more easily understood and satisfied than the complex needs of cities."[115] Significantly, by the 1960s, most car radio listeners listened alone during drive-time radio shows. These had expanded from the fifteen isolated minutes that characterized 1920s radio shows. As American cars gradually lost their tailfins, city workers drove more slowly through heightened traffic into distant suburbs, listening to hour-long shows.[116]

RADIO'S "FREE" CONTENT

> [In] 1935 . . . California high school students were already listening alone. . . . A striking difference from earlier listeners was the desire to listen alone and not be interrupted. As radio comedy programs became subjects of interest, and as drama and comedy became increasingly significant forms of programming, attentive listening became more important than interaction with family or friends.
>
> —Richard Butsch, *The Making of American Audiences*, 2000

It should be clear that in the early twentieth century, emerging technologies of consumerism reduced the number and length of human interactions while providing a variety of substitutes for human company, and that as this process continued, it was increasingly characterized by positive feedback. Isolation became increasingly worse as we relied unconsciously on new technologies to ameliorate isolation. Moreover, this transformation in American sociability is uniquely tied to the growth of cities where human contact became a source of stress that exceeded personal control. All these trends continue in our own time.

By 1909, Charles Herrold had discovered that radio enthusiasts preferred music to voice and began broadcasting classical music from his home in San Jose, California. "Doc" Herrold ingeniously overcame part of the problem of financing these first radio broadcasts by slyly attaching his arc transmitter to the power supply of the Santa Fe Railway's local streetcar lines.[117] Lee De Forest, who invented both the Audion (1906) and Triode (1907) vacuum tubes, prepared the ground for Herrold's broadcasts by making it possible to amplify radio signals. It was De Forest's tubes that freed radio from the crystal-set era of enthusiasts and amateurs and made its commercialization possible.

By 1907, De Forest understood that broadcasts would become the most profitable application for his devices. He sold rights to the Audion tube for use in radio telephony, but the agreement stipulated his own right to broadcast. At that time, AT&T had not yet acquired any radio stations. Thinking De Forest was just an eccentric inventor, the company was happy to comply. In 1915, De Forest had erected a 125-foot tower above his factory and had begun hosting nightly half-hour concerts of phonograph music. He sometimes bragged that he was the first person to advertise over the air, since during these free concerts he plugged his own radio components to an established audience of fellow radio enthusiasts.[118]

No one objected to De Forest's ads, but commercial radio advertisements were a highly contentious topic in the late teens and early twenties. Until NBC constellated into a commercial network in 1926, radio stations and their broadcasts were often funded either by local organizations (mainly businesses) seeking publicity or by radio manufacturers eager to provide free entertainment in order to encourage sales of their devices. Frank Conrad, a radio enthusiast employed at Westinghouse, used his own transmitter to broadcast music to people who owned radio sets in the Pittsburgh area. In 1920, Westinghouse seized on Conrad's initiative, realizing they might sell more radios since "people not interested in talking via radio might be interested in listening."[119] The company encouraged Conrad to establish the first commercial radio station, KDKA, and two years later, broadcasting caught on as the number of commercial stations jumped from 77 to 524 in the warm spring and summer of 1922.[120]

That same year, an AT&T station took the first step toward the commercialization of broadcast radio. On August 28, 1922, WEAF (New York) experimented with a paid announcement for a complex of tenant-owned apartments in Jackson Heights. This first advertisement for Hawthorne Court cost only one hundred dollars, but it was widely discussed and admired by broadcasters throughout America. Over the next three years, more and more of them switched to this "toll station" model and began using advertising revenue to finance better-quality programming.

Broadcasters and audiences alike acknowledged that WEAF's popularity with listeners was a direct result of its advertising revenue since it spent liberally to attract a "higher class of talent" in contrast to many other stations whose "musical talent . . . is . . . mediocre."[121] This lesson was driven home in 1925 when WEAF unveiled the (RCA) Victor Hour featuring exceptionally fine classical music by the Victor Salon Orchestra, with regular performances by stars of the Metropolitan Opera Company and guest performances by renowned instrumental virtuosos.[122]

Prior to the development of networks, a variety of advertising models tried to make radio pay. One of the most successful alternative business models for early radio also emphasized the highest level of professional entertainment. The person who made it financially viable was Sister Aimee Semple McPherson in Los Angeles, California. McPherson was unique because she fostered extreme dependence on a machine (radio) at a very early date.[123] During an Oakland revival, Rockridge Radio offered her free airtime one Sunday morning in April. McPherson developed a huge and immediate following because of this performance. The previous year (1921) had seen the first regularly scheduled religious programming at Station KDKA in Pittsburg, when the Calvary Episcopal Church began broadcasting its Sunday evening service. In 1922, commercial network radio was established, and soon after, McPherson became the first woman to preach a sermon over the air. People on the West Coast began to identify themselves as "radio converts," which opened McPherson's eyes to the enormous potential of radio, which she called "the most miraculous conveyance for the Message."[124]

In 1924, Los Angeles' population topped one million, and McPherson purchased her own radio station, KFSG (Kall Four Square Gospel). The station's audience was estimated at about thirty thousand regular listeners. The station's license application emphasized the station's "entertainment and musical impact," describing its musical programming as "the finest presented by the most talented and favorite artists" who provide "spiritual comfort for many thousands in and around Southern California."[125] With this station, McPherson became a model for all subsequent televangelists. In her hands, KFSG took faith healing to a new level. On the air, the need for professional stage management and showmanship demanded by her temple's daily live performances of faith healing disappeared. In a very concrete way, commercial radio's one-way channel prevented anyone from confirming or denying McPherson's most celebrated "cures." They seemed true, and they had the authority of radio science and licensed broadcasting behind them.

In an age of yellow print journalism, when people read most newspaper accounts critically and suspiciously, the public nonetheless accepted what they heard on the intimate medium of the radio verbatim. Early admen claimed that radio possessed "fundamental sincerity," which soon became the source for persuasive techniques in which "artifice [should] be concealed [so] that [advertisements] seemed straightforward and truthful." Before reliable speakers were developed, listeners' connection to early radio was encouraged in a very physical way by the use of headsets that isolated the listener and made him or her much more attentive to the broadcast. This substantially encouraged the audience's impression of sincerity. A decade before Orson Welles's *War of the Worlds* (1938) demonstrated how easy it was to broadcast a hoax over commercial radio, McPherson began instructing Angeleños to "kneel by the radio and place their hand on it to receive long-distance cures."[126] Throughout the City of Angels, tens of thousands of infirm, desperate, lonely, and all-too-gullible people heard and trusted McPherson's voice and touched the wooden cabinets of their wireless sets, grateful for the meager connection—human or divine—that KFSG brought to their lives.

This is the earliest example I can find of Americans pursuing an intimate, emotional, and physical relationship with a machine. When McPherson began curing people over the radio in 1924, cars had not yet been wired for sound, although telephones, of course, had been enabling people to communicate with their loved ones since the 1870s. Nonetheless, the satisfaction provided by the telephone is essentially responsive, two-way, and human, whereas broadcast radio was an entirely one-way device. McPherson began offering her profound emotional comfort through the listeners' physical connection to their personal machines late at night, when the signal was clearest and, importantly, when McPherson's listeners were most likely alone. Radio was an extremely powerful device even without the dimension of physicality. During the 1930s, radio became an altar of collective connection used with enormous success by Germany's National Socialists, who listened to radio broadcasts of the Führer during mass rallies. Perhaps intuitively, McPherson understood that radio could be made significantly more powerful and intimate by encouraging her listeners to establish a tactile, physical relationship with the device itself. It could, she claimed, "cure" them. Many believed her. This marks the very beginning of our substitution of machines for human company. KFSG was America's first electronic fetish.

Fortunately, McPherson could not repeat her success at a national level since networks had not yet been established.[127] But the idea of a network—the idea of offering advertisers the widest possible audience—may have sprung from the head of a similar radio huckster. (There was no shortage of them in the early 1920s.) This one was named Norman Baker. He owned an independent station, KTNT, in Muscatine, Iowa. A genius at garnering publicity while running various businesses into bankruptcy, Baker one day speculated about the possibility of linking a hundred independent stations in June 1926. Part of the idea was a traveling company of vaudevillians who would supply original material to member stations.[128]

Baker's idea was an advancement on the regional chains of stations that sometimes came together to broadcast a special event like the 1923 World Series, which was heard both by WEAF (New York) listeners and by the WGY audience in Schenectady. In 1925, the *Atwater Kent Hour*, which featured first-rate classical music, was broadcast on Sunday afternoons on a chain of thirteen stations that stretched from WEAF into the Midwest. That same year, President Calvin Coolidge's inaugural address was heard on twenty-four stations.[129] Norman Baker's idea was basically to make these occasional chains of stations permanent and then to regularly share programming among them.

As the head of RCA, David Sarnoff was at the apex of radio's food chain for new ideas, and Sarnoff was a very clever man. When Baker's idea reached him, he understood immediately the two main advantages a network offered: first, advertisers would jump at the chance of placing their ads with a large, geographically diverse audience, and second, the cost of developing high-quality programming would guarantee large audiences spread across a revenue base formed of many stations. A network like that could spend much more money producing good programming and still achieve a lower price per pair of ears for the mass audience they delivered to their advertisers. The advantage of a network was that it substantially lowered the cost per listener while improving the quality of programming used to attract them. This was good news. Americans had already invested hundreds of millions of dollars in radio equipment. By 1935, 70 percent of America's twenty-nine million households had one radio (there were only half as many telephones). Nonetheless, radio programming was a jumble of mixed standards. Anyone with a Victrola and a license could be a broadcaster, and by the end of the twenties, radio audiences were tired of weak signals and bad programs.

Knowing that if he could guarantee quality programming, he could also guarantee advertisers a sizeable growing audience and increase sales of RCA's radios themselves, Sarnoff moved quickly: RCA acquired WEAF on July 7, 1926. Sarnoff's negotiations offered continuous revenue to the station's former owner, AT&T, provided that they refrain from broadcasting and instead supply the phone lines connecting Sarnoff's stations in a future network. By September 14, full-page ads in newspapers across America announced that RCA (50 percent ownership), GE (30 percent), and Westinghouse (20 percent) would collaborate to underwrite a new National Broadcasting Company (NBC).

Sarnoff denied any attempt to develop a radio monopoly and instead emphasized the substantial benefits to America's radio audience: "The Radio Corporation of America . . . is seeking . . . to provide machinery which will insure national distribution of national programs, and a wider distribution of programs of the highest quality."[130]

On November 15, 1926, NBC's Red Network began its top-of-the-line entertainment with an inaugural broadcast from the Waldorf Astoria over its flagship station WEAF. This $50,000 variety show was simultaneously rebroadcast to seventeen other stations. (Six weeks later, NBC launched a five-station junior circuit called the Blue Network.) Suddenly, ad agencies had intimate access to America's homes. Immediately, they began directing their attention to women who spent most of their daytime hours alone in the home, and who made about 85 percent of the American family's purchasing decisions.

One month before the debut of the Red Network (in October 1926), the US Department of Agriculture hired fifty different women in fifty states to become the first "Aunt Sammy" (Uncle Sam's "wife") to provide homemaking and dietary tips to American women in a national program called the *Housekeeper's Chat*, which preexisted network radio. Aunt Sammy may have been based on General Mills' Betty Crocker®, who first appeared in print in 1921. The GM broadcasts began on local stations but then moved to a network model featuring only one woman, who broadcast from WCCO in Minneapolis. In 1930, NBC's rival network, CBS, invited a real person to host a new program organized like a magazine into different sections consisting of small blocks of time. These segments featuring cookbook author and cooking instructor Ida Bailey Allen could then be sold to a variety of advertisers who represented manufacturers who made products for the kitchen, boudoir, or living room, and whose low unit costs prevented them from sponsoring an entire show.[131]

Possibly because transcription recordings did not survive well, radio historians sometimes put the trend toward individualized listening a bit later, when it began to engage other family members like men and children and become truly universal. The following excerpt from a recent book describes this trend:

> From the mid-1930s onward radio manufacturers increasingly moved away from promoting familial models of listening to individualized one . . . increasingly radio listening

> was depicted in many different locations, not just the living room . . . listening outside of the family circle increasingly divided the domestic space into individualized zones of reception . . . and . . . paralleled the development of the specialized markets and programming appeals.
>
> [And] before the Second World War individualized listening in multi-radio homes was not the norm, even though more and more families owned more than one radio.[132]

On the other hand, feminist radio historian Michele Hilmes claims that lack of respect for women's programming—embedded in an overwhelmingly male-dominated industry—is responsible for our continuing misperceptions of early daytime programming and its listeners. Whatever the reason, daytime programming began in the late 1920s, and by 1930, it had divided the radio audience in two. Alone in their homes during the day, women listened to music as they went about their routines or took a break while they listened to the earliest homemaker shows and proto–soap operas.

In October 1930, Henry Selinger, station manager of Chicago's WGN, brought to the airwaves the idea of a daytime serial "used to sell products to women."[133] Despite Selinger's involvement, *Painted Dreams* was undoubtedly the unique creation of writer, director, and producer Irna Phillips, who was to become a force in radio soap operas over the next thirty years.[134] *Painted Dreams* focused on the lives of female characters like Mother Moynihan, her daughter, and their boarder, Sue Morton (Phillips herself played both mother and boarder). The show ran daily, six days a week, from October 1930 to April 1932, when a legal dispute over ownership of the series ended Phillips's involvement.[135] Fortunately, transcripts of the lawsuit provide historians with valuable clues about the production conditions of early radio shows.

At night, especially in the years between 1926 and 1932, the radio was "family" entertainment as reliable loudspeakers made the era of passing the headphones obsolete. Network musical variety shows and radio dramas now entertained several family members at once. The year 1929 was a watershed one for such family entertainment. The *Rudy Vallée Show* (a.k.a. *The Fleischmann Hour*) premiered that year, as did *Amos 'n' Andy*, *The Rise of the Goldbergs*, and *Clara, Lu, and Em*. Before becoming a network feature, *Amos 'n' Andy* had been a local Chicago show that was syndicated to independent stations through the production of transcription recordings, which captured the full fifteen-minute duration of most "live" shows and then sold them for rebroadcast. Advertisers liked this format, which provided a cheap alternative to NBC's or CBS's expensive ad rates.[136]

But already the airwaves were changing. Radio threatened the unity and sociability of the family experience of American radio on many fronts. Advertisers and networks wanted access to the largest and most powerful buying segment of the American audience. Because women listened to radio alone during the daytime, marketers had a brilliant tactical advantage over them. Ad agencies soon began exercising their power over the networks and began to first select and then design shows to appeal to a daytime homemaker audience. The first soap opera, *Clara, Lu, and Em*, switched from its evening schedule on NBC to daytime hours in 1932. Moreover, the family market for radios in America was approaching saturation. By 1930, Americans owned about half of all radio sets in the world, and the ideal of family radio was coming to an end. Faced with a shrinking market, radio manufacturers began to innovate. RCA's Radiola merged with Victrola and offered radio and phonograph combinations. But in the austerity of the Depression, few Americans could afford these devices.

Smaller radio manufacturers with much lower overheads than RCA soon found they could miniaturize the $200 cabinet sets that had dominated the market before 1929. Companies in outlying areas like Los Angeles began to manufacture radios that sat on a tabletop or sideboard. These smaller radios had names like the Tombstone or the Cathedral, but generally they were called midgets and sold in the range of thirty-five to fifty-five dollars. Miniaturization of electronic components did not become a vital issue until World War II, when vacuum tubes were used in the proximity fuses of antiaircraft shells, so the tubes these midgets contained were the same size as those of cabinet radios, but miniaturized midgets contained fewer tubes.[137] With smaller loudspeakers and fewer tubes, radio's sound changed; and for this reason we now associate the rounded, echo-laden intonations of songs like "You Oughta Be in Pictures" (1934) with this era of hard times and cheaper radios. Moreover, because the market for family radios was shrinking, the Radio Manufacturers Association began promoting the idea of placing one of these cheaper radios in every room in the house. This seemingly innocent marketing strategy was really an assault on family unity. Eventually, it established "individualized listening" as the rule for most radio audiences. Family members spent more time alone in their rooms listening to programs designed to appeal to the interests of their age group and gender. This sold more radios and more radio-advertised products, but the cost in human terms was enormous. Family members spent less time together.

The "radio-in-every-room" plan was first suggested in 1927 and first used as a marketing advantage for luxury hotels, like the Statler.[138] Radio manufacturers, of course, loved the chance to sell their devices in bundles of hundreds to large hotels or in even bigger bundles of thousands to hotel chains. It's easy to find postwar radio-in-every-room ads since, when radio manufacturers resumed domestic radio production in 1946, the campaign resumed immediately and lasted until the arrival of television in 1949. Representative radio-in-every-room ads from the 1920s and 1930s are harder to find. But in the *Saturday*

Evening Post on July 13, 1929, an Atwater Kent ad depicts four hands, each belonging to a different family member reaching for the radio dial. Characteristically, these early ads "replaced ads picturing families listening together with ads picturing them quarreling over what to listen to."[139] The rhythmical slogan—"radio in every room"—was quickly appropriated from hotel ads by radio marketers determined to sell America on the idea of multi-set homes. As *Printers' Ink* put it, "Every family was going to be a two car family. Every home was going to have a radio in every room. Every man was going to have 12 suits of clothes and 10 pairs of shoes. Every woman was going to have three complete changes of outfit every day of the week."[140]

The convenience and ubiquity of radio that came with multi-set homes meant that people could listen in comfort and solitude to their favorite shows without the distraction of human company or arguments about which show to listen to. Members of America's families responded by listening to their own shows in different rooms at widely different times. The sociable Golden Age of family radio listening, therefore, was a very short-lived period. It was followed by the greatest segmentation and isolation that occurred in the American family before the advent of television. The practice of listening alone was sometimes described as "single" or "individual listening," but increasingly after 1932, it is called "private listening." Also around this time, the word *headphones* was increasingly replaced by *earphones*, emphasizing the solitary act of listening rather than the social appearance of the device. A casual frequency analysis of Google Books® shows that these names increased with the resumption of commercial production of technology around 1948, when "private listening" spread to include record players and other electronic devices now equipped with "privacy" earphone jacks. The main point, however, is that gradually, after reducing the amount of time spent together, our solitary enjoyment of technology marked a reduction in the time spent with family members, and so it contributed to the decline in family members' reliance on and loyalty to each other.

If it did so, that was very good for business. Consumers, after all, buy and own things individually. They do not share. For marketers, it is far better to sell to a nation of individual consumers who each need a car, a washing machine, a telephone, a radio, and so on, than to market wares to a nation composed of family households where small, united groups share these items. For this reason, market segmentation, advertising, manufacturing, and corporate capitalism act as the dedicated economic enemies of familial bonds. So it is for economic reasons that the consumer life became the solo life. As Eric Klinenberg puts it: "More people live alone than ever before . . . [because] . . . today more people can afford to do so."[141] Tragically, as consumerism took hold, American values about the primacy of family ties wore away. The family had been a productive, secure unit during the agricultural period of America's history. It provided meaning and social place. Children labored and were less educated, but large groups provided security at a time when families eked their subsistence out of the land. But industrialization changed the rural-based values of the American family forever. Writing about the disappearance of work songs from the American landscape, music historian Ted Gioia observes: "For farms the most striking impact of industrialization was what it took away—namely, masses of people. Migration to the cities became an irrevocable trend in the U.S. West. Even though agricultural communities would continue to maintain vibrant musical traditions . . . until the rise of radio and sound recordings . . . these songs would no longer exert the cultural influence they . . . once possessed. From now on, city sounds would dominate the aural imagination of the working class."[142]

As they listened to radio during the Depression and war

years that followed, more and more Americans listened alone until the "individualized listening," "private listening," or "solitary listening" (as it is now known) that had become the norm for phonograph records also became the norm for radio. Solitary listening is a fundamental change in human behavior that would be impossible without technology, but it was accompanied by a further mediation, a further distancing of the human element. In the earliest stages of solitary listening, Americans still generally listened to live broadcasts of performances as they occurred in real time. This was because, until after World War II, the recording techniques available in the United States relied on primitive analog inscription methods that could capture only about fifteen minutes of uninterrupted sound. So until the late 1940s, you knew as you listened to the performers of the day in your car, your kitchen, or your living room that they were performing live somewhere at that very moment. This simultaneity of performance and reception did a lot to foster the sense of intimacy and community that early radio possessed.

During the 1930s, transcription recordings had been used to share startup radio dramas among independent stations. Their quality was inferior and declined with each play. So the first nationally broadcast exception to the intimacy of live simultaneity didn't come until after World War II. It was Bing Crosby. After Crosby won an Oscar in 1944 for his portrayal of a young priest in *Going My Way*, he became the top earner in Hollywood. His movie contract with Paramount stipulated that he make three films a year for $150,000 each, and his annual recording royalties from Decca amounted to about $250,000. Crosby was a modern star. He liked to work on film sets and in recording studios, but he found the weekly round of live studio audiences exhausting. As the host of NBC's *Kraft Music Hall*, he was a tireless professional, but these weekly shows paid only $7,500 each.[143] NBC adamantly refused to let him prerecord the shows, so Crosby took the fall of 1944 off and rethought his career before approaching ABC and offering to work for a new sponsor if they'd allow him to prerecord. ABC jumped at the chance to sign a performer of Crosby's stature and—provided he could maintain his ratings—agreed to allow him to prerecord his shows on 16-inch, 33.5-rpm lacquer discs, which were then edited and rerecorded to produce a thirty-minute show. The problem was that Crosby was a perfectionist, and during the lengthy editing process, a lot of distortion was introduced to the transcriptions.[144] Still, as *Billboard* reported when Crosby's new show, the *Philco Radio Time* show, debuted in October 1946: "The fact that the show is transcribed has virtually no negative effect on the program's appeal."[145]

Nonetheless, a new technology was in the pipeline. A graduate engineer called Jack Mullin returned to California after enjoying an interesting war with the US Signal Corp in Europe. During his years in England, Mullin had listened to the stunning high fidelity of music broadcasts over German stations like Reichssender Hamburg, the broadcasting home of announcer Lord Haw-Haw. When Mullin consulted friends in British army intelligence, he found they were similarly puzzled by German broadcasts, but for a very different reason: "Certain German leaders seemed to be on the air around the clock delivering live speeches."[146] Gradually, the Allies learned that Germany had made stunning advances in recording technology during the 1930s, and that in 1932, inventor Fritz Pfleumer had granted patent rights to the process of making magnetic tape to AEG (Allgemeine Elektricitäts-Gesellschaft, or German General Electricity Company), which, since 1933, had been one of the principal sources of corporate funding for the fledgling National Social Party. Mullin learned that German broadcasts had been recorded on a plastic ribbon impregnated with iron oxide made by the I. G. Farben subsidiary BASF. He also learned that, since 1935, BASF tapes were designed to be played on a German-manufactured reel-to-reel recording device capable of maintaining a constant playback speed. This device was called the AEG Magnetophon. In 1939, BASF refined its recording tape, switching its basic component (ferric oxide) to a higher-fidelity variant.

In early May 1945, immediately following the war, Jack Mullin (a newly minted colonel) was assigned to the Paris detachment of the US Signal Corps with orders to investigate German uses of electronic technology. He began collecting German Dictaphones® and wire tape recorders, but none of the hundreds of machines he found were capable of the fidelity and duration of Germany's wartime broadcasts. It was the Allied capture of Radio Luxembourg in September 1944 that revealed a secret recording technology developed at Berlin's State Radio Company (Reichs-Rundfunk-Gesellschaft). When he arrived in Paris, Mullin knew that in 1941 engineers Hans Joachim von Braunmühl and Dr. Walter Weber had developed a recording technique called AC Tape Bias, a revolution in the fidelity of recorded sound. Mullin also learned that AEG had quickly capitalized on this invention by developing a special studio version of Braunmühl and Weber's recording machine (model R22A) whose "recording head field was augmented with a high-frequency, AC bias signal, which assured a recording of extraordinary low distortion and . . . noise."[147] It was this device that had broadcast Adolf Hitler's addresses around the clock throughout the Axis for the duration of the war.

Unfortunately, the OSS kept a tight grip on the Luxembourg machines in order to operate Radio Luxembourg as an Allied propaganda vehicle. Moreover, AEG's main factory and the BASF plant at Ludwigshafen near Mannheim had been destroyed by strategic bombing raids late in the war, so Mullin was hard-pressed to find a working Magnetophon. Eventually, he learned that a station in Frankfurt was still using the Nazis' high-fidelity tape recorders in its local music broadcasts. These he confiscated for the Signal Corps. Then, luckily, in nearby

Bad Nauheim, American forces seized two more suitcase-sized studio high-fidelity recorders, which were good-naturedly consigned into Mullin's care. Mullin took these machines back with him to Paris, and for the remainder of his European tour he disassembled and studied them.[148] Meanwhile, postwar Mannheim developed a substantial black market where Mullin acquired fifty reels of BASF recording tape. In an era before Bubble Wrap®, Mullin packaged the components and tapes carefully in hand-knitted, US Army–issue socks and shipped them to his home in San Francisco in eighteen small parcels labeled "war memorabilia."

As he made his way back to California aboard ships and trains, Colonel Mullin carried one more package containing the low-noise heads for both recording machines. At home in San Francisco, Mullin took his treasure to Bill Palmer, head of W. A. Palmer Films. Palmer hired Mullin immediately. When the machines were reassembled, Palmer and Mullins demonstrated them at the annual convention of motion-picture engineers in October 1946 by making a crystal-clear recording on the spot of pianist José Iturbi and violinist George Stoll playing with the MGM Symphony Orchestra. Crooner Merv Griffin soon learned about the German tape recorders and paid handsomely to record *Songs by Merv Griffin* (1946), the first disc ever mastered on tape. On October 1, 1947, Bing Crosby used Mullin (his new sound engineer) and the Magnetophon machines to inaugurate the era of taped shows on the nationally broadcast *Philco Radio Time.*

Bing Crosby's use of the technology was an enormous success, and soon the Minnesota Mining and Manufacturing Company (later 3M) refined and improved BASF's plastic recording tape, while the Magnetophon machines themselves were reverse-engineered and reproduced by the US firm Ampex. The first Ampex recording clones were commercially available for movie and radio use in 1948, and this year marks the end of most live sound performances and the real beginning of radio archives. Recording tape (with its low-noise tape and long-length features) revolutionized network radio by making it possible to broadcast at uniform times across the continent. Bing Crosby was heard at 10:00 p.m. on the East Coast and at 9:00 p.m. in every other American time zone. Before the war, listeners in New York might relax by listening to a variety show after dinner at 7:00 p.m., just when network listeners in Los Angeles were getting home from work and preparing dinner. By providing control over the timing and quality of broadcasts, tape facilitated larger audiences and better advertising dollars. The possibilities of rebroadcasting quality tape recordings of popular broadcasts further brought down the production costs of quality radio.

So, by the 1950s, when the majority of America listened to music or drama, they listened alone to prerecorded productions. The simultaneity of radio's live Golden Age had ended, and the only living thing left in the channel of communication was the solitary consumer. Audience reactions to studio-recorded performances were usually added after the fact from a file of prerecorded applause, but it was Jack Mullin himself who invented the laugh track in 1947 by storing audience responses to a particular comedian for use with a considerably less funny performer later on. By this time, we were well on our way to living only through mediated experiences of the physical world.[149]

SCREENS

> In general . . . I would be inclined to let [the child] spend as much of his evening with television . . . as he chooses. If the rest of the family is driven mad by having to watch or listen to a child's programs . . . it's worthwhile to get him a set for his room.
>
> —Benjamin Spock, *Baby and Child Care*, 1955

It is possible that the "one owner-one operator" model of modern electronic consumer technology is intrinsic to all consumer devices. This was certainly the case with portable electric hand-tools (like handheld power drills), which predate radio and began to appear toward the end of World War I, but there are also a few other precedents in the area of personal electronics that predate radio. Portable, mass-produced sound devices begin with the introduction of Höhner harmonicas to the American market in 1862. Then headphones appeared in 1880 as a solution to the problem of switchboard-room noise for telephone operators—and although they were personal devices, they were not yet retail items. Phonographs, however, were very retail-friendly, and as they became cheaper, they, too, moved from being group-oriented devices situated in the parlor to machines enjoyed by individual listeners shut off in various rooms throughout the American home. Thomas Edison's ten-dollar spring-driven cylinder gramophone, which appeared in 1900, forced gramophone manufacturers to lower their prices and make the machines more accessible. In the next few years, the music recording industry took off. Later, as we've seen, cheaper, more portable radios resulted in more and more people listening alone. This trend from initial group use to solitary or individualized use continues in the later technological developments like television, personal computers, and the Internet.

Television copied radio's marketing strategy of placing advertisements specific to the interests of demographic "clusters" (men, women, and children) whose members listened to radio individually in different locations within the family home. Television was developed by the Radio Corporation of America (RCA) under the patronage of David Sarnoff, a protégé and personal friend of Guglielmo Marconi, who taught the young Russian-born street urchin radio telephony. As a form of naval communication, early radio was—as Raymond Williams points out in *Television: Technology and Cultural Form* (1974)—an individual means of communication like the telegraph or telephone, "oriented toward uses of person to person, operator and operative." There was "nothing in the technology to make [mass broadcasting] inevitable."[150]

Sarnoff changed radio completely by imposing on it an impersonal broadcast model with highly controlled content "for transmission to individual homes."[151] This gave him an expansive and reliable market for RCA radio sets, broadcasts, and advertising time and brought with it enormous personal power. Like Edison, Henry Ford, and Steve Jobs in our own era, Sarnoff was a transitional visionary whose role in creating consumerist society has gone largely unnoticed. Nonetheless, the "individualized listening" or "solitary listening" experiences of all contemporary segmented markets, which are the truest characteristic of media networks (radio and television), originated in the lonely adventure of this young Marconi operator as he listened to ship transmissions through "cans" (headphones) in the radio sheds scattered along the docksides of the lower boroughs. When the time came to build his networks, Sarnoff knew that radio's Golden Age experience of family "togetherness" (the word had not yet been invented) would be easily replaced by the more powerful and intimate experience of solitary listening, provided that broadcasting content was carefully tailored toward each specific group of listeners.

Television's earliest stages repeated those of radio, but its adoption was greatly accelerated. By the end of its first decade, one in four Americans had a TV: this is about double the number of radios purchased during the first decade of commercial radio.[152] At first, there was a novelty period when people watched TV in public spaces, and this was followed by a brief period of family viewing. Soon, however, TV audiences became jaded, and rapt attention to the tube faded as TV became the familiar background to American life. It was a device that was always on. By the mid-1950s, family TV viewing averaged about five hours a day.[153] By 1955, most shows were taped, and the period of live television—like that of live radio—had come to an end.

Many people have written powerful books about the source and disastrous effects of TVs powerful attraction. My favorite is *The Plug-In Drug* (1977) by Marie Winn (who is living comfortably in New York City, and who graciously but firmly declined to be interviewed). As good as these books are, it would be a mistake to blame "television addiction" alone for the decline in social capital that occurred in America in the 1950s. As one contemporary critic has it: "Television cannot be considered the smoking gun or prime suspect or mysterious X-ray in the decline of American communities but, at best, a contributing factor in the changes that have occurred."[154]

Instead of blaming television for the disappearance of American community spirit, it's much more accurate to say that the war's end set in motion widespread sociological changes in which TV participated, much as flour or sugar participate in baking a cake. Following their victories in Europe and Japan, Americans wanted more than anything to reunite the nuclear family and get back to "normal"—whatever "normal" was. This commonplace sentiment gave rise to odd forms of what some historians have called the "domestic containment" of the 1950s.[155] Despite full-time employment during four years of war, most women returned to their role as homemakers as upwardly mobile second-generation families left the city center for pastoral suburban addresses in developments like the various Levittowns. Their homes, the postwar ranch houses of suburbia, had "no hall, no parlor, no stairs and no porch."[156] The American porch, which, in an earlier age had invited informal visits from passing neighbors, was replaced by a private patio at the rear of the suburban house. This marked "a real shift . . . in the way in which . . . lives [were] now centered inside the house rather than on the neighborhood or community."[157]

Inside the homes of suburbia, in a repetition of the radio-in-every-room plan, American families were soon encouraged to purchase more than one television set. In 1948, Motorola introduced a "portable" (twenty-six-pound) set. This soon became America's favorite second set. By 1952, TV ads showed family members dispersed throughout the home, watching television alone or in small, isolated clusters.[158] Individualized TV watching was "ironically . . . presented as a way to preserve family unity" since it prevented arguments about what to watch.[159] The shows most characteristic of the era—*I Love Lucy* (1951), *The Adventures of Ozzie & Harriet* (1952), *Make Room for Daddy/The Danny Thomas Show* (1953), *Father Knows Best* (1954), *Leave It to Beaver* (1957), and *My Three Sons* (1960)—valorized patriarchal control. At the same time, they constructed a wish-fulfillment world of family "togetherness." Togetherness itself was an ideological construct of the emerging television era; the word was first coined in a 1954 *McCall's* magazine article describing the nation's wish that the deprivation and emotional isolation of the war years be resolved in a utopia of abundance and familial harmony throughout America.[160] In reality, in ranch houses throughout America, people increasingly watched TV alone, and these periods of solitude lasted for longer and longer stretches of time.

Here, then, is one of the real sources of damage to social capital by any personal technology in which we overindulge. Like TV, activities such as playing video games or surfing the Internet clearly displace other activities from the limited ecology of our available waking hours. There is good evidence to show that excessive TV viewing increases aggressive behavior in children, and that such excessive use reduces creativity in adults and cognitive flexibility in children. But what TV does most and best is to displace our choices for other activities in much the same way as an invasive species displaces the established flora and fauna of any ecosystem it enters. Time spent watching television alone is time *not* spent doing other things with other people, and this includes interacting with friends and family members or playing community sports or even learning how to read.

The habitual use of television isolates people, and such habituation is a regular feature of its use. An elegantly constructed (but hard to read) study from British Columbia showed TV's displacement effect as early as 1986.[161] Community interaction in an isolated valley town identified only as "NoTel" was carefully documented before the arrival of a television transmitter in 1973. After a single channel became available to residents, community involvement in sports and clubs shrank remarkably. The results of this study have been borne out by many similar studies in subsequent decades. But the best we can say is that *for some reason*, television is a compelling diversion that tends to become habitual. When it does so, it displaces more sociable activities and leads to increasing isolation. Not surprisingly, as people turn into couch potatoes, they increasingly watch TV alone.

STARS

> Despite the lack of communicative give and take, the persona who is the focus of a parasocial relationship becomes integrated in the audience member's social circle.
>
> —Austin Sarat, *Studies in Law, Politics, and Society*, 2008

Devices like televisions are not intrinsically bad. Rather, technological inventions contribute to human isolation through excessive and unconscious use. As isolation increases, human beings typically make substitutions "for human contact . . . called parasocial relationships."[162] Alone among American subcultures, the Amish appear best able to recognize this danger. They debate the adoption of each new technology because they are concerned about its impact on their community's life. While the rest of us indulge to excess, the Amish accept few technological diversions that offer substitute satisfactions for human company. Although Amish people still "visit" each other faithfully, most other Americans were trained, during the twentieth century, to accept and practice technological indulgences that replace visits and friendship. Throughout history, isolation has been exploited by ascetic nuns and monks—a word derived from *monos*, meaning "alone"—to develop a deeper relationship with God. All para-social relationships share the same basic neurological mechanism as ascetic or mystical isolation: our brain chemistry requires relationships, and when they are absent, we "make do," as neuroscientist John Cacioppo terms it, by projecting human qualities onto nonhuman entities. Prominent among the modern technological or mass-media satisfactions of anthropomorphic projection are the prosthetic friendships that developed simultaneously with the emergence of Hollywood's "star system." Although there were stage "stars" before the arrival of electronic media, there is a considerable difference between modern stars and the actors and actresses of the era before film. Nineteenth-century stage stars were known to the public by their full or last names (for example, Mr. Richard Mansfield; Mr. Harry S. Northrup). But the theatergoing public knew very little about (and had little interest in) stage actors' private lives. In those days, there were no "media friends." How different is our attitude today toward "Brangelina," Lindsay, Britney, Johnny, Jack, Zack, Kanye, Kobe, Meryl, or whomever.

Knowledge about the private lives of media stars provides modern audiences with supplementary or substitute satisfactions for the friendships they *do not* find, foster, develop, or nurture during the time of their daily engagement with personal technology. Neuroscience has revealed that isolated individuals are much more given to developing "insecure, anxious attachment styles" and that these people are also more likely to form "perceived social bonds with television characters."[163] Television's "companionship substitution" gained its popularity by ameliorating the lack of friendships in our increasingly rootless society. Television, as Vance Packard pointed out in 1972, provided America with "instant neighbors like David Frost and Lucille Ball."[164] Sadly, one of the most popular themes of very successful TV shows is the audience's longing for friendship, which is gratified through the portrayal of tightly knit groups of characters in serials like *Friends*, *Cheers*, or *Seinfeld*. What is even sadder is the commonplace use of the words *friend* and *friendship* in theme songs used to publicize children's shows. Poignantly, the lyrics of "Hey, It's Franklin" directly address the children of the show's audience, declaring Franklin's willingness to "spend" time "with you."

This important connection (between isolation and anthropomorphism) underlies the prosthetic, one-way relationships between real human beings and media representations of fictional humans. Such "para-social" relationships were reinforced by the emergence of movie studios in the years 1909–1914. But the first media star was actually a singer who rarely appeared in films. From 1902 until his death in 1921, America voraciously consumed the petty details of Caruso's life: his womanizing, his social appearances, and his daily routine. In so doing, they began the first mass-media parasocial relationship with this Italian tenor whose rendition of "O Sole Mio" caught America's deepest yearnings in the early years of the new century. Not by coincidence, the "star system" began to emerge in Hollywood at this same moment. By 1909, the crudities of early film production and early film acting were becoming resolved as film became an increasingly competitive business. As one film historian puts it: "Film acting was evolving from the stylized pantomime of French movies then considered to be most advanced. . . . Simultaneous with the improvement in acting were advances in photography. Flickers and jumps were largely overcome, and the shadow images on theatre screens began to flow smooth and sharp. Film storytelling also acquired clarity and force."[165]

In 1910, American audiences responded to all these changes by becoming curious about the actors who appeared in the productions of the ten American film companies licensed to use contemporary filmmaking patents. The best of these companies was Biograph, whose innovations included studio lighting, cross-cut editing, and comedic chase scenes. Biograph's formidable director, D. W. Griffith, trained a generation of silent-film actors, but their identities were kept from the public in an effort to make film audiences focus on the satisfying quality of branded "Biograph" films. This changed when the company fired its most popular actress in 1909. Known to America only as the "Biograph Girl," Florence Lawrence was Canadian-born, but her looks typified the Harrison Fisher era of American beauty (as perhaps Drew Barrymore does today). Desperate to establish a reputation for his new company, Independent Motion Pictures (IMP), Carl Laemmle hired Florence Lawrence in 1909 and gave her screen credit while simultaneously billing her as "America's most popular moving picture actress." Responding to a rumor that she had been murdered in St. Louis (a rumor Laemmle himself may have started), Miss Lawrence traveled to the city to prove it wasn't so. There, in a brilliant publicity coup, she was mobbed. The crowd stole items of clothing from her. She fainted. After that, her fame was ensured. America adopted her as a personal favorite, and men and women wrote letters to her as though she were their intimate friend.

At the same time, although they were not yet called stars,

other famous "picture players" began emerging as print organs began to support and capitalize on the new kind of celebrity. In the spring of 1910, at the *New York Dramatic Mirror*, Frank E. Woods established a Moving Picture Department that reported on motion-picture actors and identified them by name. *Moving Picture World*, which had begun as an industry organ in 1907, became increasingly focused on screen actors' personalities and lives, and Carl Laemmle, having learned a thing or two from promoting the Biograph Girl, devoted himself to popularizing a new star, Mary Pickford. In the years before the beginning of World War I, Florence Turner, Broncho Billy, Tom Mix, and Charlie Chaplin would emerge as early American "stars" in a system of media friendships built on mass popularity. The fame of these "stars" was supported and encouraged by the print publicity of newspapers and movie fan magazines that began to emerge in increasing numbers.

The year 1907 was a pivotal one in terms of laying the foundation of the star system. Between 1907 and 1908, film production shifted toward narrative forms and away from the documentaries that had predominated since the early days of the kinescope. As this happened, the form changed from a medium of attractions, sensations, and location shots to a medium of story, personality, and studio-centered production. The new form was more predictable and could be produced with greater reliability for less cost. As modern techniques "took," both camera work and acting changed. The mise en scène now allowed for increasing subtlety in actors' expressions and began to emphasize details, gestures, and facial expressions. As directors acquired increasing skill, interior psychological reality could be represented through montage and close-up sequences. The stylizations and conventions of stage acting could not accomplish any remotely similar intimacy. Of course, this invited the audience to focus on the person and personalities of the actors appearing on the screens before them.[166] After 1913, stories about actors' personal lives off-screen began to circulate regularly in the popular press, perhaps as a way for fans to test the screen performance against the "real" character of their favorite actors. As fan magazines and publicists proliferated, technologically achieved stardom became the first stage in substituting prosthetic friendships for human connections focused on human beings . . . stars.

No one could know that the next step would make machines themselves substitutes for human company. . . .

CHAPTER 2

WIRED FOR SOUND*

Walkin' around with my head full of music
cassette in my pocket and I'm gonna' use it
Ster-EE-Oh!
Out on the street, you know
WOH WOH WOH
I'm wired for sound.

—Cliff Richards, performing "Wired for Sound," words and music by B. A. Robertson and Alan Tarney, 1979

MUSIC *IS* TECHNOLOGY

As mobile technology invaded the public spaces of our cities, music, the simplest, most innocent and most characteristic of human pleasures, was completely transformed. Today, plugged into an iPod® at the gym or listening to a drive-time radio show alone during your commute, you might sometimes wonder (as I do) "what is music" or "how does it take the edge off of loneliness, anxiety, and sadness?" These questions are almost as old as music itself. But since Sony's introduction of the original Walkman® in December 1979, new questions have emerged, including

- Has modern music become an enjoyable alternative to social interaction and have headphones become a public sign that we don't want to interact?

- Does an iPod (or any headphone device) insulate us from too many contacts, too much urban stimulus?
- Do city dwellers rely on solitary music during moments alone because solitary listening is a palliative (soothing or comforting) technology?

The Walkman began both as a reaction and as a market alternative to the first "portable" stereos that went on sale in America in 1976 and quickly achieved a reputation for obnoxiousness. Perched on the shoulders of an angry underclass, these twenty-pound monsters had a profound sociological impact. In the warm months of the early eighties, in large cities like New York, the police issued about one summons a day related to the loud playing of these devices. They also confiscated a machine every three days.[1] The boogie-box, or boom box, was "a big, though portable stereo cassette player . . . [with] . . . only one volume setting—*loud.* It played only in places that should be quiet, such as parks, and in places that are already too noisy, such as streets, buses and subways. Nobody ever asks the fellow who totes it to turn it off. That's because he's usually eight feet tall and weighs 400 pounds. If he's small, he is generally believed to conceal a knife in one pocket and a zip gun in the other."[2]

Compared to the "box," the smaller, cooler, and more personal Walkman offered a very different and very private musical alternative. Retailers described it as a "unique product for personal gratification."[3] Private indulgence in personally selected music was the Walkman's most attractive feature, and the practice of making personal, pirated music mixes began in earnest in 1979 in order to accommodate the Walkman craze. In 1980, a product called the "bone-phone" was marketed briefly as an alternative to the Walkman's isolating supra-aural headphones, but it faded quickly because bone-phone listeners wore the device like a collar around their necks and remained engaged with their surroundings as the music played. From the beginning, few Walkman owners wanted musical accompaniment for a sociable stroll through the city. They were seeking refuge in a musical bubble. For this reason, competing models often had names like the "Intimate" or the "Solo." Also, because enjoying personal music became a totally exclusionary experience, Sony CEO Akio Morita discontinued the second headphone jack that had been available on the original Walkman (TPS L2) as it had on some of Morita's transistor radios (the Sony TR55, TR7, and TR63) during the 1950s.[4] It was now clear that Sony customers wanted isolation and a comforting *respite* from the intrusions of the distractions of the noisy city, so the sleeker, all-metal second model of the Walkman (WM 2), which debuted in 1981, no longer had two headphone jacks. The Walkman, in fact, was a refinement of the "Isolator," the short-lived 1925 thinking cap or helmet that eliminated distractions in the immediate environment. Instead of a helmet, Walkmans used music to eliminate distractions. As recording historian Evan Eisenberg observes, in the cacophony of cities, "music becomes a substitute for silence."[5] Many contemporary journalists welcomed the portable refuge proffered by Sony's Walkman, including Pulitzer laureate George Will, famous for his acid prose:

> Some sociologists and . . . cranks are quite cross about the popularity of the Walkman. They say the device is "isolating" and prevents people from "relating." I say: Yes . . . isn't that great? Leaving aside the fact that a walk with Bach is bliss, who wants to "relate" to strangers in the street or . . . on airlines? Who does not want to be isolated from the blather and screech of metropolitan life. Walkman is the civilized answer to something that should be illegal, those 20 pound stereo "boxes" carried by young men with strong backs and bad manners . . . that pummel the ears of anyone within 50 yards.[6]

The movement from the intrusive social use of the boom box to the personal enjoyment of the Walkman, from the use of music as communication (albeit unpleasant communication) to the palliative (soothing or comforting) use of music, was anticipated in a famous passage about consumer music written by Theodor Adorno, who died in 1969, ten years before the Walkman's debut: "It [consumer music] creates an illusion of immediacy in a totally mediated world, of proximity between strangers, [of] the warmth of those who come to feel a chill of unmitigated struggle of all against all."[7]

Remarkably, the movement from music as a group activity to the lonely simulation of togetherness through prerecorded headphone sound repeats the actual evolutionary history of music itself. New interdisciplinary research into music's origins shows that the first purpose of music was undoubtedly social and communicative. Increasingly, neuroscientists, anthropologists, and paleopsychologists in new fields called "bio-musicology" or "music cognition" agree about the broad outlines of a theory identifying music as one of humankind's most formidable genetic adaptations. We can now say definitively that hominins (a recent term meaning "humans or their ancestors") used music to control interpersonal distance by promoting separation or unity. They did this in a variety of ways: early primate calls most closely resembling music act as warnings intended to repel competitors for space or mates. Mainly, though, human music extends the use of patterned sounds and often deploys it to achieve "social cohesion." In other words, listening to music collectively unites groups, reduces individual stress, and erases ego boundaries in order to facilitate the emergence of group identity. Furthermore, music can also move social groups to achieve a collective effort through uniform, rhythmic, and regulated cooperation, a social phenomenon that actually repeats the synchronous, pulsative release of the neuropeptide oxytocin during primate grooming and human musical behaviors.

Music's encouragement of social cohesion is one of its most ancient attributes. Researchers in the small subfield of archaeoacoustics have determined that Neolithic cave paintings cluster around points of resonance where—presumably—our male ancestors assembled, sang, worshipped, and prepared themselves for group hunts.[8] The main point, however, is that the social poles of repulsion and attraction remain with us as the deepest purposes embedded in music's origins. This remains true, even though there are practical difficulties with any attempt to describe how any tool, any skill, any body of knowledge like music was originally acquired; how its uses then multiplied; and why we now continue to maintain its active presence in the extensive repertoire of adaptive behaviors that we vaguely call technology. One of the clearest expressions of the view that, like all technologies, the nature and purpose of human music has mutated and expanded over millennia of use appears in a recent study by Aniruddh Patel, a cognitive neuroscientist who studies music's impact on the brain: "Technologies invented by humans have become intimately integrated into the fabric of our life, transforming the lives of individuals and groups. This never-ending cycle of invention, integration and transformation . . . has ancient roots. I believe music can sensibly be thought of in this framework . . . as something we invented that transforms human life . . . as with other transformative technologies, once invented and experienced it becomes . . . impossible to give . . . up."[9]

Other ancient technologies obey the rule that, over time, as we confront new challenges, the purposes of our skills and tools change. Our oldest known technology, stone tool making, began the "stone age" around 2.6 million years ago, but it has largely fallen out of humankind's everyday technological vocabulary. Next to it, the controlled use of fire is recognizably our oldest, still extant technology. Its use involves such an extensive body of applications and knowledge that it's difficult to recognize which of its many uses came first: warming us on frigid nights; supplying personal and community security from nocturnal predators; extending the productive working hours of daylight, or cooking raw food to make it more digestible *and* to make those who eat it less susceptible to disease. Of course, fire does all these things and much more: it can purify water; it can clear land while simultaneously making it more arable. It can prevent infection and stop bleeding from a bad wound. It can preserve food and make it more flavorful. It can signal others from a great distance. It can dispose of garbage and the dead.

Fire is a powerful technology because our reasons for and methods of manipulating it have expanded like a coral reef adding layers of use over tens of thousands of years. Fire brought with it a greater degree of comfort, and it preceded the development of clothing, which would have been unnecessary for our hirsute ancestors. Because fire has the most visible applications of any human tool set, we often think of it—casually and incorrectly—as our oldest technology. No other species manipulates fire. There are no precise dates available for when we began to manipulate it, but the earliest suggested date of 1.6 million years ago is remarkable for its antiquity.[10] By this time, early *Homo erectus* (sometimes called *Homo ergaster*) had emerged. *Erectus* combined a number of adaptations that had been set in motion by bipedalism (the ability to walk upright on two legs).

There are many explanations for bipedalism: some think it enabled us to pick low-hanging fruit; some imagine it facilitated seeing over the tall grass of the African savannah; others argue that it was a more economical form of transportation that required fewer calories and therefore made foraging more productive. By far the most creative explanation of bipedalism is that it developed as a means of reducing our ancestors' exposure to the African sun when bipeds from wooded areas increasingly made their way into open, sunnier habitats. Even today, hyperthermia remains a very real danger, killing more human beings annually than any other external cause. By "standing tall," early hominins could "stay cool" and limit the risk of overheating their bodies by exposing less body area to the intense sun once they had left the shade of the forest canopy.[11] This development was eventually followed by the nearly complete loss of body hair, an adaptation that characterizes our unusual primate subspecies. We are the naked ape. Ironically, our incipient hairlessness may have also made early human beings receptive to the use of fire as a tool for nighttime heating because after our naked ancestors lost their body hair, they had no defense against the swift drop in temperatures that followed sundown on the African savannah. By standing up to cool down, we began a process that would make the progressively less hirsute hominins welcome the use of fire as a means of providing community warmth all night, every night.

As we'll see, the emergence of every technology, including music, is full of such reversals and ironies.

DISTANCE GROOMING

> The more primitive a society, the greater their finesse in intonation and sound perception.
>
> —Iegor Reznikoff and Michel Dauvois, "La dimension sonore des grottes ornées," *Bulletin de la Société Préhistorique Française*, 1988

Did bipedalism actually encourage music?

The ability to walk upright brought with it many changes as significant for our species as fire use and subsequent hair loss. Bipedalism demanded that we develop larger brains, which were needed to balance while standing upright: bigger brains were also needed to regulate the simultaneous, rhythmic use of the large muscle groups required for walking and running across the wide area needed to feed groups of *Homo erectus*.[12] Bipedalism facilitated both foraging and hunting because it freed the hands to gather food and to manipulate weapons, tools, and instruments *while* the body remained in motion. Bipedalism also changed the location of the connection between spine and skull, reshaping the entire skull and forcing the human larynx to sink deeper into an elongated throat, where it became capable of producing many more varied, sonorous, and mellifluous sounds.[13] This is the first preparation our species made for extending the range of primate music. But even as bipedalism increased the range and nature of human sound, it may also have increased the need for such sounds.

The oldest known musical instruments are the bone and ivory flutes discovered in fragments in the caves of Swabia during the late 1990s by Maria Molina and other members of Nicholas Conard's archaeological team. At most, they are about thirty-seven thousand years old. Music, however, is much older. Zoologist Thomas Geissmann observes that the "human voice is often identified as the most ancestral instrument used in music."[14] Archaeo-acousticians Iegor Reznikoff and Michel Dauvois make the lineage of music explicit when they point out that "eventually . . . instruments were introduced to supplement the (human) voice."[15]

The best guess today is that long before language appeared (no one can say how long), vocal music began as a fundamentally interpersonal and communicative activity. Nonmusical vocalizations are common among mammals and primates, and Darwin himself noticed that "gibbon-apes . . . [produce] true musical . . . singing."[16] Darwin felt that music was part of male courtship display, but since his time, this view has been challenged by other theories about the adaptive potential of music and how it contributed to the natural selection of *Homo erectus*.

Each of the four species who emit musical calls (gibbon apes, titi monkeys, and the prosimian indris and tarsier species) share one other important characteristic: these four species are also the only known monogamous primates. Their primate songs are territorial and lay claim to a currently occupied area while simultaneously discouraging others from entering it. Once again, stereo boom boxes were used this way when they first emerged in the late 1970s. The "box" phenomenon was described in its time as "the ultimate in galling urban experiences—the kid with a blasting portable radio."[17] But long before personal stereos and entirely without the assistance of a Marantz Superscope (1976) or a Sony CF-520 (1978), gibbons were able to define and defend both their foraging space and their mating partner using only their powerful, beautiful, natural voices. Anthropologist Dean Falk paraphrases the message of gibbon song in this charming way: "This is my territory, *and* my mate. I'm healthy and strong as you can tell from my wonderful singing voice—so keep away."[18]

Similarly, all other primate vocalizations are used across distance. The most basic calls are alarms that warn members of the same species of a predator's invasion of their communal territory. Nonetheless, all primate vocalizations are used to control either territory or distance between groups and individuals. Such calls communicate, but they are prelinguistic because there are no identifiable, repeated words or grammatical structures. Melody, intensity, and repetition alone are used to convey meaning. Some calls repel: these are noisy, of short duration, and rise quickly. Other calls attract: these have a long rising sound, and their duration is elongated. In 1989, Stanford child psychologist Anne Fernald discovered that "motherese" followed four basic intonation patterns throughout all human languages.[19] More recently, a fascinating study at the University of Bremen connected the rhythms of a variety of animal calls to the patterns of four types of human songs, including lullabies, songs to attract attention, songs of praise, and warrior songs. Beautifully—Elegantly—Simply. The deep structures of human music derive from the patterns of animal vocalizations.[20] This and other evidence about the social nature of music led many theorists to speculate that music primarily concerns "social cohesion"; in other words, it helps "cement social bonds between members of ancestral groups via its role in ritual and in group music making."[21] Still, the most convincing and most interesting explanation that has emerged from the group of ideas concerning music's adaptive origins is the "putting the baby down" hypothesis. The outlines of this theory have now been refined for over a generation by Dean Falk with supporting evidence from Ellen Dissanayake (Dis-en-ai-a-kuh), who provided Falk with her initial inspiration.

Continuity between animal vocalizations and human music seems especially remarkable when we consider short-distance vocalizations used during mother-infant separations. There is a wide variety of such "contact" or "isolation" calls, and these are not limited to primates. As Dean Falk points out, lost or separated infants of many species give distinctive "calls that are recognized by mothers as coming from their offspring. House-mice pups produce ultrasonic calls . . . infant opossums make sneezing sounds, baby horseshoe bats produce broadband calls, [fallen] birds . . . emit isolation peeps . . . dolphin infants produce isolation whistles . . . golden potto infants produce clicks and tsics . . . baby aye-ayes emit eeeps or creees . . . squirrel monkeys produce easily localized and individually recognizable isolation peeps . . . chimpanzee infants utter hoos."[22]

Proponents of "putting the baby down" believe that human music likely arose from these calls as another result of the most radical change that took place in our ancient African ancestors. Bipedalism, once again, freed the hands of foraging mothers to collect food. In order to achieve bipedalism, the pelvic girdle changed in shape, which restricted the human birth canal, allowing only the passage of immature babies whose skulls were not yet fully developed. The natural selection for this mutation was absolute and quite brutal. As childbirth became more difficult, those women whose babies were born at a slightly earlier time survived better. Anatomical changes gradually developed until *Homo erectus* infants were characteristically born at a stage *before* the dimensions of their brains and skulls matured. Consequently, bipedalism resulted in the exaggerated and prolonged helplessness and dependence ("altriciality") of human infants. As a result of their children's premature birth and postponed maturity, human mothers created more sophisticated strategies to facilitate infant-mother bonding. Moreover, both because human babies were immature and because human mothers walked upright, human babies could not cling to their mothers' backs or underbellies like primate babies could. Instead, *erectus* babies had to be carried. For this reason, during foraging, human mothers needed to develop new strategies to soothe, comfort, and placate their babies, who had to be "put down" in order to free their moms to forage or to continue work while baby slept (although this last point is still a very controversial one). Perhaps this is why human beings generally respond more favorably to female rather than to male voices, and, in turn, this may be the reason that the most successful virtual robots, like "AMTRAK-Julie" or the iPhone's® "Siri," are female.

Unlike our primate ancestors, as we became human, physical contact between mother and infant probably became radically reduced, so perhaps we are doomed to live dissatisfied as creatures who experience a primal longing as part of our evolutionary development. Sometimes I wonder if this fact explains the misplaced materialism of our growth economy. Do we compensate for a deep emotional dissatisfaction by displacing it with acquisitions and greed? Whatever the answer, our ability to bridge the widening gap between mother and infant was supplemented as vocal communications—song and, eventually, language—became increasingly sophisticated. Recent research has shown that Mom's comforting voice releases the trust hormone oxytocin into the bloodstreams of pre-teenage girls after a stressful event, no matter whether Mom is present and huggable or merely delivering her reassurance over an iPhone.[23] In this way, linguistic behavior clearly extends the touch and grooming techniques that many mammals use to promote "cooperation," the unique characteristic both of oxytocin's release and its sociobiological function.[24] It is fascinating to note that while a mother's reassuring—though distant—voice can reduce the stress hormone cortisol and increase oxytocin levels, a text message (however reassuring) is not sufficient for this purpose.[25] (In fact, it is easier to lie, and—apparently—lying is more common when text message is the medium of communication. Perhaps the absence of oxytocin's bond facilitates the activity of telling a lie.[26])

The recently discovered fact that oxytocin release follows vocal reassurance both in person and over a cell phone (but not via text messages or e-mails), confirms the basic tenets—if not the precise claims—of a loosely related family of communication theories called, successively, "social presence theory" (SPT), "media richness theory" (MRT), and "media naturalness theory" (MNT). These protean sets of ideas all share the attempt to "rate" the communicative effectiveness of various technologies for business purposes. They began modestly long before the Internet existed.

In 1976, the British Post Office sponsored research into the effects of telephony and telephone conferencing, which resulted in a pivotal study called *The Social Psychology of Telecommunications*.[27] This influential work claimed that the social impact or effectiveness of a communicative medium depended on the "social presence" permitted to its users. Social presence among users increased according to the degree of acoustic, visual, and physical contact inherent in the medium. It was assumed that the greater social presence among users translated to greater immediacy, intimacy, warmth, and rapport. For these reasons—at the time—telephoning clients was assumed to be infinitely superior to writing business letters or memos.

A decade after their first appearance, these ideas were revised by changing the emphasis from the phatic (or emotional) function of language to the semantic. Assuming that reducing uncertainty and equivocality are the main goals of communication, management professors Richard Daft and Robert Lengel claimed that the virtue of what they called "rich" media was not so much the "social presence" it contributed to participants but rather the medium's capacity to reduce ambiguity. Once again, these ideas privileged vocal and visual media over written ones for complex messages or interactions.[28] Unfortunately, many of Daft and Lengel's ideas are linguistically naïve. The social identity model of deindividuation effects (SIDE) theorists soon pointed out that meaning in business communications often is a strategic construct deliberately created to achieve a specific effect.

At the turn of the millennium, a graduate engineer and managerial IT specialist at Texas A&M University reexamined Daft and Lengel's ideas, noting that there was little empirical data to support many of MRT's central assumptions. In two extremely influential papers, Nereu (Ned) Kock followed an inspired impulse to examine the face-to-face origins of hominid communications.[29] Kock then rated of electronic communicative media based on the certainty that

> natural communication involves at least five key elements: (1) a high degree of co-location, which would allow the individuals engaged in a communication interaction to see and hear each other, as well as share the same environment while

> engaging in communication, (2) a high degree of synchronicity, which would allow . . . individuals . . . to quickly exchange communicative stimuli, (3) the ability to convey and observe facial expressions, (4) the ability to convey and observe body language, and (5) the ability to convey and listen to speech. Given this, we can define the naturalness of a communication medium created by an e-communication technology based on the degree to which [it] selectively incorporates [these] elements.[30]

Significantly, without prior knowledge of "putting the baby down" or the new research about oxytocin release being provoked by listening to a mother's voice over an iPhone, Ned Kock was able to develop a powerfully descriptive communicative media theory that would accommodate these new data. When I first discussed the idea for this book with David Suzuki in 2009, he interrupted me excitedly and led me into a conference room that Cisco Unified Videoconferencing systems donated to his foundation. Cisco really is the next best thing to being in the same room as your conference partners, but for those of us who can't afford a million-dollar investment, the next-best device is simply the telephone, as urban sociologist Alladi Venkatesh observes. "The telephone is used in strong network relationships (contacting significant others), in local contacts, and in urgent situations. Of the different modes of communication available . . . the telephone is regarded as the most personal."[31]

The vocal behaviors that accomplish "distance grooming" over cell phones include canned songs and, of course, Mom's speaking voice, which begins as baby talk. Baby talk is a specifically human group of prelinguistic utterances developed to accomplish the task of bonding mother and infant across the gulf of physical separation. Mothers themselves share this opinion. Research at the University of Surrey has shown that all of the ninety-one mothers surveyed sang (privately) to their babies despite the explicitly expressed belief (by exactly half of the moms) that they lacked good "singing voices." Nearly one-third of the mothers agreed that it was easier to sing to an infant than to speak. When these women were asked "why they sang," common responses included the beliefs that singing soothed or entertained the infants or made them react and interact with their mothers' presence: "Other reasons have been more reflective of mothers' states, in as much as singing helps them to relax themselves and to feel calm. One response has stated that singing takes the frustration out of feeding time; that it makes for quality time, where you can 'cut off.'" "Quality time" was a term also voiced by participants in the Sound Start Project in relation to singing at home. Other responses to the open questions are demonstrating an awareness of maternal emotional support through singing; as in "*it reassures (the infant) of my presence*" (emphasis added).[32]

If this is an important first indication of the validity of "putting the baby down," there are other, more convincing connections between singing (music) and the mother-infant bond. Premature infants especially seem to benefit from music. Playing prerecorded music stabilizes oxygen-saturation levels in babies' blood, enhancing the development of premature infants. Premature female infants also respond so well to a combination of massage and music that they are discharged an average of eleven days sooner than other preemies. Recently, researchers have learned that premature infants listening to live lullabies sung by a female vocalist gain weight at an accelerated rate, presumably because their rate of rhythmic sucking increases in response to the songs.[33]

If it seems clear that babies are attuned to music, baby talk is the most likely candidate for an immediate precursor to human song. In 1997, independent scholar Ellen Dissanayake had this realization about music's origins. Despite Darwin's idea that music is simply "sexual display," Dean Falk, an anthropologist who participated in one of Dissanayake's earliest workshops, seized on the concept that "baby talk" (elsewhere called motherese or infant-directed speech/IDS) is the most obvious and economical precursor to music.[34] At first, Dean Falk found considerable resistance to her suggestion that motherese preceded music. Falk's recent book, *Finding Our Tongues*, expands on Dissanayake's thesis that an "entire package of [rhythmic premusical] behaviors—vocal, visual, and kinetic—(not just talk or singing) was the origin of music [and that music] itself [was] simultaneously [an undifferentiated form of] music/dance."[35]

Falk believes that motherese is the origin of music *and also* the most likely precursor for language itself. This notion is a radical departure from traditional linguistics. As a consequence, during the nineties, Falk encountered considerable resistance to these ideas from linguists. This resistance persists in popular books that ridicule her idea by calling it the "Ronettes Theory" of musical origins.[36] Eventually Falk began to wonder if her and Dissanayake's theory was "poorly received partly because [it] emphasized the role of women and infants—rather than men—in human evolution."[37] It doesn't seem impossible that gender politics would intrude on a debate challenging the precepts of any academic field, including linguistics. To an outsider, though, Falk's difficulties in finding a sympathetic reception among linguists fall neatly into the description of "paradigm shift," described by Thomas Kuhn in *The Structure of Scientific Revolutions* (1962). In Kuhn's terms, during the late '90s, Falk's anthropological theory of the origins of language and music was "incommensurable" with the established paradigm of linguistics. They were talking to each other while embedded in different and mutually exclusive gestalts. A "shift" was needed before scientific progress could occur.

That shift lasted an entire decade, during which extensive medical research by a team led by Sandra Trehub confirmed aspects of "putting the baby down" with quantifiable and convincing data. Trehub's work reveals that maternal music is intrinsically interesting to infants (much more interesting than maternal speech).[38] Trehub's group was able to show—definitively—that infant stress-arousal levels (as indicated by the presence of cortisol in their saliva) dropped and stayed low for a prolonged period of time after their mothers sang to them.[39] The comforts of music, in other words, are quite real, and recently born infants are even more predisposed toward maternal music than they are to human language. More recent (2002/2009) experiments have focused on the neuropeptide oxytocin, a difficult substance to study since it is a large molecule that disintegrates rapidly, and also because it is secreted in pulses, so its blood-concentration levels are unstable and many blood samples are required during an experiment.[40] Nonetheless, the connections between oxytocin, music, and public health have become a current topic in Sweden, where choral activity plays an important social role. Two Swedish teams involving registered nurses have been able to handle the tricky demands of the subjects' blood work and have thus confirmed that *both* participating in music and simply listening passively to it facilitate oxytocin release.[41] As primates groom each other, they experience bodily warmth and social cohesion brought on by oxytocin release. Humans have similar experiences when we give and receive backrubs or hugs. In addition, whether we are alone or in a group, and whether our music is live or canned, when we listen to it, we get a reassuring fix of the unique love-and-trust hormone, oxytocin. Music is grooming at a distance. It facilitates oxytocin release.

PALLIATIVE MUSIC

> Music listening increases oxytocin secretion . . . this effect seems to have a causal relation from the psychological (music makes people feel good) to the physical (oxytocin release) . . . these positive effects are sufficient to suggest the proposed regimen of music listening after open-heart surgery.
>
> —Ulrica Nilsson, PhD, RNA, "Soothing Music Can Increase Oxytocin Levels during Bed Rest after Open-Heart Surgery," *Journal of Clinical Nursing*, 2009

Today, it's almost anticlimactic to suggest that music offers us a reassurance of human care and company, a guarantee that, even though we are isolated or separated from those we love most, nonetheless, we are not alone. "Grooming at a distance" is still grooming: it prompts a release of oxytocin while simultaneously reducing cortisol levels that produce stress. Recently, a dramatic shooting in Mexico highlighted music's ability to calm and reassure children when a drug cartel in Monterrey killed five people at a taxi stand near Alfonso Reyes elementary school. As soon as the shooting began, teacher Martha Rivera Alanis ordered her charges (five- and six-year-olds) to lie on their kindergarten classroom floor while bullets whizzed outside the windows. Once on the floor, Rivera Alanis led the children in a rousing chorus from their favorite TV show, *Barney and Friends*. In a cell-phone video made of events inside the classroom during the shootings, the expressions on the children's faces go from alarm to pleasure as their teacher begins to lead them in the song.[42]

Although it is incidental to the original group functions of music, the use of music to provide confidence, reassurance, and comfort during stressful events begins with participatory group songs like Lillebjørn Nilsen's "Barn av regnbuen" (Children of the Rainbow), recently performed by forty thousand Norwegians outside of an Oslo courthouse during the trial of Norwegian mass murderer Anders Behring Breivik. The same confidence and reassurance provided by such group performances transfer from participatory group events to the solitary pleasure of listening to Bach or Keith Jarrett during your commute. For want of a better term, I call the musical soothing that occurs in the absence of bonding or "social cohesion," the "palliative" use of music. It is unique to urban life, and—as a mainstream activity—it dates from the earliest decades of the twentieth century onward. Since the development of recording technology, anyone has been able to use music to soothe and comfort himself or herself whenever he or she is alone. The skill required to play a simple instrument like the forty-thousand-year-old bone flute Maria Molina discovered in southeastern Germany has been replaced by the on-and-off switch or successive generations of recording technologies. Since 1879, we have been able to divert ourselves by listening to sounds and songs over a coin-operated phonograph. Since 1979, we have been able to comfort ourselves on the move by deploying headphones (and, later, earbuds) while navigating the rugged and uneven urban landscape between our islands of social acceptance and familiarity. The technologies of mobile, personal music that we accept today as affordable luxuries are actually an important part of human social life embedded in our primate biochemistry. Unfortunately, we no longer enjoy music primarily at group gatherings but in the algid spaces of our cities in the fleeting moments between work and home. If musical culture began as communicative song deep in our hominin past, in the twentieth century, it became a lonely and isolating solace for the modern iMan.

ACCESSIBILITY IN AMERICAN MUSIC

> I hear America singing, the varied carols I hear,
> Those of mechanics, each one singing his as it should be,
> blithe and strong.
> The carpenter singing as he measures his plank or beam.
> The mason singing as he makes ready for work,
> or as he leaves off work,
> The boatman singing what belongs to him in his boat,
> the deckhand singing on the steamboat deck.
> The shoemaker sitting as he sits on his bench, the hatter
> singing as he stands,
> The wood-cutter's song, the ploughboy's on his way in the
> morning, or at noon-intermission or at sundown,
> The delicious singing of the mother, or of the young wife
> at work, or of the girl sewing and washing.
> Each singing what belongs to him or her and to none else.
> The day what belongs to the day—at night the party
> of young fellows, robust, friendly.
> Singing with open mouths their strong, melodious songs.
>
> —Walt Whitman, *Leaves of Grass*, 1869

No one knows when we began making music for merely personal pleasure, but music has always offered solace and comfort to the solitary. Since mothers were *probably* the first to sing to their children, they may also have been the first to use song for other purposes, including singing for their own pleasure. We now know that grieving mother primates created symbolic tools like dolls to help them cope with the loss of a child.[43] Perhaps solitary music began in a similar way as a coping mechanism to ease the grief of a dead child's memory. Alternatively, perhaps a more mature child, unwillingly separated from his or her mother, began to sing spontaneously to comfort himself or herself (this behavior would have made the child more likely to be found, and such a successfully rescued child could have passed along more musically adapted genes). However it began, solitary song was once, to be sure, a very new way to use music. Still, it was not a radical departure. Despite music's origins as a social and communicative medium, and despite the fact that *when it is shared* its effects are generally more satisfying, clearly music has the potential to soothe and comfort either one person alone or many people together. When we are happy (perhaps to make ourselves happy), we sing alone in the car, in the shower, or on the decks of small, affordable sailboats on a bright, calm sea. We also sing in the company of others at sports events, in churches, in temples, in school assemblies, and while driving the car when suddenly our shared favorites reach out to us from the radio. On all these occasions, music is buoyant and comforting. It is comforting to sing. It is comforting to dance. This is true even if we do it badly or if we are compelled to do it. Music is contagious fun, and, like sex and pizza, bad music is often better than no music at all.

Although it is difficult to document, it is for precisely this reason that popular music found an enthusiastic welcome on the American frontier. In the lonely wilderness, music offered its comfort to the loneliest and bravest pioneers. Davy Crockett, for example, was a renowned fiddler. Unfortunately, paper, ink, and literacy were in short supply in the early days of the wilderness, so very few writers recorded the phenomenon of homespun frontier music. Only occasionally did visitors leave us an impression of early American diversions in a prose snapshot of frontier life. Here is the intrepid and highly educated Englishwoman Harriet Martineau writing about the reassurance and comfort of human-made sound in the American wilderness one year after Crockett's death at the Battle of the Alamo in 1836:

> All travelers in the White Mountains know Ethan A. Crawford's hospitality. He cannot be said to live in solitude, inasmuch

> as there is another house in the valley. . . . Crawford's is a virtual solitude except for three months of the year . . . [so] we were little prepared for such entertainment as we found. After a supper of fine lake trout, a son of our host played to us on a nameless instrument, made by the joiners who put the house together and highly creditable to their ingenuity. It was something *like the harmonica in form* [this in 1837!] and the bagpipes in tone; but, well-played as it was by the boy it was highly agreeable. Then Mr. Crawford danced an American jig, to the fiddling of a relation of his. The dancing was somewhat solemn; but its good faith made up for any want of mirth. He had other resources for the amusement of his guests; a gun wherewith he was wont to startle the mountain echoes, till, one day, it burst: . . . also a horn, which blown on a calm day, brings chorus of sweet response from the far hill sides.[44]

Martineau's description captures an essential difference between European and American music. In her native England (and in Europe generally), the most powerful social institutions (church, court, and state) used and required music for their rites and observances. Consequently, the spectrum of European musicianship included many professionals who enjoyed patronage and support during the widespread practice of a prestigious art form. North America, on the other hand, lacked similar sponsorship, so "the creation of a diverse musical life on these shores" relied on the entrepreneurial skills of the transplanted musicians themselves.[45] Competent European immigrants were compelled to find ways to market their services to an enthusiastic but often unsophisticated populace. Centuries before access to local newspapers or magazines (and well before radio and television), music was the most prevalent choice among a limited selection of pervasive daily American diversions like playing cards or horseshoes.

Many people sang or played their instruments daily at their workplaces, their homes, their choirs, or social gatherings.

Consequently, the few skilled musicians in America became teachers of music and retailers of instruments, instruction booklets, and sheet music. Demand was great, and these businessmen-musicians "taught Americans that they could have music in their homes if they made it themselves."[46] In pursuing music as a diversion, Americans became accustomed to an attitude of democratic access to music that originated in the can-do, do-it-yourself attitude Martineau described in 1837. To meet the American combination of modest skills and widespread desire to create and enjoy music, music publishers emerged. But it was a long road to the professionalization of popular music that characterizes the refined consumer products of Broadway and Tin Pan Alley. Even as popular music emerged, other vernacular traditions of music became increasingly established among diverse American groups: regions, races, and professions all developed characteristic song-forms since "songs—short, melodious, [and] simple to perform . . . appealed to amateur performers."[47]

The most distinct example of a vernacular tradition of music was one that emphasized democratic access for all Americans. This was the shape-note movement that began simply as a means of promoting widespread literacy of musical notation. For similar reasons, Noah Webster instituted his spelling reforms by publishing his famous dictionary in 1828, but the reformed spelling movement was based on observations Webster made in an earlier essay about orthography published in his *Compendious Dictionary of the English Language* in 1806. Where did Webster get the idea that literacy might be encouraged by promoting a simpler notation?

Noah Webster is famous as a lexicographer, but first and foremost he was a publisher whose career lasted sixty years. In the 1780s, Webster became one of three Americans to receive copyright protection for works printed in the United States. Among this select group of American publishers was Andrew

Law, an ordained Calvinist minister. Law was not only Webster's publishing colleague; he was also a Connecticut neighbor (or fellow "Connecticuter"). Law's efforts to spread religion using sacred music had led to a combined career as a singing master and tune book publisher in Cheshire, Connecticut, about thirty miles from West Hartford, Webster's family home. Law's first book, *Select Harmony*, appeared in 1779. In 1794, Law published three volumes of *The Art of Singing*; volume one is the *Musical Primer*, the first printed attempt to teach Americans how to read music.

Law's explanation of his religious project is as straightforward as the man: "The harshness of our [American] singing must be corrected. Our voices must be filed. Every tone must be rendered smooth, persuasive and melting."[48] But Law found that ordinary musical notation was too cumbersome and abstract for many of his pupils. Learning to read music requires substantial simultaneous intellectual effort as music students struggle to acquire technical skill. So Law devised a simplified musical notation based on the four musical syllables used by eighteenth- and early-nineteenth-century music teachers to teach singing. Today we are all familiar with the seven-syllable system (do, re, mi, fa, so, la, ti) made famous by Julie Andrews in *The Sound of Music*. In Law's time, this system contained only four syllables: fa, so, la, and mi. To each of these notes, Law assigned a respective shape—square, oval, triangle, diamond—while eliminating the five-line format that has been characteristic of musical notation since its introduction in sixteenth-century France.[49] In British English, this five-line format is called the *stave*, but since the publication of Webster's *American Dictionary* (1838), it has become common knowledge that Americans use the word *staff*. Like Law before him, Webster was attempting to reform a system of symbolic notation, and to make it more relevant and accessible to Americans who had already developed their own idioms.

Unfortunately, although Law patented his shape-note system in 1802 and revised the 1803 edition of *The Music Instructor* to demonstrate his method, he was not the first to print or copyright shape notes. In 1801, another shape-note system appeared in a Philadelphia songbook, William Little and William Smith's *The Easy Instructor*. Soon after, in the better-settled and educated areas of New England where musical education and instruments were readily available, as were imports of European music, a controversy erupted when musical sophisticates criticized shape notes as a lowering of musical standards suitable only for rubes and bumpkins. For this reason, early in their history, shape notes earned the first of a long line of pejorative nicknames, including "buckwheat notes" and "dunce notes." Nonetheless, *The Easy Instructor* enjoyed enormous popularity, and a second edition was published in Albany in 1805.

Later, as religious reformers in the Northeast replaced even the most beautiful of the homespun American compositions with traditional European hymns, access to print became more widespread. Revivalists in the South and West availed themselves of the opportunity to publish shape-note collections, which began to appear throughout the rural reaches of America.[50] As this happened, shape-note hymns began to emerge as a distinct folk tradition marked by a grassroots egalitarianism among its participants. Song collectors and book buyers were both practitioners and social equals, so shape-note music was accompanied by a kind of class leveling and an attitude toward other music that was immune to snobbery or prejudice.[51] Characteristics of shape-note singing (especially harmonies sung at a higher pitch than the main melody) have been blended into many other American song styles, including bluegrass and the "flatfooted" jubilee-style gospel quartets that would inspire Roy Crain in 1926 to form the Soul Stirrers, a founding influence for secular "soul" music as it began to emerge from gospel. (The Soul Stirrers also influenced the later emergence of a capella, doo-wop, and Motown.) Sam Cooke was a late member of the Soul Stirrers. As with soul, doo-wop, and Motown, the best Cooke songs retain the spirituality of traditional origins while expressing modern themes that go beyond religious orthodoxy to express the spiritual paradoxes of ordinary secular life during the great African American migration to America's northern cities:

> It's been too hard living but I'm afraid to die
> 'Cause I don't know what's up there beyond the sky.
> It's been a long time comin' but I know
> change gonna come. Oh yes it will.[52]

Shape-note music's wide but subtle influence is a direct result of its peculiar poly-melodic beauty and its impact of many voices on the community of singers. During its heyday—before 1870—the distinctly American issue of democratic access to music that underlies this innovative notation system spread to the actual practice of shape-note singing and determined the format of its performance. The far-flung geography of shape-note publications (Cincinnati, St. Louis, Philadelphia, West Virginia, South Carolina, and Georgia) was responsible for the many regional names shape-note music took, but despite the variety of names, and the fact that it was sometimes sung in German, the performance of shape-note singing became and remained uniform to this day. Today, groups in Alabama, the Carolinas, Georgia, Missouri, and Tennessee still meet and use the songbooks in the same traditional way.[53]

Whether you call it fa-so-la singing, character-note singing, patent-note music, brush arbor music, Sacred Harp music, Harmonia Sacra music, or "hominy soaker," *all* shape-note singers sit down to sing. The songs are loud, and the style is nasal, involving many sliding notes or "portamenti." Members keep time with a chopping motion made by the right hand as the music sweeps over and transports its participants, who face inward along the four equal sides of a hollow square that contains a temporary leader at the center. Although non-singers may sit outside the square to listen, the music is not directed toward uninvolved audience members. In fact, only the central leader is positioned to hear all the song's parts in perfect balance, so the leader is essentially the audience. Still, within the square of participants, anyone can lead, and all participants take turns leading. So although each song is supervised by an individual, the supervision is short-lived and the individual remains one member among a group composed of his or her equals.[54]

Because of the essential democracy of its performance, in shape-note singing all ordinary social and musical hierarchies shift as roles, opportunities, and benefits change with each song. It is a fundamentally social form of music that attempts to balance leadership privilege with group access and participation, or to reconcile the individual with and within his or her community. It is a musical model of a Utopian America, a historical embodiment of Jeffersonian democracy and community from a time when the trust and respect Jane Jacobs describes were the common and essential elements of society. Today, it is a lovely, haunting anachronism and a concrete proof that at least one aspect of music is its power to create "social cohesion"' among hominins.

If shape-note music was an effort to simplify musical notation in order to democratize America's access to music, the same urge led to an indigenous American sheet-music industry. Sacred Harp songs were collected for participants in locally published "anthologies" or "collections," a form of music publishing that is distinct from "songsters," since these books contain both words and music, while songsters were like broadside ballad copies reproducing only the lyrics of a song. But even as the shape-note form emerged, America was exploring another form of music publishing, and eventually "sheet music" would dominate a new consumer area called the home music trade. The folio pages of sheet music, of course, are designed for music racks in parlors. They are large and not durable or easily portable. Individual sheets sold for twelve and a half cents (a shilling or one bit) per page. Most songs were two pages, so in their sheet-music form they cost twenty-five cents per copy. Two bits, of course, would buy any American a shave and a shoeshine. If the two bits spent for a good song seemed insignificant at the moment of purchase, it was nonetheless more than ten times the price of other popular copies of the song, so sheet music was well suited both to the consumer's budget and to the income of American printer-publishers.[55]

The sheet-music industry required access to music lessons and a greater availability of musical instruments. Both were difficult to find in the America of 1800. Only one American in five thousand bought a piano in 1829, but by 1910, that ratio had changed to one in two hundred and fifty. As the century progressed and the national economy grew, there was much more disposable income shared among an emerging middle class, while indigenous manufacturing increased people's access to all kinds of consumer goods. American piano manufacture began in 1825 when Alpheus Babcock of Boston patented a pianoforte with a metal frame that would expand or contract in exact proportion to changes that ambient temperatures created in the lengths of the piano's strings. The tuning of Babcock's piano was (fairly) immune to American seasonal changes and to the changes that took place when instruments were shipped from cool, humid Massachusetts across the Appalachians or into the deserts of the Southwest. Soon the demand for "Boston" pianos inspired another manufacturer, Jonas Chickering, to open a piano factory near Babcock's plant. By 1851, Babcock, Chickering, and their competitors produced nine thousand pianos each year in the United States.[56]

As the price of pianos dropped, music literacy increased and music lessons became cheaper and more readily available. John Hill Hewitt (1801–1890), a second-generation American musician and a failure at everything but songwriting, became a music instructor and then the author of many popular songs. Hewitt was the first composer to develop a distinctly American song style, and it was tailored to appeal to his clients and their families, the wealthy upper-middle class of Georgia and South Carolina. In the 1820s, American domestic space was being redefined. During the coming decades, the middle class established rigid lines that defined gender roles within the family unit. Private space emerged out of the development of the nuclear family whose haven was the family home, which was divided into major zones of society, privacy, and service, with each zone further divided into rooms or subareas with specialized functions.[57] Increasingly, the parlor became the area for music within the family home, and women became the family's musical practitioners. This "private" music was quite different from "the noise, excess, unrestrained emotionalism, and showy professionals of much public music [which] was thought inappropriate for such a new sphere . . . [so] a form of popular music came about . . . that treasured reserve and sentiment, was without ostentation, and could be performed by the competent amateur."[58]

John Hill Hewitt was ideally suited to appeal to nineteenth-century middle-class sentiments while teaching middle-class women piano and flute. He was a dashing figure who had failed out of West Point in 1822 after fighting duels, impersonating officers, taking part in a student rebellion, and failing final exams in both math and chemistry. West Point nonetheless introduced Hewitt to Dubliner Richard Willis, the school's bandmaster and music teacher who had worked as a researcher for Thomas Moore, the most influential popular songwriter of the early nineteenth century. Through Willis, Hewitt became intimately acquainted with all seven volumes of Moore's *Irish Melodies* (1808), and their influence is pronounced in a variety of ways throughout Hewitt's songs, including their simple, romantic narratives, their use of major keys, and their unvarying rhythms.[59] Of course, all these characteristics make the songs easy for amateurs to play.

John Hewitt returned to New England when his father became fatally ill in 1825. In Boston, he met his younger brother, James, who had taken to music publishing. James Hewitt reluctantly agreed to publish "The Minstrel's Return'd from the War," a romantic ditty in which a bugler breaks a promise to his beloved to never to return to war and then gets killed. This became America's first hit song (Hewitt's original tune is now used to support "If You're Happy and You Know It . . ."). A prolific composer who had written musical plays, Hewitt had at last found his calling, and he set to work learning the sentiments that best appealed to his audience. He kept abreast of stylistic innovations and adapted his work to the emerging song market as Americans increasingly became consumers of music. During the next decade, Hewitt enjoyed many more hits, including "The Mountain Bugle" (1833) and "The Knight of the Raven Black Plume" (1835). For establishing an ideology of the private sphere as it developed in nineteenth-century America, there is no more important lyricist than John Hewitt, whose sheet-music sales were not bettered until the arrival of Stephen Foster. By 1848, when Foster's "Oh! Susanna" finally outsold "The Minstrel's Return'd from the War," a closed loop had been set up between printed media, its marketplace, and the emerging middle-class and their daughters and parlors.

Sheet music became America's most economically important music because its per-page cost stayed more or less the same throughout the nineteenth century, as refinements in printing increased and as the middle class (who used music as a means of self-definition) expanded. As the century progressed, sheet-music publishers made more and more profit per page because the proportions of their economies of scale continued to grow. Consequently, profitability led to competition, and competition led to more selection—more music—as music historian Richard Crawford describes: "Having produced no more than 600 pieces between 1787 and 1800, the [sheet music] trade by the late 1820s was turning out that many titles per year, growing to 1600 annually in the early 1840s and 5000 in the 1850s."[60]

The accessibility of this private music was shared by another, more pervasive and public instrument whose earliest appearance in American is not well documented, and yet, it filled the air surrounding working Americans of the nineteenth century wherever they were. In the fields, in the forests, on the plains, at sea, or on riverboats, in the ragtag back lots of American cities, or in the nighttime repose of the bivouac, harmonicas brought more music to more people than any instrument that had ever come before.

The first recognizable ancestor of the harmonica—called the aura—was patented in Germany in 1821. It was a simple device in which fifteen steel reeds were placed side by side. Easy to make, to master, and to produce, it attracted international attention. In Boston, an inventor and instrument maker named James Bazin came into contact with "free-reed" instruments made in France through an article in the local press. He used this knowledge to develop a sliding-scale pitch pipe under contract to some local teachers. Then he developed a "reed trumpet," using the same principles. This reed trumpet still exists and is "essentially a . . . harmonica albeit one where individual notes were selected by a revolving mouthpiece."[61] Use of the reed trumpet was unfortunately quite cumbersome, so, by 1830 or 1831, Bazin developed a horizontal blow-type harmonica that he began producing in small quantities and selling (for about a decade) through John Ashton, a local music distributor. Only one of Bazin's harmonicas still exists (at the

Boston Museum of Fine Art). It consists of fifteen steel blow-type reeds arranged horizontally. All things considered, it is in pretty fair shape, but unfortunately its sliding silver mouthpiece disappeared at some point during the last 180 years.

As a marketing ploy to provide his instrument with cachet, Bazin claimed his instrument was as French as he was: "I found that though I could not dispose of the article at any price as an original invention, I could scarcely supply demand for it at three times its cost when it appeared to be . . . an improvement on a foreign one, the fact of its having come by way of Paris . . . [established] its claim to be received in good society."[62]

This misunderstanding about the national origins of the harmonica might seem to explain why—in the southern United States during the nineteenth century—the harmonica was often called the "French harp." Actually, though, Bazin is not responsible for the name. The origins of this puzzling term date to the Civil War period when good German harmonicas suddenly became readily available to Union troops stationed in New Orleans. Early in 1862, Matthias Höhner signed his first export agreements with suppliers in the United States.[63] After Admiral David Farragut took the city on April 29, 1862, the contents of Confederate music stores throughout the parishes were designated contraband of the war and seized, since many New Orleans music shops had published songs in sheet-music form that championed the Confederacy and ridiculed the Union cause. One publisher, German-born Philip P. Werlein had a shop on Camp Street with a selection of German-made harmonicas that were in great demand by the musicians who played in the city's bars and bagnios, or bordellos. Werlein was the first Southerner to publish a version (albeit a pirated one) of black-faced minstrel Daniel Decatur Emmett's "I Wish I Was in Dixie's Land" (1859). In the early years of the war, Werlein published versions of Emmett's song with propagandistic lyrics, including "The War Song of Dixie." Consequently, after the city surrendered, the Union confiscated Werlein's complete inventory, and his store remained closed until 1865.[64] Among the occupying Union troops, the confiscated German harmonicas went on sale almost immediately for the alarming price of three dollars, the same amount of money it cost to visit a "Cyprian," or working girl, and the name "French harp" probably derives from the instrument's association with prostitutes and prostitution.

New Orleans's unique history had included the transportation from Paris of eighty-eight female convicts (many of whom were prostitutes) in 1721. Of course, once they arrived, they set up shop establishing New Orleans as the oldest North American center for the oldest profession. Long before prostitution was confined to Storyville in 1894, New Orleans's working girls were sprinkled liberally throughout the city's parishes. In 1862, at the beginning of the Union occupation, Cajun and Creole prostitutes still often spoke French (patois) and the "French fever" (syphilis) was quite common among them. Finding a bordello in those days was as easy as following the sound of the band music wafting through the streets, and some Northern soldiers naively believed they could avoid contracting the French fever and other STDs by requesting oral gratification, a service for which New Orleans was notorious. Eventually, a unique kind of New Orleans bordello would emerge, called a "French House," which specialized exclusively in providing fellatio to all comers. The best-known of these houses was called Diana and Norma's.[65] Nonetheless, during the Union occupation of the city, "playing the harmonica" often referred to some very unmusical activities. A Union soldier might request to leave his post to "practice his harmonica" or to approach a working girl in a bordello or on a street corner by asking her to "play him a lively tune." Our wide variety of contemporary expressions that use "French" as a code word for fellatio expanded greatly during this period. These expressions are still with us and now include the verb to French (someone);

a French date; a French kiss; a French lay; a French massage; a French trick; and simply a French or a Frenchy. The southern regional name for the harmonica most likely became French harp or mouth harp because of this association, although, like the history of other slang terms associated with prostitution ("the Big Apple," for example), the original meaning became increasingly obscure as the unwritten language of the streets adapted to new pressures and new concerns.[66]

Bazin was familiar with the free-reed principle and used it in his harmonica. He refers to the German origins of the instrument in an article written in 1880. But he is unaware of a significant German manufacturer's modification (around 1825 or 1826) that mounted twenty reeds in a frame of ten holes. In this patented design by Richter, two reed plates were mounted on either side of a cedar comb whose hole segments formed separate channels for each two-reed pair. The notes of Richter's harmonica resembled those of a piano and were designed to enable the player to produce simple melodies. This is the key to the harmonica's enduring success. In the middle of this instrument was a full diatonic scale. Gapped scales appeared on either side. When blown, the reeds produced the major tonic cord; when drawn (or sucked) the reed produced the dominant seventh. This became the standard configuration for all subsequent European harmonicas.[67] For generations, the harmonicas blow and suck features and the range of its scales were the acknowledged source of superiority for these German instruments. It was also the reason they were so widely coveted in the United States, where German-made instruments were sometimes called pocket pianos. During its nearly two-hundred-year history, the humble harmonica has been called many things, including aura, band-in-a-pocket, Blues Harp, Blues Burger, Breath Harp, Cookie Cutter, Gob Iron, Fist Whistle, French harp, Harp, Harpoon, Lady Shaver, Lickin' Stick, Mississippi Saxophone, Moothie, Mouth Harp,

Mouth Organ (after the German name *mund-aeoline*), Pocket Piano, Tin Biscuit, Tin Sandwich, Toot Sweet, and Snort Organ. Its many names are as much a reflection of its widespread popularity as of its powerful and colorful regional history, especially in the United States.

The fact that Bazin knew of and began making free-reed instruments like the harmonica as early as 1831 is significant because in nineteenth-century America, German harmonicas were luxury items imported in small quantities by local music stores until Matthias Höhner's relatives began bringing them to America in 1862. The earliest German harmonicas were Richter's (after 1826) and Gebruder Ludwig's (after 1844), but there were also those by Weiss or Koch, who, like Höhner, were located in Trossingen. American harmonica history generally focuses on events after the Civil War. Nonetheless, demand for harmonicas in antebellum America was so great that inventors like Bazin began making free-reed, blow-type harmonicas in the 1830s, as did others.

Previously, Harriet Martineau described for us a homespun harmonica-like instrument that she encountered in the wilderness of Tennessee in 1837, indicating the reassuring and comforting role that human-made sound played in the American wilderness. This is a further sign that the American market for harmonicas (and music) was vast. The appeal of this unpretentious instrument was that it was small, portable, and relatively inexpensive compared to a piano. It was also easy to master, and so it became a ready accompaniment to folk and working-class songs, as well as an individual diversion and distraction that filled life's spare moments much as we now use our iPhones. Abraham Lincoln was an enthusiastic if somewhat ungifted owner of a Höhner harmonica. During the presidential campaign of 1864, Henry Whitney describes Lincoln waiting in a carriage while amusing himself privately with the instrument before delivering a speech: "He had in his hand a small French harp which he was making the most execrable music with."[68]

Following the Civil War, manufacturing turned away from armaments toward new domestic products, including toys and luxury items. Harmonicas became popular on the frontier in the late 1870s, and Billy the Kid and Wyatt Earp were known to play the instrument, guaranteeing the instrument's future popularity with American boys. But harmonicas remained a bit pricey until the late 1880s, when American-made instruments became so cheap that their ownership and use exploded into a runaway fad. Domestic manufacturers brought the price of American-made harps down to the level of candy bars or molded-leaden toys, and by the mid-1880s, most boys were desperate to own one, as this article from 1884 indicates:

> Up the Bowery recently . . . three little boys rushed along with harmonicas in their mouths and molasses candy in their fists. . . . A ragged little fellow rushed forth from a store against a fat old gentleman knocking him over. The f.o.g. picked himself up with a naughty word, just in time to see the urchin scurrying off down the street with a mouth organ held aloft triumphantly in his hand. The reporter stepped into the store when the boy had issued and asked ". . . the cause of the boy's excitement?" "The harmonica," replied the proprietor. "A newsboy that ain't got a harmonica is a small potato. The craze for them is something astounding. I sell hundreds of them every week. Newsboys, workingmen, girls and women all buy the harmonica. That little newsboy that just rushed out . . . has to take home all his earnings. A gentleman handed him 10 cents this morning for picking up a dropped handkerchief, and in less than five minutes he was here."
>
> "Do you sell a harmonica for 10 cents?"
>
> ". . . I do. We have them for a dollar; but a 10 cent one is as good as a dollar one. We used to sell the small one for twenty-five cents. Since the reduction to ten cents we have sold large quantities of them . . . we seldom sell any other than a 10-cent mouth organ. The newsboys get considerable music from these toys."[69]

FACTORY WHISTLE, FACTORY NOISE

> As production processes became increasingly mechanized—and . . . noisier— . . . the workers were forced either to sing outside the factory walls or to change the music inside from the active singing to passive listening. . . . The only remaining option was . . . for the music to halt. . . . And this too, frequently happened.
>
> —Ted Gioia, *Work Songs*, 2006

The harmonica was simply the most versatile of a variety of portable, accessible, and low-skilled instruments that preceded it. Jew's harps and single-note whistles were the most plentiful of these simple folk sound-makers until the harmonica's arrival, but there were also ocarinas and comb-kazoos, Irish penny whistles, and homemade fifes or flutes. Generally, such instruments would be found in the company of the fiddle, and domestic fiddle makers date from earliest years of the emerging colonies when other homespun instruments like the banjo appear in a variety of nonstandard forms.[70] In addition to these well-known folk instruments, there are lesser-known ones, like the bones, clappers, or spoons; the use of a scrub-board as a trap drum; and the single-string washboard bass. Like Bazin, many people were trying to invent new instruments to serve the musical needs of the new nation. Benjamin Franklin invented one called the glass harmonica that has since disappeared. Another thing that has almost completely fallen out of the American musical repertoire is unassisted "whistling," a practice that, in modern times, carries connotations of rusticity and therefore also of simplicity or even mental disorder. Nonetheless, as a spontaneous and personal musical practice, whistling used to be as common as song in the workplace and public spaces of America's fields and small towns. "Whistling," observed the *Washington Post* in 1896, "is an entirely American custom. It matters not what the melody is (but it is usually a cheerful one), it always impresses one with the feeling that one should not allow anything to worry him, but just be happy anyway, and, in fact, before this particular melody or omnipresent whistle has passed for the instant out of your hearing, you find yourself buoyant in spirits in spite of the attempted anxiety."[71]

Participation in such spontaneous public music was ubiquitous in every demographic group of nineteenth-century America, but whistling, harmonicas, improvised instruments, and work songs were especially prominent in the cultural life of African Americans, despite the fact that in the 1830s (after Christianity was introduced into slave communities), many previous forms of song and dance were suppressed. Increasingly, spirituals became the dominant form of black music, but because black work songs (especially field songs) were such serviceable tools, they persisted. Of course, literacy was also suppressed among America's slave population, so there are very few accounts by African Americans themselves about why they enjoyed and practiced this music and eventually mutated in the eight- and twelve-bar blues, R&B, and rock 'n' roll. Perhaps the most authentic comments by African Americans about the purpose of their work songs are contained in the first chapter of Bruce Jackson's *Wake Up Dead Man*, a fascinating investigation into the origins of the blues. This following excerpt details Jackson's interviews with Texan convicts sentenced to hard labor. The power of music to set a rhythm for intense, repetitious physical labor, to coordinate a group work effort, and to make time pass pleasantly is reflected in the explanations that these unlucky men gave him for singing while they worked: "When they're not singing, every man has probably got his lip stuck out 'cause he's got time to think. *All you got to do is concentrate on your song and your rhythm and the time goes by* (my emphasis). . . . When you workin' in union in a line everybody carries his part . . . when you workin' in union and singin' in union it makes it a lot easier all 'round."[72]

Of course, African American music had enormous influence on all subsequent American forms, but nineteenth-century habits of singing at work were not confined to black field hands. In a valuable book simply called *Work Songs*, musician and musicologist Ted Gioia devotes a chapter each to the American work-song traditions of hunters, farmers, shepherds, textile workers, sailors (including fishermen), lumberjacks, cowboys, miners, and prisoners. Prior to the introduction of tractors, combines, steamships, chain saws, and jackhammers, songs reverberated throughout the American landscape during working hours. Unfortunately, the noise of the Industrial Revolution and large urban centers was destructive to the spontaneous practice of any music. As city centers grew and industrialized, their soundscapes changed. Industrial noises increasingly polluted the atmosphere of factories, making work songs impractical. Ironically, noise-suppression edicts like the one issued by New York police commissioner Theodore Bingham in 1908 were mainly directed against the singsong cries of street barkers who composed clever, homemade jingles to sell their wares:

> Blackberries, blackberries fresh an' fine,
> I got blackberries fresh from *DEE-vine*!
> (my emphasis)[73]

In America's factories, noise was the most obvious enemy of work songs, but there were more subtle enemies, including pacing, efficiency practices, and a reduced labor force. In a famous essay called "Sailor Songs" in *Harper's* magazine in 1882, William L. Alden, the journalist who brought the sport of canoeing to America, lamented that the sheer noise of steam engines killed the sea shanty: "In place of a rousing 'pulling-song' we now hear the rattle of the steam-winch; and the modern windlass worked by steam or the modern steam-pump, gives us the clatter of cog wheels and the hiss of steam in place of the wilder choruses of other days. Singing and steam are irreconcilable."[74]

Noise was only one factor that eliminated the production of music from worksites. Another was the acceleration of industry. Rural textile mills were once powered unreliably by water: the role of music at this time was to fill in the dead spaces. Workers brought their instruments to the mill to play during breaks caused by low water, as Ethel Faucette, a millworker, long ago recalled: "We run by water then, and when the water'd get low they'd stop for an hour or two . . . [then] . . . a gang of boys would get their instruments and get out there in front of the mill and they would sing and pick the guitar and banjo, and different kinds of string music. Get out there in front of the mill under two big trees, get out there in the shade and sing . . . maybe they'd stand there an hour or two and the water'd gain up and they'd start back up."[75]

Perhaps the most powerful adversary of work songs was the attitude adopted toward labor with the rise of corporate capitalism. In 1864, the Thirteenth Amendment defined and outlawed the "involuntary servitude" of slaves. Henceforth *all* labor had quantifiable monetary value. The new attitude demanding compensation for all labor is made clear in an 1865 letter from Jourdan Anderson, an escaped former slave responding to his Tennessee master's written (in 1864) suggestion that he return to service in the South:

> [W]e have concluded to test your sincerity by asking you to send us our wages for the time we served you. This will make us forget and forgive old scores, and rely on your justice and friendship in the future. I served you faithfully for thirty-two years, and Mandy twenty years. At twenty-five dollars a month for me, and two dollars a week for Mandy, our earnings would amount to eleven thousand six hundred and eighty dollars. . . . We trust the good Maker has opened your eyes to the wrongs which you and your fathers have done to me and my fathers, in making us toil for you for generations

> without recompense. Here I draw my wages every Saturday night; but in Tennessee there was never any pay-day for the negroes any more than for the horses and cows.[76]

As the conviction "all labor deserves remuneration" took hold throughout every class in America (after the Civil War), there was a burst of labor union organization. Then, in 1868, the Fourteenth Amendment instituted a new period of capitalism characterized by depersonalization and limited liability in which corporations were afforded the rights of citizens. The Knights of Labor would form in Philadelphia the following year, but before unions became abstract entities representing the rights of an economically defined workforce, companies became abstract economic entities responsible only to their shareholders. These embodied businesses or "incorporations" began to treat their workforce as just another business expense devoid of human needs and concerns. It is for this reason that Peter Berger observed, "technological production brings with it anonymous social relations." Where once slaveholders (in order to deprive slaves of just compensation for their labor) promoted an ideology identifying African Americans as subhuman beasts of burden, devoid of souls and incapable of genuine humanity, the new corporate ideology introduced "scientific" techniques of management to minimize its labor costs. Not surprisingly, individual workers were no longer treated like animals but like interchangeable, replaceable machinery even by their unions. Increasingly, anonymous economic relationships replaced the socially defined relationships of an earlier era, leading to a decline in social bonding and trust. Trust, in fact, would become an increasingly abstract notion throughout the twentieth century as human relationships became quantified objects of temporary value in the ubiquitous exchanges between capital and labor. Not surprisingly, in the early years of the new century, images of robots and artificial humans made inroads over slaves or sharecropping minstrels as society's preferred image of the unknown "other" or exploited underdog.[77]

To say that this economic environment was hostile to the work song is a profound understatement. The exclusion of work songs is one of the final stages of what Peter Berger memorably describes as "the segregation of work from private life."[78] Songs and singing were displaced into the hours after work or into the meetings of the newly organized labor movements like the Knights of Labor and (after 1905) the International Workers of the World (IWW; also known as "Wobblies"). Both organizations advocated the eight-hour working day and resisted the ruthless quantification of labor of which Taylorism and Ford's assembly line are late developments. Textile workers especially developed a strong tradition of union songs that resisted the exploitation of workers in their rapidly industrializing sector. The ability to create "social cohesion" or solidarity among workers was especially visible during the famous textile strike in Lawrence, Massachusetts, in 1912, described here by Pulitzer laureate Ray Stannard Baker (pen name David Grayson), cofounder of *American Magazine* and confidante to President Woodrow Wilson: "It is the first strike I ever saw which sang. I shall not forget the curious lift, the strange sudden fire of the mingled nationalities at the strike meetings when they broke out into the universal language of song . . . not only at the meetings did they sing, but in the soup houses and in the streets. I saw one group of women . . . peeling potatoes at a relief station suddenly break into the swing of the '*Internationale*.' They have a whole book of songs fitted to familiar tunes."[79]

The songbook Baker mentions was the *Little Red Songbook*, whose fourth edition (published in 1911) included such songs as Joe Hill's famous "Preacher and the Slave," from which came the still-popular phrase "pie in the sky." Despite the socialist and labor orientation of the *Little Red Songbook*, this song collection is still a perennial American favorite, and it has been reissued in nearly forty American editions since 1909. The groundswell of support among working-class Americans for organized labor in the first decade of the new century provoked staunch resistance to the Wobblies by the popular press *and* the US government. This opposition was clearly funded and directed by business concerns, and it included several murders. In 1914, activist songwriter Joe Hill, a central figure who brought credence and support to the IWW, was charged and later executed on small evidence for the murder of a grocer and former policeman in Utah. In 1916, a group of deputized businessmen in Everett, Washington, attacked a striking group of Wobblies during a strike and are known to have killed five of them, although six more went permanently missing. In 1917, in Butte, Montana, a member of the IWW's governing board was lynched by masked men who identified themselves as vigilantes but who were probably company goons in the pay of the Anaconda Copper Mining Co., which was then the focus of an IWW strike action.

In factories during the era of these disputes, songs became an emblem of worker unity. Anywhere where the habit of workplace singing continued to exist in spite of the noise of industrialized worksites, it was discouraged. A direct result of this was that workers now wanted music more desperately than ever. In other words, the time was ripe for the complete commercialization of music. Songs became a commodity because, as Berger explains: "there must be a private world in which the individual can express . . . elements of subjective identity . . . denied in the work situation."[80]

Around the turn of the century, more than ever before, musical taste was allied to personal identity, and the song production exploded, creating, among other things, Tin Pan Alley. Workers looked for music outside of the workplace in economical settings like saloons, vaudeville stages, nickelodeon theaters, or phonograph parlors. Only in rare industries like cigar manufacturing were phonographs played to comfort and entertain the workers while they labored. Many have observed the coincidence between the mechanical reproduction and conveyance of music and the historic moment when workplace singing was discouraged and effectively shut down: "The spread of the new technologies involved in the dissemination of music—by radio, phonograph, Muzak, and so on—during the years between World War I and World War II happened almost simultaneously with the decline in singing by workers. It was almost as if workers were unwilling to give up their musical traditions until some adequate substitutes were provided."[81]

Of course, in an age when social relationships were reduced to economic transactions, these "substitute technologies" changed music from an active group activity to a passive and marketable (or consumable) product. It was during this process that "solitary listening" became the dominant means of experiencing music. The new technologies of music effectively moved personal music into America's private spaces. Apart from single-occasion performances of live music, what was left in public or the workplace was, after 1930, piped musical radio or, after 1934, motivational Muzak® designed to speed up and placate sedentary workers.

STARS, MUSIC, AND PERSONALITY

> The effect of song hits . . . —their social role—might be described as . . . patterns of identification . . . comparable to the effect of movie stars . . . magazine cover girls and . . . beauties in hosiery and toothpaste ads. . . . Hits . . . appeal to a "lonely crowd" of the atomized . . . those who cannot express their emotions and experiences.
>
> —Theodor Adorno,
> *Introduction to the Sociology of Music*, 1976

Even as the spheres of music and work became mutually exclusive, the economic forces of industrialization and urbanization exacted enormous further costs on the psyches of ordinary Americans. Historians recognize a major change in the dominant personality type following the Civil War, but the forces of change had been gathering for some time, and the storm did not pass until the twenties. These same sociocultural forces had a profound impact on the consumption of American music, entirely transforming the experience of listening from a participatory group activity to a more sedentary and often solitary one.

In his popular book *American Nervousness* (1881), neurologist George Beard identified a troubling contemporary mental condition named "neurasthenia," a disease whose symptoms resembled those of modern depression. In the same vein, psychologist William James later identified a different malady that he called "Americanitis," a term repeated in Annie Payson Call's book *Power through Repose* (1891), where it is described as "a chronic state of nervousness," the "constant tension of so many muscles not in use," and their "habitual over-contraction."[82] Popular tonics containing powerful narcotics (including Coca-Cola® and Rexall's Americanitis Elixir) were publicly embraced as treatments for this condition, and it was described in a number of popular self-help essays including William Sadler's *Worry and Nervousness, or The Science of Self-Mastery* (1914). Sadler's popular book provides puzzled readers with a relationship between James's Americanitis and Beard's neurasthenia. They are, according to Sadler, merely as stages of the same malady: "Our modern methods of work and habits of living may have something to do with the alarming present-day increase in . . . nervous disorders. . . . The American people, especially, are more and more addicting themselves to a combination of mental habits and physical practices which are directly and indirectly responsible for increasing nervous tension . . . laying the foundation for those typical cases of nervous collapse commonly spoken of as 'nervous breakdown,' 'neurasthenia,' etc."[83]

It's hard to appreciate the pressure America experienced at the turn of the century, but the society was at a point of crisis comparable to the upheaval following the 9/11 attacks. It was perhaps even more insidious and threatening since there was no hostile, personal enemy—Osama bin Laden or his al Qaeda fanatics—challenging America. Instead, it was as though life's goalposts had suddenly moved and ordinary people were at a loss for how to locate them. Artists who experienced this shift would become the "lost generation" of Parisian expatriates, while intellectuals would become—among other groups—the Chicago School, which included an assortment of sociologists like Louis Wirth who tried to explain the new way of life in terms of "urbanism" or "urban alienation."

The most powerful analysis of the changes taking place in the American personality during the decades spanning the turn of the century had to wait for the clarity of hindsight with the appearance of a modest essay called "'Personality' and the Making of Twentieth-Century Culture" (1979). In this pioneering essay, cultural historian Warren Susman ingeniously examined changes in the advice and terminology of self-help books from the 1880s onward. His essay concretizes the replacement of American ideas about "character" by an ideology expressing the belief that "personality" was interior, individual, and subject to self-willed transformations. Clearly, a great leveling of authority and traditional values had been set in motion by the Civil War burning down the deadwood that obstructed modern culture. The forces of science, industry, the economy, and immigration swelled into the antebellum vacuum. As this happened, the homogeneity and bedrock beliefs of the socially constructed selves of respectable Victorian America were challenged at their most fundamental level, and the new—consumerist—society with its new demands and pressures emerged. Throughout this process, the American self, as a historian of psychology puts it, was "in the process of being configured into a radically different shape . . . the focus on this new self was a response to the condition of being lost in the crowd, overlooked in the crush of humanity recently assembled in the large cities. In the turn-of-the century world, individuals appeared to be feeling lonely and isolated, hungry for attention and positive regard. There was a pervasive sense that others would not find one interesting and attractive unless one worked at it."[84]

During this psychological transformation, the ordinary anchors of everyday life fell away for many working Americans. Family, community, tradition, and certainty were shaken apart by the economic force of the new—urban, postindustrial, and corporate—brand of capitalism. The sense of a person's self, which had previously been socially defined, moved into the interior of each individual's life and mind. Gradually, another concept of the self emerged as capitalism moved into this new stage, and sales or leisured consumption replaced the older emphasis on production and honest, hard work. This transition marked a shift toward a new type of person, one "predicated on the effectiveness of sales technique or the attractiveness of the individual salesperson. Personal magnetism replaced craftsmanship; technique replaced moral integrity."[85]

The pervasive anxiety of this era led Americans to look for leadership anywhere they could find it. Three new areas promised relief. First, a new, popular psychology of personality offered to teach Americans how to transform themselves into people with "an intensely private sense of well being." Self-pleasure and self-satisfaction now became the purpose of individual existence rather than a by-product of a well-lived life, and this ideology conveniently dovetailed with the new consumerism.[86] Not surprisingly, then, a second transformative force emerged as the emerging field of advertising co-opted psychology and drafted psychologists like John B. Watson, A. A. Brill, and Sigmund Freud's brilliant nephew Edward Bernays into its well-paying service. On the advice and example of these men, copywriters began to suggest to consumers that they could transform their position in the social and business hierarchy by buying and displaying the correct products and behaviors. The new generation of ads was highly motivational. In Bernays's clever hands, advertising would soon be turned to political and propagandistic purposes. The new advertisements promised to transform lives and threatened dire embarrassment and humiliation if consumers did not buy the manufacturers' wares. But advertisers were also careful to associate the new products with fantasies of personal contentment and well-being. The Constitution guaranteed Americans their right to freedom in order to pursue happiness, and by the turn of the century, Madison Avenue was rapidly finding convincing ways to make consumers believe that happiness could be purchased. Democracy, in other words, was becoming commercialized and privatized even as it was being made more trivial. It should not surprise anyone that this was the era that created the "star personality" as a model of the new mix of "traits that made for economic and social success in the new century."[87] Stars are the third area to which America looked for leadership out of its crisis in belief. And since music publishing and recording technology had reached higher levels of sophistication than had Hollywood or the kinescope, the first American mass-media "star" was a singer who was so famous that (like Elvis, Sting, or Madonna after him) he was known only by one name.

Caruso made nearly three hundred recordings between 1902 and 1920. His 1907 recording of "Vesti la giubba" from *Pagliacci* was the first phonograph disc to sell over a million copies. It seems natural to claim that the source of this aria's universal appeal in 1907 is its subject matter. "Vesti la giubba" is about carrying on a public performance of the self after the interior character has been devastated and demolished. Its English title is "Put on the Costume," and Caruso's success inspired a rewrite as the Motown hit "Tears of a Clown" by Smokey Robinson in 1967. Undoubtedly when Caruso sang the original words in Italian, listeners of his era felt a pain common to their generation:

I no longer know what I say, or what I do!
And yet it's necessary . . . make an effort!

Bah! Are you not a man?
You are a clown!

. . .

laugh, clown, so the crowd will cheer!
Turn your distress and tears into jest,
your pain and sobbing into a funny face—Ah!

. . .

Laugh at the grief that poisons your heart!

Because of Caruso's universal appeal, Victor Records used him in an international advertising campaign strategized by Edward Bernays that lasted two decades. Modern celebrity evolved during this period, and the star system of film emerged, copying and supplementing the lessons Victor learned as Caruso's stardom was meticulously constructed. The essential component was publicity, since stardom both for recordings and for films depended on print notices. Stories about stars increased people's fascination for them and created a demand for more stories and for more appearances of the star on disc or in film. These stories became increasingly intimate as the illusion grew that the audience knew these people as intimately as real friends.

Before the end of World War I, Victor was only the 174th largest company in the United States. Nonetheless, they supported the country's fifth-largest magazine advertising budget.[88] Advertising generated interest, and interest demanded news. Until his death in 1921, Caruso was always big news. He began working for Victor in 1903, six years before the date traditionally offered as the beginning of Hollywood's star system, usually marked by the fame of the "Biograph Girl," Canadian belle Florence Lawrence, the first movie star to be known by name. Years before the appearance of the film star, Caruso had achieved permanent international recording fame by forcing his operatic colleagues to follow him by recording on gramophone discs. From Victor's use of Caruso, Carl Laemmle learned to manipulate the preexisting fame of a hired performer to publicize any company that was farsighted enough to buy his (or her) contract. Like Caruso in 1903, the Biograph Girl in 1910 was already famous for promoting another company. By cleverly manipulating the publicity around her, Laemmle ended her anonymity, changing her name back into Florence Lawrence, the film star who now worked *not for Biograph* but for Universal Pictures. After Lawrence left Universal, Laemmle repeated the process with others until the film star was accepted as a natural and important part of American life.

It began one April afternoon in Milan in 1902. After a triumphant performance at La Scala, Caruso recorded ten operatic arias for the Gramophone and Typewriter Company. Even before the discs went on sale in London, news of them convinced the leading international opera stars who were to appear at Covent Garden with Caruso later that season to sign similar recording contracts. After such prestigious singers began recording, other renowned artists did too, and Caruso's fame was ensured. He was the first "recording star," and after him the recording industry took off. In 1902, Caruso's recordings were available in London for a mere 10/– (50p), but by 1904 the best recordings had more than doubled in price, costing a guinea.[89] By 1907, the first million-selling disc was produced, featuring, of course, Caruso. Meanwhile, Victor progressively manufactured an increasing fascination with the Italian tenor's "remarkable personality" through a campaign of print advertisements. They began by using carefully designed portraits that emphasized the "elegance" of all those who recorded for Victor's premium Red Seal label.[90]

Caruso's career marks a turning point in many things, but his most significant accomplishment was as an emblem of the changes taking place in the American personality, because he would become, first and foremost, an American star. During the early years of the new century, ideas of celebrity were changing to accommodate a cultural shift from an older, self-reliant agrarian "character" needed to stay the course during a lifetime of frontier challenges and stern social responsibility. The more modern notion of "personality" was better adapted to individual citizens making their way through the varied contexts of city life. Fascination with Caruso's personality and rags-to-riches financial success reflects this shift and provides the first example of a mass-media para-social or one-way friendship.

Caruso was recruited for Victor's prestigious Red Seal label by Eldridge Reeves Johnson, a general factotum at Emile Berliner's disc gramophone business, who bought the company in 1901 after Berliner himself was forced to withdraw. Confronted with intense competition from Thomas Edison's National Phonograph Company and Edward Easton's Columbia Phonograph Company, Johnson took advice from the advertising industry's leading minds and forged a "two-pronged marketing strategy based . . . on serious musical recordings and . . . on an unprecedented commitment to advertising."[91] Edward Bernays manipulated public opinion in favor of Victor and Caruso, but Johnson also had expert technical help. Frederick Gaisberg, the preeminent recording engineer of his day, worked for Columbia and for Berliner before Johnson's takeover. It was Gaisberg who realized that the limitations of contemporary recording technology were unfriendly to the piano music that was then America's favorite. Mark Hambourg, one of the most famous concert pianists of the day, described recorded piano music as "thin and tinny, like the plucked string of a banjo or guitar," and Sergei Rachmaninoff thought his cylinder recordings for the Edison Company sounded like balalaika music.[92] In 1904, two player-piano companies went toe-to-toe with Edison and Columbia by introducing a new device. Welte and Sons and Aeriol both introduced Pianolas, which sounded like real pianos played by live, on-site pianists. These reproducing "player" pianos catered directly to the American taste for piano music while offering much better fidelity than either the phonograph or gramophone.

Confronted with such competition, Gaisberg cleverly ducked the problem and in so doing changed America's musical taste. If he avoided piano music, Gaisberg knew he could manipulate the fidelity of voice recordings by selecting singers with loud voices and by placing the "collecting horn" a short distance away from them. Without any change to the primitive analog recording technology then available, Gaisberg's experience alone provided fairly good sound reproductions of all the leading opera stars who had been pressured to record by Caruso's bold move onto disc. These included a who's who of contemporary opera targeted for recording contracts on the recommendation of conductor Landon Ronald (later Sir Landon), Victor's new musical adviser. This famous company included Suzanne Adams, David Bispham, Emma Calvé, Pol Plançon, Antonio Scotti, and Anton van Rooy. Capitalizing on Caruso's fame, in 1903, Johnson signed Caruso to an exclusive and highly publicized contract with Victor. The

Italian tenor was, according to Gaisberg, "a recording man's dream . . . we . . . were always on the hunt for just this type of voice."[93] With Caruso's help over the next three decades, Victor recordings established themselves as the best sound reproductions of the world's most serious musical artists. They operated their premium Red Seal label at a loss in order to publicize their less expensive Black Seal discs to a larger mass audience. All the while, Victor's advertising, marketing, and publicity strategies became increasingly expensive and sophisticated as their experts acquired knowledge about what they were selling and how best to sell it.

Caruso's charisma was accompanied by his enormous vocal talent, but both charisma and talent were displayed to the American public by a canny marketing effort that was ubiquitous in turn-of-the-century America. Ads for Victor/Caruso appeared on streetcars, in shop windows, and in magazines and newspapers. Johnson's "total-exposure" strategy led the *Musical Courier* to identify Victor as early as 1907 as "a brilliant . . . exponent of modern advertising."[94] Nonetheless, Johnson was careful to keep Caruso out of film, especially the new synchronized sound films or photo-scenes pioneered by Alice Guy, head of Pathé's Gaumont studios between 1905 and 1907. Until 1914, Caruso was reproduced only on Red Seal discs, although—beginning in 1908—these were sometimes used as film soundtracks. Nonetheless, emerging movie executives were acutely aware of Caruso's stardom and his business success. Through the recording medium, he provided listeners with a "sense of human contact" and made his audience "feel they knew him."[95] Besides hiring and making stars, the head of Universal Studios, Carl Laemmle, emulated Johnson in many things, including disguising the name of his company to distributors by naming some of its subsidiaries "Gold-Seal" and "Victor" to make them appear like independent film companies.

In 1910, Victor's company magazine typically advised its

representatives to "push Caruso—push his great big name (the biggest in the musical firmament). . . . He is the one great artist who stands alone."[96] The measure of Victor's success is Caruso's lasting immortality. He has become exactly what Victor's billing claimed for him: "The voice of the century." Caruso sang only in Italian, and yet his fame is truly global. Today, nearly one hundred years after his death, when the radio surprises us with the opening strains of "Santa Lucia" or "O Sole Mio," we still recognize his distinctive voice and recall his name. Most people who once took a film course can still recognize the face of Florence Lawrence, whom Carl Laemmle turned into the first silent movie star to possess name recognition, but Caruso's voice is downloaded daily through iTunes®, and he is still seen by multitudes on YouTube. The enduring popularity of Elvis and Michael Jackson teach us that para-social relationships—the mass-media friendships that developed to console lonely consumers—do not need to end in ordinary death. Like the prophets of previous ages, mass-media "stars" sometimes ascend into the firmament and endure there permanently, like Polaris, a comforting beacon of orientation to the lonely and lost. This is exactly what happened to Enrico Caruso on August 2, 1921.

CANNED MUSIC

> Today the magic of music unadulterated by humdrum human contact can be enjoyed by almost anyone at any time.
>
> —Timothy Day, *A Century of Recorded Music: Listening to Musical History*, 2000

The year Caruso died, a passionate young pianist named Theodor Adorno (who had graduated at the top of his class one year before) was taking private lessons from German composer

Bernard Sekles. Decades later, as a prominent member of the Frankfurt School, Adorno would condemn the consumer music that emerged in his lifetime as a "rip-off" because it was "a fraudulent promise of happiness which, instead of happiness, installs [only] itself." He wrote bitterly, describing the commercial misuse of the "social function" of music: "The feebler the subject's own sense of living, the stronger their happy illusion of attending what they tell themselves is other people's life."[97]

Adorno went on to write a famous passage often quoted by sociologists of music eager to describe the mobile isolating nature of personal music devices:

> By circling people, by enveloping them . . . and turning them as listeners into participants [consumer music] contributes ideologically to the integration which modern society never tires of achieving in reality. It leaves no room for conceptual reflection between itself and the subject, and so creates an illusion of immediacy in the totally mediated world, of proximity between strangers, of warmth for those who come to feel the chill of the unmitigated struggle of all against all. Most important among the functions of consumed music . . . may be that it eases men's suffering under the universal mediations, as if one were still living face to face.[98]

The illusion of proximity and warmth that all music perpetuates has been the objective of all manufacturers of prerecorded music. For lonely hominins (including modern men and women), music is distance grooming. The makers of player pianos achieved the illusion of human connection through prerecorded music in 1904, when, as economic pressure squeezed ordinary Americans, new technologies provided compensations or replacements for the participatory music we had lost in our workplaces or on the homestead porch. Edison courted this same market by producing a low-cost spring-driven phonograph in the early years of the century. Better fidelity, better verisimilitude, and a better illusion of human proximity and warmth lay at the higher end of the market, and the search for complete verisimilitude would continue until the '60s, when live audiences could, for the first time, no longer distinguish between live or prerecorded music used in performance.

The beginnings of palliative prerecorded music were small. By 1903, Victor's Red Seal campaign was in full swing. Until that moment, live piano music had occupied a privileged position as the high-water mark of musical culture. It was everyone's favorite, even though popular songs were a ubiquitous genre. Unfortunately for phonograph manufacturers eager to cater to popular tastes, piano music didn't lend itself to primitive analog recording technology. This gave piano manufacturers as well as manufacturers of "automatic pianos" an enormous edge in supplying the public with music at the very moment it was being displaced from the lives and worksites of ordinary Americans. Pianolas, of course, didn't require the years of practice necessary to make a competent operator for the piano forte, but early Pianolas were like calliopes, tinny-sounding things whose relentless cheeriness could not satisfy a customer's desire for genuine human connection through human-made music.

For this reason, in 1904, two companies introduced various models of what are called "reproducing pianos," automatic or player pianos that "reproduce" the human intonation or style of a gifted pianist. Apparently ignorant of the Greek meaning of *photo*, the European manufacturer of these instruments, Wente-Mignon, played on the word *photograph*, claiming that their "recording mechanism *phototones* the playing note for note—instantly. [The pianist's] touch, shading, accentuation, expression—everything that characterizes the individuality of the artist is faithfully reproduced."[99] This is catalog copy, of course, written at the enthusiastic beginning of the advertising age, so it is reasonable to wonder just how accurate it is . . .

In his book about player pianos, musicologist Brian Dolan offers a memorable anecdote that demonstrates the very real technical accomplishment of the best automatic pianos after 1904. Dolan's friend Lisa Fagg is a biologist with an affinity for flea markets. One day, as she rifled through some market stalls, she heard strains of piano music that took her back to her childhood, when her grandfather, J. Lawrence Cook, filled her family's Harlem parlor with a steady stream of favorites as he practiced his craft recording and editing piano-roll music. Cook was America's most prolific Pianola artist and produced somewhere between ten and twenty *thousand* individual piano rolls over a fifty-year career. He had a distinctive style, but he was also a gifted mimic. He edited and revised the rolls of more famous pianists, including Fats Waller. It is now known that many so-called Waller rolls are actually collaborations or imitations performed by Cook.

As Professor Fagg explored the flea market, she became increasingly aware of the period piano music that flooded the space around her until recognition finally dawned. Suddenly she exclaimed, "That's Grandpa!" and raced toward the source of the music, a reproducing piano playing in a booth that specialized in antique piano rolls. Thrilled and amazed, Fagg introduced herself to the proprietors, who told her that her grandfather had been employed by QRS Music Roll Company to select, edit, and produce piano rolls and that there was even a special JLC interest group in America that sold, traded, and collected his rolls. Fagg has since posted a memoir of this incident on the Internet, and Dolan observes that player pianos "had a long history of spreading music around before the gramophone and radio were used to popularize music."[100]

The reproducing-piano industry reached its peak in 1925,

when American manufacturers of reproducing pianos made and sold nearly two hundred thousand instruments.[101] It was the year before David Sarnoff created network radio, and, as if in anticipation of the new medium, recording technology changed radically with the introduction of electrically amplified microphones and electrical recordings that captured and reproduced a much larger frequency range than did analog technology. Victor released its first electrical recording in July, a spectacular performance of Saint-Saëns's *Danse Macabre* conducted by Leopold Stokowski. This record was made at the Philadelphia Orchestra's home venue, the Academy of Music, a hall modeled on La Scala. The new recording technique meant that musicians no longer had to huddle around a sound-collecting horn. Instead they could play for Victor's (and later NBC's) microphones from their regular positions just like a live performance. When played back on an electric gramophone, such recordings offered a wonderfully expansive alternative to the piano roll.[102] Steady improvements in the range of recorded sound continued until, in 1945, the first full-frequency recordings (ffrs) technology was released for public use. By the 1960s, there was no longer any discernible difference between the fidelity of prerecorded music and live music, a fact demonstrated when Acoustic Research Inc. presented a string quartet in a series of "live versus recorded" concerts in which musicians mimed the performance of their own prerecorded music, and listeners were unable to detect the moment of the switchover.[103]

SOLITARY (ACOUSMATIC) LISTENING

> I always think about how I'm in my room alone writing it, and eventually most people listen to music alone. . . . So there's actually a quiet little direct line between writing and listening.

> It's a strange bubble of solitude, because you're linked, but you don't know each other, yet you're communicating.
>
> —John Pareles, "The Bounty of Solitude" (interview with Leslie Feist), *New York Times*, 2011

Phonographs and gramophones brought with them remarkable changes. As fidelity increased, music recorded on discs changed from a single performance that was overheard and "captured," becoming a document that could be edited, redrafted, and refined many times before its release. But, in addition to changes in the production of most music, there was a radical transformation in its reception by an audience. Just as radio later encouraged solitary listening, the gramophone, too, encouraged the habit of savoring music alone.

In 1877, Alexander Graham Bell invented the telephone, a device that could minimize human loneliness and separation by delivering personal reassurance across great distances. One year later, Edison announced his working phonograph, a device that could minimize human loneliness and separation by delivering personal reassurance across time.

Improved "gramophone" technology emerged gradually, but once Leon Glass combined the device with a nickel slot machine in 1889, factory, office, and sweatshop workers could all summon music on demand. They no longer needed to painstakingly learn to play an instrument or seek out someone who had. Just as business letters came to the ears of female typists, Edison's ear tubes delivered popular songs. Droves of paying customers hunched over playback machines in public parlors near ferry, trolley, and rail terminals. After the Chicago World's Fair (1893), listening to music on gramophone slot machines became a national pastime, and music changed from do-it-yourself, shared entertainment into a consumer product created by technical specialists as well as by musicians. A new kind of listening—acousmatic listening, or listening to music with no visible source— became the strangest feature of music in the burgeoning machine age. Oxford musicologist Eric Clarke claims it is less peculiar to watch a silent film than to listen to disembodied music because "vision is the socially dominant sense in our culture. . . . To leave that sense 'dangling,' as acousmatic listening does . . . is perceptually incongruous."[104]

In phonograph parlors and nickelodeons, people with ear tubes clustered around the new devices while avoiding the awkwardness of eye contact. Relief for this minor social discomfort came soon after, when gramophones became available on easy credit terms. By 1901, spring-driven models could be purchased for one dollar per week. The uncomfortable sensation of listening to disembodied music in public or in company was suddenly ameliorated by the relative portability of gramophones. Even models with large amplifying horns could be wheeled into separate rooms where listeners could enjoy music all by themselves. Though it now seems odd to say so, those who listened to short popular songs alone on their gramophones were cultural revolutionaries. They initiated a psychological change as far-reaching as the one Walter J. Ong described in *Ramus, Method, and the Decay of Dialogue* (1958) as the shift between oral and scribal culture. Indeed, solitary listening had an impact as profound as that of widespread literacy after Gutenberg. Like a reader, the solitary listener is part of an abstract, far-flung audience that reaches far beyond the here and now of a live performance. "Solitary listening," writes Mark Katz, historian of recording technology, "is now the dominant type of musical experience in most cultures."[105]

I feel the meaning of this development has been long overlooked. Where Gutenberg freed middle-class Europeans from the mediation of the educated classes (aristocrats and clergy), recorded music freed lonely Americans from the silent tyranny of their own company. "Silence," as George Prochnik recently observed, "is for bumping into yourself. . . . People seek to avoid that confrontation."[106] Where reading made people more capable of purposeful and extended linear thought, solitary listening reduced their span of concentration and made them less tolerant of boredom. Where reading deepened character, solitary listening ignored character altogether. The texture of live music yielded to the low-fidelity, three-minute span of the gramophone. At the same time, popular ideas about music changed. Long and complex structures were abandoned for the livlier form of disposable pop songs. Still, people could play whatever music they wanted, whenever they wanted it, enabling them to use music as a diversion from the harsh, persistent internal voices that nag those struggling in a difficult new environment. Music lifts one's spirits, offering diversion, escape, and comfort. Industrialization needed music for these purposes, if not others, and the gramophone served it up, hot and ready, encouraging people to get up and dance to ragtime's new sounds. Lonely and bored teenagers fell into dancehalls where they spooned and rubbed themselves against likeminded strangers in the American night. The star system that film studios had invented to deepen audience loyalty soon came to promote pop music, first on the gramophone, then on radio. A large number of the Hit Parade high-fliers of the 1930s and 1940s originated in film; "Over the Rainbow" from *The Wizard of Oz* being only the most famous of many hundreds. From film and radio, music moved eventually to television. Like solitary listening, the stars ameliorated America's loneliness without offering reciprocity. We became one-way intimates with the talking heads we saw on movie screens or with the voices we heard over the airwaves, and sadly, we never interacted with them.[107] At first, the deeply antisocial character of such solitary listening prevented its widespread acceptance. It implied, as Eric Clarke writes, "a visible withdrawal from the social context and immersion in an intensely private world that people may find unsettling or offensive."[108]

When did this change happen?

In 1923, essayist Orlo Williams observed, "We think, people should not do things 'to themselves' . . . they may not even talk to themselves without incurring grave suspicion." Amusingly, Williams's descriptive use of pronouns recalls the taboo against onanism. Clearly, he was worried that if he were seen listening to his gramophone alone, others would think him wildly anti-social or crazy. He wrote, "If I were discovered listening to the Fifth Symphony without a chaperone . . . my friends would fall away."[109] In fact, this is exactly what happened to social circles in the remainder of the 1920s and throughout the rest of the century. The friends of solitary users of personal technologies fell away, not because they thought users were crazy. As people spent more and more time with technology, they spent less and less time with friends. Devices like the phonograph afforded the opportunity for musical expression to ordinary nonmusical people who no longer enjoyed the presence of music at work or in the public spaces of cities. During the twenties, the permissibility and desirability of being alone to listen to music took hold after fairly good *electrical* recordings made orchestral music increasingly available in 1925. As this happened, a minor fad called "shadow conducting" overtook American music enthusiasts. Mark Katz brilliantly documents this phenomenon in *Capturing Sound*, when he observes that by 1926 many members of the Minneapolis Phonograph Society privately practiced the "exhilarating . . . indoor sport" of "shadow conducting."[110] More poignantly, musicologist Richard Crawford recalls that in the early forties, his own father

> would go into a room of our house that was glassed in, with opaque glass, and I would hear music coming out of that room. If I stood outside I could see the shadows moving inside the room. Now my father worked in a foundry in a supervisory capacity and was not a musician in any sense . . . I eventually put together what he was doing . . . when I saw him walk

> into the house . . . with a baton. He was going into that room, turning on the record player and conducting. I imagine . . . it was a very important experience for him.[111]

Apparently, the phenomenon of shadow conducting lasted a good many years. A 1930 issue of *Disques* describes the practice, saying, "It would . . . be a gross exaggeration to sa that any appreciable proportion of *phonograph* users practic 'shadow conducting.' But it would not be an exaggeration to say that a great many people 'shadow conduct' mentally."[112] In 1959, *Records in Review* observed that "*shadow conducting* is a harmless enough eccentricity and has even numbered among its practitioners such renowned professionals as Toscanini and Beecham. This disc is, however, purely for the home time-beater."[113]

In correspondence, Professor Crawford tells me that his father first came into contact with orchestral music between the ages of nine to nineteen (from 1918 until about 1928). Duri this period, the family had a Sunday ritual that included a we trip to the Michigan Theater, which possessed a full orche Crawford recounts that "as well as accompanying the [s movie [the orchestra] played selections . . . from . . . orchestra menu. . . . [and] Dad got to know this repertoir a spectator . . . one of his heroes was the Michigan Theate orchestra conductor . . . 'Ed [Eduard] Werner.'"[114]

Crawford does not know when his father began the habit of "silent conducting" but mentions the possibility that the opaque windows of the library in the house they took possession of on Pearl Harbor Day in 1941 may have been designed to ensure privacy for this very purpose, and that when his father went into the

> "library," turned on the phonograph, and conducted records of music he knew by ear and loved, he was in earnest, in a kind of musical choreography that gave him pleasure. . . . [It

> never occurred] to me to ask if the opaque glass that substituted for the library wall had been put in so that he could have his esthetic moment in privacy. Private it was, though. . . . [F]or him, the conducting was a self-driven, private activity that allowed him to narrow the gap between him and the music, which he loved but had no skill in the making of.[115]

The shift toward social acceptance of the selfish and solitary enjoyment of electronically rendered music seems complete by 1931. That year, an anonymous editorial in *Disques* celebrated the impersonal experience of guiltlessly listening to music: "Alone with the phonograph, all the unpleasant externals have been removed: the interpreter has been disposed of; the audience has been disposed of; the uncomfortable concert hall has been disposed of. You are alone with the composer and his music."[116]

So, by the early years of the Depression, solitary listening had become commonplace in America and elsewhere in the Western world. Unemployed millions made their way through a decade of hard times, cheered on by the sponsored entertainments of network radio, exemplified by Yip Harburg's popular anthem "Brother, Can You Spare a Dime?" Americans now listened to network radios alone in their cars or over one of several midget sets distributed—to maximize listening privacy—throughout the home. Perhaps as a legacy of the war after 1948, headphones became an increasingly common way to listen to discs, and as a reflection of this change a new word—*earphones*—became their most common appellation. But it was the debut of stereo recording in 1954 that brought a degree of verisimilitude to recorded music that made it nearly invisible. Because "stereo" created the impression of space and depth, recorded music—especially when one was listening through stereophonic earphones—came much more vividly to life. In the late '50s, a music lover could tune out the world and surround himself or herself with the convincing virtual space of a musical performance. At the office or in any public space while appearing attentive, the owners of transistor radios could tune in and drop out for the first time. Surreptitiously, ears containing monaural earphones were simply turned away from company to catch the news, ball games, or a favorite song. In the years since 1954, technological advances have increased the fidelity and volume available through earphones, allowing us to tune out the real world completely: a recent study of injury-related traffic deaths related to earphone use reported that of the 116 pedestrian fatalities attributed to earphone use between 2004 and 2011, 55 percent involved trains. For at least 29 percent of those deaths, the train sounded a warning signal before striking the pedestrian.[117]

Moreover, around the time earphones became commonplace in the early 1960s, urban man developed a new strategic behavior for dealing with a constant stream of unwanted micro-interactions with strangers. Metropolitan life constantly and overwhelmingly confronts us with choices about engagement. As we step into the crowded street of any city, we are subjected to the glare of countless strangers. In the late 1920s, beachgoers in New Jersey began emulating movie stars by purchasing and wearing Sam Foster mass-produced sunglasses, but it is said that film actors began wearing custom-made "shades" much earlier, first to protect their eyes from the glare of arc lamps on movie sets, then soon afterward to avoid eye contact with their curious and demanding public, since "dark glasses . . . allow the wearer to stare at another . . . without that other being sure he is being stared at."[118] This was the first behavior for "dimming the lights" when confronted with the glare of strangers' attention in public.

By the 1960s, sociological research began to focus on behaviors surrounding the human gaze as Americans developed specific techniques for minimizing the psychic energy required to move safely through the urban grid. Fresh from the wilds of Winnipeg, sociologist Erving Goffman noticed an unusual phenomenon in 1963, around the time Americans began deploying monophonic earphones in public as a distraction from their immediate surroundings. Where Victorians would greet each other formally as they passed, Goffman describes the accepted and more modern practice of "civil inattention." This involved looking at strangers briefly to investigate and acknowledge them in a shared public space before turning one's gaze away to prevent the impression of intrusion or hostility: "One gives another enough visual notice to demonstrate that one appreciates the other, is present (and that one admits to openly to having seen him), while at the next moment withdrawing one's attention from him so as to express that he does not constitute a target of special curiosity or design."[119]

Of course, this elaborate two-step behavior is obviated by modern MP3 (or AAC) players. In the twenty-first century, glaringly white Apple® earbuds inform all those who observe us in public that we are disinterested, musically inclined, nonthreatening people, while Bluetooth® Wi-Fi earpieces convey a slightly different, more aggressive message: far too busy, don't dare disturb. Once again, interaction with a device prevents and is preferable to risky, energy-consuming interactions with strangers. We have been conditioned for over a hundred years to risk interpersonal contact only through the mediation of machines. We trust machines much more than we trust human beings. Through the faint distance grooming of music listened to through earbuds, our machines provide us with an oxytocin surge that is much more reliable than most interactions with human beings, even if it invites comparisons with babies' pacifiers. Earbuds are pacifiers for adults. We pay handsomely for them.

CHAPTER 3

TRUSTING MACHINES

> He has worked with machines all his life, he has tooled cars to the point where he has felt they respond to his care, he has known them and slept beside them as trustingly as if they were hunting dogs, he knows a thousand things about the collaboration between a man and a machine. . . . He has spent his life with machines, they are all he has ever trusted.
>
> —Norman Mailer, *Of a Fire on the Moon*, 1970

It now seems reasonable to claim that we rely on the voice-sounds of cell phones and the music-sounds of MP3 players to provide a sense of connection that warms us *chemically* in the interpersonal frigidity of the modern city. It also seems reasonable that the portable sound technology we use to "self-groom" or to "distance groom" has played a role in acclimatizing modern city dwellers to an increasing level of interpersonal frost. But why, when, and how did we first begin to prefer the use of technology to solve our problems rather than choosing the traditional activity of trusting and interacting with other humans who might already be known to us? Whose competence and commitment could therefore be predicted to some extent? Human trust is hardwired into our neurological machinery via the mirror neurons that were discovered in the 1990s and through the strange chemical, both hormone and neurotransmitter, oxytocin, about which we know so little. Nonetheless, in a very real sense, we are trust machines.

What happened that caused us to prefer the activity of trusting machines to the action of trusting others?

TRUST IN TRADITIONAL SOCIETIES

> Complex societies, it must be emphasized, are recent in human history. Collapse, then, is not a fall to some primordial chaos, but a return to the normal human condition of lower complexity.
>
> —Joseph Tainter, *The Collapse of Complex Societies*, 1988

Jane Jacobs observed that the trusting relationships of small neighborhoods break apart when ergonomic city districts are violently reconfigured to better serve the automobiles crisscrossing a metropolis. Nonetheless, in the biggest *cultural* picture possible, the historical progress of industrialization and modernism has demanded from its very beginning that human trust be transformed. What began in our hominin past as an experiential, interpersonal emotion based on human contact and reinforced by brain chemistry becomes, in the urban grid, an abstract practice that facilitates larger and larger social systems. Buying Christmas presents for my family from a neighborhood merchant I know well is a very different experience from typing my credit-card information into the open box of an online website representing an organization in the Midwest and trusting them to send my purchased goods by courier or post in ten days' time. In the first instance, I may enjoy passing the time of day with a known personality or be concerned that he or she might shortchange me; while in the second, knowing my transaction is purely informational and will only take seconds, my concerns are quite different. Perhaps I worry about the security of the vendor's website and wonder if my financial information or even my "identity" (a strange word choice for abstract numerical information) will be stolen. Recently, the personal information of twenty-four million customers at Zappos.com was copied, taken for no doubt nefarious fiduciary purposes. In our time, the simple act of buying shoes has become so fraught with risk that new applications (Mint or Adaptu) allow you to check your account balances and transaction records automatically on the fly. In this way, the complexity of modern life advances every day, requiring more and more "system trust" and less trust in individuals. In addition, when I shop online, I am usually an international customer, so I am often concerned about delivery dates and reliability since the Canadian Post Office (Postes Canada) rarely delivers my goods in the same timely way I have come to expect from the US Postal Service. The unreliability of Postes Canada has become such a problem that I now rent a mailbox in an American border town and cross the international boundary every time I order a hard-to-find book or disk. I also know that if things go awry in the modern processes associated with shopping that it will probably be much more difficult to achieve appropriate redress. *So* each time I shop on the Internet, I must decide how much confidence I can realistically place in abstract organizations and their promises of safe, secure, reliable, and timely service. Moreover, I expect the abstract form of trust I deploy online will deliver a much smaller neurochemical reward than a human interaction might, but more of that later. . . .

For North Americans, the origins of the change in the nature of trust go back 150 years.

It seems trivial to write that the scale of destruction achieved during the Civil War forced profound cultural changes on America at a very deep level. But perhaps the deepest level of all was the transformation that took place in the practice of interpersonal trust and interpersonal relationships. The emergence of a national paper currency in 1861 posed a formidable challenge in a divided country whose only national currency had previously been coins. While coins are never worth very much each, they are at least worth the weight of the metal of which they are composed. During the Civil War, the value of copper rose sharply, so there was a corresponding shortage of pennies. This cannot happen with paper money since paper is so plentiful that it is rarely a strategic resource.

In the United States during the 1860s, as the nation shifted to nationally printed paper money, both the coinage and then the paper currency began to bear the motto "In God We Trust." This phrase became the abstract symbol of an emerging national economy in and through the activity of "trusting" a divinely protected national currency. Treasurer Salmon P. Chase understood the symbolic and financial necessity of switching to a paper currency, and his innovation quickly became an emblem of the Union's durability and reliability. Another significant change during this period was the US mail, whose reliable service became bankable in the second year of the Civil War. From 1862 to 1869, the postal service developed "rolling sorting stations" between major cities, which significantly reduced the time required to deliver a letter or parcel. The benefits to national commerce were immediate and lent considerable credibility to the commercial utility of Lincoln's Union. The efficiency of the US Post Office was a nationally recognized symbol of American society working well. Significantly, Aaron Montgomery began the first mail-order catalog (which would become Montgomery Ward) in 1872. Hammacher Schlemmer was a New York tool supplier that had achieved a national reputation during the Civil War by minting its own "rebellion tokens" or "copperhead" coins to supplement the Union's shortfall. In 1881, they issued their first mail-order tool catalog. So, by the time they moved into mail order, Hammacher Schlemmer had achieved a reliable "brand identity" or system trust among their potential customers. Other catalog businesses had to build such brand identity and trust, as did Richard Warren Sears and Alvin C. Roebuck after they began their famous catalog in 1888. As commerce became a truly national enterprise from coast to coast, it strengthened and structured the vastness of the Union while familiarizing Americans with the new practice of impersonal, modern trust. This familiarity facilitated all later developments including self-service, coin-ops, and online shopping.

Also, as society relied more and more on technology and the impersonal processes it created, the world's image of America changed from a nation of can-do innovators into a collective name for a centrally organized and quite diverse continent (even though manifest destiny was never fully realized). Simultaneously, as abstract conceptions of trust emerged, they challenged and replaced those of older, premodern cultures like that of the American South. It is a cliché, of course, that Dixieland represents a traditional culture where "olden times . . . are not forgotten," but the American South truly was a premodern or traditional society distinct from the rapidly modernizing and much more technologically developed North. Sociologist Anthony Giddens has described the values and beliefs of these older cultures that depended on kinship relationships and well-defined local communities to organize social ties, but it is interesting that the first attempt to distinguish between types of large, anonymous, modern communities and smaller, traditional ones first became an important theme of sociological investigations during the generation that followed the Civil War. In 1887, Ferdinand Tönnies suggested that "the most modern Gesellschaft [advanced-society] type state, the United States of America, can scarcely lay claim to anything like a true national character, nor does it wish to do so."[1]

Undoubtedly Tönnies was attempting to account for the changes taking place in his own country following the Franco-Prussian War of 1870, yet significantly these changes paralleled those in the United States as the North struggled to change and subsume the South during the Reconstruction period. Tönnies's ideas are embedded in their era. In 1865 and again in 1870, a terrifying and costly technological war led to the economic union of widely different societies. In America, the South was forced to rejoin the North; in Europe, five years later, Krupp supplied armaments that guaranteed the technological superiority of an alliance between Prussia and three culturally distinct states of northern Germany. This led directly to a final victory over the French Empire and to the birth of modern Germany, an unusually diverse nation. "We have," wrote Tönnies, "a *community* of language, custom and belief; but a *society* for the purposes of business, travel or scientific knowledge [in which] commercial partnerships are of particular importance."[2] To describe this emerging new order, Tönnies distinguished between *Gemeinschaft*, an older, smaller form of human social grouping characterized by highly developed, long-term interpersonal relationships, and *Gesellschaft*, a society in which "individuals [live] alongside but independently of one another." "In Gemeinschaft," he wrote, "we are united from the moment of our birth with our own folk for better or for worse [but] we go out into Gesellschaft as if into a foreign land."[3] "Community [Gemeinschaft]," wrote Tönnies, "is old," but "society [Gesellschaft] is new, both as an entity and a term."[4]

Although it is infrequently mentioned, trust is at the heart of Tönnies's appositional distinction, and as we'll see, the transformation in trust during this period had an enormous impact on America's perception of technology. In 1887, Tönnies believed that only in the small, closed socioeconomic context of Gemeinschaft does the virtue (and genuine human pleasure) of human trust emerge, because it is based on continuous affirmation, understanding, shared experience, and natural instincts or emotions. The cohesiveness of such communities is what creates trusting relationships, which in turn promotes further social cohesion. In words that resemble Jane Jacobs's later observations about trust in small city neighborhoods, Tönnies writes: "Neighborhood may be compared to kinship in much the same ways as the marriage bond may be compared to the relationship between mother and child . . . [in] all relationships based on affinity (rather than consanguinity) the tie has to be underpinned by living together and shar[ing] habits. . . . Shared memories generate gratitude and loyalty; the concrete reality of such connections must manifest itself in mutual trust."[5]

Later Tönnies would specify that in Gesellschaft, by contrast, confidence in someone is by its nature very impersonal and based mainly on reputation. This kind of modern trust is involved in elaborate forms of economic cooperation, and it leads to a surge in professionalization since the professions exist mainly to provide confidence in the judgment and actions of unknown (and interchangeable) individuals. Generally, Tönnies warns, only a naïve person will rely uncritically on such a poor manifestation of trust based on reputation alone. More sophisticated, modern people will be inclined to doubt, question, and challenge all strangers' qualifications right from the outset. Tönnies could easily have been describing the distinction between Southern honor-based culture and Yankee entrepreneurship. *And* since increasing complexity continues to enter human lives globally, his binary distinction has had a long influence in the study of modern culture.

Increasing social complexity is a defining characteristic of modern culture, and a later theorist of trust would point out it is the ongoing purpose of human trust to reduce social complexity by raising our tolerance for (the) uncertainty of future outcomes. Nonetheless, there is a difference between traditional and modern trust. Niklas Luhmann noted that in modern societies, social order no longer depends on the personal version of trust that characterized small, traditional societies like the assortment of communities that comprised the American South in the decade before the Civil War. Instead, Luhmann proposed larger, less personal societies encourage a kind of abstract "system-trust," which also reduces social complexity—once again—by raising our tolerance for (the) uncertainty of future outcomes. Ironically, however, in a kind of Malthusian dilemma, as complexity is increasingly resolved by abstract trust, society is freed to become more complex, requiring a greater and greater extension and abstraction of trust.[6] I find it fascinating that a common delusion among schizophrenics is the technological fantasy of an "influencing machine" possessed of an ever-increasing complexity, which allows "enemies" to direct and control the victim's thoughts.[7]

In our own era, Anthony Giddens provides the most detailed view of the distinction between trust in traditional and modern societies. As director of the London School of Economics, Giddens came into close contact with Saif al-Islam when the son of the ill-fated Libyan dictator, Muammar Muhammad Abu Minyar al-Gaddafi, was a doctoral candidate at LSE. Friendship with Saif must have provided Lord Giddens, an eminent sociologist, with some practical firsthand knowledge of traditional cultures, but his seminal study of trust, *The Consequences of Modernity*, was published twenty-six years before he visited Saif's father in his tribal tent south of Benghazi.

Giddens characterizes four major differences between modern and premodern trust. The older practice of interpersonal trust, Giddens says, relies on kinship, community, (religious) cosmology, and tradition. All these elements were in play in the premodern culture of the American South, but—interestingly—when they are contrasted with emergent, modern, technological Northern culture, the meaning and the necessity of America's ongoing reliance on technology becomes quite clear.

In *Albion's Seed* (1989), historian David Fischer established that the American North was settled by Puritan, Quaker, Dutch, and German farmers who came and worked the land before eventually migrating to cities. Characteristically, these settlers from England and the Continent cooperated fairly well (as farmers generally do). Moreover, as part of their Protestant heritage, they had recently rejected the ancient and traditional authority of Catholicism and felt themselves quite "modern" in worldview. A shared emphasis on education allowed them to build a new society that valued all types of professional expertise from the tradesman to the inventor or the engineer. National origin was of less importance in America's industrialized North than the skill set you had to sell.[8] This attitude, in turn, contributed to one of America's most profound and productive contradictions: that despite a prolonged, diverse, and violent history of prejudice, principles of individual liberty, even to the point of religious and racial tolerance, were embedded at the bedrock of the laws of this emerging society.

By contrast, Grady McWhiney, historian of the American South, established that another group, this one with Celtic origins, settled farther south in a land unsuitable for intense forms of agriculture. (Celts did not become farmers until a decade after the invention of the cotton gin in 1794.) In *Cracker Culture* (1988), McWhiney identifies a group of Scots-Irish herders who immigrated to America from the late seventeenth to early nineteenth century and came from places like Ulster or the Scottish highlands and lowlands. McWhiney is careful to distinguish this group from the later nineteenth-century immigrants like the educated Scots Presbyterians or the deeply Roman Catholic Irish who fled their homeland during the potato famine.[9]

These people were herders, and they clustered in groups of extended family clans whose main form of justice was *lex talionis* (retribution or revenge). Psychologists Richard Nisbett and Dov Cohen's fascinating study of the psychology of Southern culture describes the place as a *Culture of Honor*, which developed quite differently from the North: "The South differed . . . in a very important economic respect and . . . this has carried profound cultural consequences . . . the southern preference for violence stems from the fact that much of the South was a lawless, frontier region settled by a people whose economy was originally based on herding . . . [in] herding societies . . . a threat to property or reputation is dealt with by violence."[10]

Retributive violence, of course, is an especially bad judicial strategy in dense and modern population areas where people are focused on manufacturing, industry, or commerce. In order to accommodate these purposes, a more abstract form of justice was developed. But in the South, conditions were different, and the culture of honor was sustained even as the Northern states developed into a more modern, impersonal society.

The means of achieving such violent *talionic* justice in the South was primarily the blood feud or family feud. The word *feud* itself derives from a thirteenth-century Scottish term, *fede*, meaning "enmity" or "hostility." The best-known feud is undoubtedly the thirteen-year conflict between the Hatfields and the McCoys in the border country of Kentucky and Tennessee from 1878 to 1891. This feud resulted in a dozen violent deaths and many more injuries.[11] Generally, the social impact of such conflicts is to impress on every witness that a "threat of deadly consequences for family members [is] the primary means of maintaining [social] order."[12] In describing the transformations that have taken place in the human behaviors of "trust" since the age of such feuds, Giddens writes, "Kinship connections are often a focus of tension and conflict . . . however many conflicts they involve and anxieties they provoke . . . kinship can usually be relied upon to meet a range of obligations more or less regardless of whether they feel personally sympathetic toward the individuals involved. . . . Kinship . . . provides a nexus of reliable social connections which . . . form an organizing medium of trust relations."[13]

In addition to the importance of kinship relations among premodern people, Giddens identifies loyalties that result from membership in the local community as an important formative nexus for premodern trust. Unlike the North, few major centers of population developed in the South, and these either came late or derived from the early establishment of port cities. The prohibitive geography and low population base of herding cultures presents genuine obstacles to regional social development. Giddens points out that "the large majority of the population were relatively immobile and isolated . . . locality in pre-modern contexts is the focus of and contributes to ontological security in ways that are substantially dissolved in circumstances of modernity."[14]

As a result of continuous contact among the few inhabitants of a given community, trust naturally develops among them.

Giddens's last two determinants for premodern trust can be considered together. Religion and tradition seem to have quite similar functions. In homogeneous premodern settings, religious cosmologies and cultural traditions provide continuity across time, and time itself is past oriented. History and precedent have enormous influence on contemporary cultural issues.[15] Both are long-range ways of organizing groups of people across periods that are longer than any one human life. Giddens writes that "tradition is routine. But it is routine which is intrinsically meaningful."[16] Religion is potentially more meaningful than tradition since "deities and . . . forces provide providentially dependable supports."[17] Nonetheless, in premodern cultures, both religion and tradition are often personified in a relationship with an unimpeachable religious functionary, who explains the cosmology of the community's beliefs in ways that "inject reliability in the experience of events."[18] Giddens suggests that religion may be "connected psychologically to trust mechanisms" through the "personages . . . forces it represents" and that because of this religious trust, therefore, resembles what he elsewhere terms the "basic trust" invested in "parental figures."[19] In a comparison of the antebellum South and the emergent modernity of the northern Union, Giddens's observations are confirmed again and again. In the South, religious functionaries championed their communities' most heinous beliefs and traditions, including slavery, against the criticisms of Northern abolitionists whose best view of Southern culture was that it was extremely backward. Things came to a head in November 1860, of course, when an abolitionist president was elected to office. In response to this election, Southern ministers preached and then published antiabolitionist sermons, which became bestsellers throughout the South. The best-known of these is probably Benjamin Palmers's "Slavery a Divine Trust, Duty of the South to Preserve and Perpetuate It: A Sermon Preached in the First Presbyterian Church of New Orleans, La., Nov. 29, 1860." A few short weeks before the first eleven states left the Union, the author of this tract observed that Southern statesmen were currently forming a government "to uphold and perpetuate what they cannot resign without dishonor and palpable ruin."

MODERN TRUST

> The change to urban life has affected deeply the customs, the habits, and the thoughts of the people. . . . Modern concentrations of vast numbers of people in cities has led to the organization of industrial corporations with hundreds and frequently thousands of employees. . . . More government is demanded . . . the fear is that these tendencies are going too far, that the worker is being made into a machine, and that so much effort is given to developing his material side, that the moral and spiritual sides are forgotten.
>
> —Robert Ridgway, "ASCE President's Annual Address," *Proceedings of the American Society of Civil Engineers*, 1925

In the Northeast, a very different—much more abstract and impersonal—system of trust was evolving, one that replaced long-term relationships and, too often, personal contact itself. Very different patterns of social organization were required for the larger society resulting from the exponential industrial and commercial expansion that characterized the emerging continental economy. The "American system of production" was emerging and had not yet been adopted by the rest of the world. Bertram Wyatt-Brown casts the beliefs of America's industrial heartland in sharp contrast to those of the South on the eve of war: "Behind [their] differences lay the bourgeois and highly institutionalized nature of Yankee culture. In the rapidly modernizing North, the strength of other institutions lessened personal dependency of family and community opinion, especially in cities, which absorbed a large share of the Northern population. Even the few Southern cities that existed were more rural in culture and milieu than were their Yankee counterparts."[20]

Fundamental to this emerging system is what Anthony Giddens calls "modern trust" or "system trust." I believe this is ground zero for our contemporary isolation and reliance on technology. As modernism evolved, kinship relationships and the homogeneity and traditions of long-established local communities were replaced by the casual friendships and by the fleeting partnerships of heterogeneous urban dwellers. One strange symptom of this transformation in human trust is a marked increase in serial killings in the United States after the midcentury. A popular history of murders in the United States cites the example of Herman Webster Mudgett, claiming that "the latter part of the nineteenth century produced one of America's worst mass and serial killers."[21] But Mudgett had plenty of company, including the Bloody Benders, Jane Toppan, the (Austin) Servant Girl Annihilator, Alfred Packer, and Johann Otto Hoch. The electric chair was developed and first used to eliminate this new crop of murderers in 1890. Moreover, Eric Monkkonen, a historian of public policy, has described the development of municipal police forces throughout the later nineteenth century as a symptom of the transformation in trust then taking place in America's cities. In the expanding metropolis, urban police forces were increasingly founded to protect citizens from each other as "U.S. cities increasingly became cities of strangers . . . in an age when unprecedented numbers of migrants came from greater distances and different cultures, perceptions of transience could easily be heightened. And when cities became large, one's daily chances of interactions with strangers became certain. Urban dwellers shared the same spaces and many customs, yet they often did not know one another. Intimacy of place, experience, and attitude became radically severed from mutual trust in the second half of the nineteenth century. Onto the streets of these complex and unnerving cities walked the newly uniformed police."[22]

A further contemporary symptom of the transformation in trust is the profound change that took place in the primary associations with the word itself. Standard Oil's general counsel Samuel C. T. Dodd exploited "trust" laws previously used to protect the property of elderly or incompetent citizens. Dodd cleverly evaded anticompetition legislation with a new form of corporate organization based on administration by a "board of trustees" rather than by a tycoon-proprietor like the man who had hired him, John D. Rockefeller. These trustees administrated but did not own the corporation's holdings, and this exempted the company they administrated from antimonopolistic prosecution. Dodd's model of distancing legal responsibility from administrative decisions became the organizing principle for all large corporations in the 1880s. Even the antitrust Sherman Act of 1890 did little to change America's perception that the economy was controlled by large monopolistic corporations. "Trust" became an epithet and "shorthand for almost any large business corporation regardless of its size."[23]

In the twentieth century, the transformation of trust, the most fundamental human/hominin behavior, was so profound that Anthony Giddens returns to it in volume after volume during the 1990s. His most readable and thoughtful study on the subject is *The Transformation of Intimacy* (1992), in which he writes:

> Kinship was once seen as naturally given, a series of rights and obligations which biblical and marriage ties created. Kinship relations, it has been widely argued, have been largely destroyed with the development of modern institutions . . . in the separating and divorcing society, the nuclear family generates a diversity of new ties associated, for example, with so-called recombinant families. However, the nature of these ties changes as they are subject to greater negotiation than before. Kinship relations often used to be a taken-for-granted basis of trust; now trust has to be negotiated and bargained for, and commitment is as much of an issue as in sexual relationships.[24]

Although a negotiated form of interpersonal trust remains after kinship is deconstructed by modernity, nonetheless, it is rarer and harder to achieve than the trust characteristic of traditional societies. In other words, as we moderns lost the habit of trusting others, the activity of trusting became more fraught and less frequent, and we relied on distractions and diversions to deflect the emptiness of an untrusting world. Interpersonal cooperation became increasingly obsolete as the traditional community dissolved. As our emerging modern world expanded toward its current global scale, interpersonal distance created a "transformation in intimacy," the very topic Giddens investigates. The cooperation of traditional societies changed into the competition of modern society.

In every context of everyday life, this transformation can be observed, compared, and "analysed in terms of the building of trust mechanisms."[25] Specifically, Giddens continues, "Trust in abstract systems provides for the security of day-to-day reliability, but by its very nature cannot supply either the mutuality or intimacy which personal trust relations offer. In this respect traditional religions are plainly different from modern abstract systems because their personalized figures allows for a direct transfer of individual trust. . . . In the case of abstract systems, by contrast, trust presumes faith in impersonal principles."[26]

Abstract and secular systems like the "corporation," the "labor union," and the "stock exchange" appeared in the nineteenth century. These systems have since "provided a great deal of security . . . which was absent in pre-modern" times, but, nonetheless, "trust in abstract systems is not psychologically rewarding in the way in which trust in persons is."[27] Gradually secular organizations replaced religion as the primary means of organizing and stabilizing human relationships across time. Increasingly, too, these relationships were monetized and hence subject to free-market competition. The phrase "caveat emptor" had ushered in the modern era for American capitalism after the *Laidlaw v. Organ* decision in 1817, but by the 1860s, market competition had accelerated so that "the basic problem of legal thinkers after the Civil War was how to articulate a conception of property that could accommodate the tremendous expansion in the variety of forms of ownership spawned by a dynamic industrial society."[28]

Competitive and financial values intruded into all aspects of human interaction, and, oddly, we became poorer for it. As we became mobile, economic beings tied to a series of productive cities, we lost our closest trusting relationships with kin, religion, and tradition. Because they were tied to distant communities, these relationships were inadequate to support our forebears in the wider, urban horizon to which they migrated. The relationships of hearth and home were simply too cumbersome to transport or sustain over long distances, although we quickly invented new technologies—the photograph, the telephone, and the voice recording—to attempt such sustenance. Very quickly our primary relationships with kith and kin were displaced by new, less satisfying, more abstract, and more transitory relationships formed in the urban crucible. As we adapted, we learned how to compete better and how to cooperate *and to commit to each other* less.

Moreover, around the middle of the nineteenth century, British engineer Henry Bessemer discovered that simply by blowing hot air across molten pig iron, he could *usually* burn away its silicon and carbon impurities, creating structural steel in a cheap and fast one-step process. After 1858, structural steel became plentiful in Great Britain where the prototype skyscraper, a ten-story building unremarkable by today's standards, was erected in Liverpool in 1861. In America, Alexander Lyman Holley adapted the Bessemer process, and as structural steel became more common in the United States, skyscrapers followed.[29] Modern human society quickly became more urban and sky-bound, and as this happened, it also became much less *autochthonous*, or connected to specific physical landscapes and to the communities they contained in emotional and spiritual ways. Pedestrian traffic on the sidewalks of the vertical city intensified, of course, but this simply promoted interpersonal coldness, as did the rush to compete for economic survival.

In the premodern South, friends, neighbors, and relatives had un-self-consciously "hollered" out their greetings and news to each known, familiar, and more or less trusted neighbor in a uniquely American verbal behavior (hollerin') that preceded the rebel yell and promoted "social cohesion," the kind of cooperation typical of small, precapitalistic communities like Appalachia. Like the banjo, this practice had

African origins. Originally, Southern field cries were "made by the voice of one lonely worker to a companion hundreds of yards away in another field."[30] Eventually this practice spilled out of the farm field and came to convey news and greetings. It was originally called "negro yodling," "Carolina yelling," "corn-field or cotton-field hollerin'," "whooping," or "loud-mouthing," but it was common among Southern rural people irrespective of race. A roving reporter from the *New York Daily News* encountered it among a gang of black railroad workmen in 1853: "Suddenly one raised a shout as I had never heard before, a long, loud musical shout rising and falling and breaking into falsetto, his voice ringing through the woods in the clear frosty night air like a bugle call. As he finished, the melody was caught up by another, and then another, and then several in chorus."[31]

The practice of hollerin', however, would have been grotesquely misplaced in the vertical city. As Mark Twain recorded in the 1880s, pedestrian traffic there resembled a scene from *Metropolis*. Strangers brushed past masses of fellow strangers staring straight ahead in complete silence at regular intervals during the ordinary working day. Gradually a new sociological phenomenon emerged, that of the "civil inattention" described by Erving Goffman (in 1963) as the first generation of electronically isolating mobile devices—transistor radios—emerged.[32] All this happened at the moment society became focused on time, money, and the future. Curbstone brokers began selling shares in small companies immediately after the Civil War, and by 1908 the New York Curb Market Agency had standardized the practice of selling "securities"—stocks, bonds, and "futures"—among its members. Eventually, this practice would become automated in an abstract system that entirely eliminated the necessity to trust a personal but potentially unscrupulous broker. At roughly the same time, futuristic fiction became mainstream. The best-known speculative fiction of the period is Edward Bellamy's bestseller *Looking Backward* (1887), a book that prefigures the futuristic writings of H. G. Wells, especially his nonfiction bestseller *Anticipations* (1901). But Bellamy was not alone in writing futuristic works in America during the 1880s. Other books included American publications of the anonymous New Zealand novel *The Great Romance* (1881), John Macnie's *The Diothas* (1883), and Laurence Gronlund's *The Coming Revolution* (1880) and *The Cooperative Commonwealth* (1884). By the end of the nineteenth century, the future rivaled the past as a focus for contemporary speculation. This was an entirely new shift in imaginative thought.

MODERN ALTERNATIVES TO TRUST: PROFESSIONALIZATION

> It was the American universities that took engineering away from rule-of-thumb surveyors, mechanics and Cornish foremen and lifted it into the realm of application of science. . . . The European universities did not acknowledge engineering as a profession until long after America had done so.
>
> —Herbert Hoover,
> *Memoirs: Years of Adventure, 1874–1920*, 1951

A critical symptom of the nineteenth century's transformation of intimacy was the expansion of the "professions." Whereas premodern people, in times of crisis, vested their confidence in a reputable, familiar, and reassuring shaman, warlord, or priest, moderns put their trust in the knowledge and behavior of an abstract profession whose trained, objective "expert" (a "professor" or, later, a "professional") acted as an impersonal gateway to the collective expertise of a particular science or body of law. This is exactly what Luhmann and Giddens mean when they say "system trust" lacks "mutuality and intimacy":

Personal concerns and considerations are externalities to be avoided by the skilled professional. He or she is "trustworthy" only because each professional "discipline" is an abstract embodiment of knowledge represented by interchangeable experts trained or "disciplined" to obey its rules. In military terms we respond to a professional as we would to an officer of a superior rank, "we salute—or respect—the office, not the man." Moreover, all professions have explicitly formulated injunctions against "becoming (too or overly) personal" and insist that practitioners "remain professional" during interactions with clients. An important step in achieving the social acceptance necessary to establish a profession is formulating explicit "codes of ethic" that stipulate the ways in which a practitioner "maintains objectivity" or "distance" in representing the interests of his or her clientele. The absence of any close, personal relationship, according to the ideology of the professions, is the best guarantee that each client will be well served. It is also a symptom of the transformation that took place in human trust: moderns were required to invest confidence in temporary leaders who were personally unknown to them.

Until these changes took hold, our modern dichotomy between the words *amateur* and *professional* did not exist in the early nineteenth century. At that time, being an "amateur" simply meant to be an enthusiastic lover or appreciator of a particular discipline. An amateur scientist interested in electromagnetism might still attempt experiments and make cutting-edge discoveries that attracted the notice of more advanced practitioners. There was not yet a discipline-driven disdain for the curious or the self-taught. And there were not yet any laws that compelled citizens to use professional services to access a whole range of services from medications to electrical connections. Consequently, this was an age of remarkable innovation and invention, and, to some extent, because of this, the transitional period between premodern and modern America resembles our own innovative era, which owes its existence to the democratization of expertise facilitated by the Internet. In that bygone time, modern-day hackers would have been inventors.

In nineteenth-century America, a variety of occupations professionalized to accommodate the expansion of society and the economy. This was a century-long process that was not complete until about 1910, when the US Census first registered the occupation "engineer." That year, when there were over ninety million Americans, the engineering profession was well advanced, with about forty thousand people describing themselves as engineers. Nearly a century before, in 1817, United States Military Academy West Point was founded to supply the United States with the civil engineers George Washington longed for during and after the Revolutionary War. One of General Lafayette's officers, a military engineer and artillerist, Louis de Tousard, left French service after Louis XVI's execution in 1793. Because he resigned his commission, he could not be recruited as an instructor at the prestigious École Polytechnique, which opened in 1794. Instead, in 1795, Tousard joined the newly formed US Corps of Artillerists and Engineers, and by 1798, he had completed a blueprint for West Point called "Formation of a School of Artillerists and Engineers," which he sent to James McHenry, the secretary of war.

In 1804, Napoleon transformed the École Polytechnique (which the French simply call "X"—pronounced "eeks") into the leading military school of its day, and the American military establishment began paying strict attention to Tousard's proposal. They laid plans to graft the excellence of French training institutions onto the American military, but the War of 1812 intervened. By 1815, a site had been selected, and Major Sylvanus Thayer was chosen to organize the new school. He was sent to France to study the curriculum and methods of both

"X" and the Artillery and Engineering School at Metz. Thayer returned to America in 1817 with a library of twelve hundred technical books and a small corps of French-trained engineers who taught a very select group of cadets fencing, drawing, mathematics, engineering, and the French language. Usually the development of training schools and the compartmentalization of subspecialties develop late in the evolution of a new profession.[33] In America, however, Sylvanus Thayer was able to reverse this process of development and jump-start the acceptance of engineering as a profession in a nation that already had a vigorous mechanical-shop culture. The impact these men had on the emerging economy was enormous: "Working so closely with private enterprise enticed many officers to resign and take more lucrative positions in civilian life. One-fourth of former officers in the antebellum era later worked as civil engineers. These defections gave rise to criticism of the academy and its curriculum. One historian correctly . . . wrote that before the Civil War, West Point produced more railroad presidents than generals."[34]

Although Britain and Germany had already developed formidable traditions of engineering, neither had organized their engineering schools by the time Thayer graduated his first class of recruits in the early 1820s.[35] America's first popular songwriter, John Hall Hewitt, failed to graduate in the class of 1822. Thayer didn't care. He was training engineers, and his was an egg-breaking form of pedagogical brutality well-suited to a military school. In his point-driven meritocracy, engineers were West Point's most elite product. The line officers who graduated from the school, especially in the first three decades, were—simply put—the worst engineering students. These men were called "goats," and a tradition would develop (after 1907) of an annual football game played in senior year between the "goats" and the "engineers." Famous goats include such formidable military minds as William Tecumseh Sherman and Ulysses S.

Grant.[36] Others who failed their exams and did not graduate included Edgar Allan Poe and James McNeill Whistler, whose father *was* a graduate. In later years, Whistler would sometimes remark that "if silicon had been a gas, I would have been a Major General."[37] John Tidball, who was a goat and a graduate, became a courageous line officer, distinguishing himself at Gettysburg before becoming a major general in 1865. Tidball graduated in the class of 1848 and later described the engineering curriculum as resembling the rigor of a Jesuit education. Perhaps he was correct in guessing that the French officer training that served as the model for West Point owed much of its severity to the demanding pedagogical practices of the Soldiers of Christ, who permeated French institutions of higher learning at the time: "We were taught with every breath we drew . . . the utmost reverence for this [order-of-merit] scale; it becomes a kind of fixture in our minds that the engineers were a species of gods, next to which came the 'topogs'—only a grade below the first, but still a grade—they were but demigods . . . the line was simply the line, whether the horse, foot or dragoon, . . . for the latter a good, square seat in the saddle was deemed more important than brains. These ideas were ground into our heads with . . . Jesuitical persistency."[38]

The Thayer method was extremely effective, even it was unimaginative. Thayer's pedagogical philosophy aimed for complete uniformity of product, since in that age, uniformity was a fetish of the French military, which pursued it in everything from "uniforms" to ordnance. At his artillery school, Tousard had learned what was alternately called the "uniformity system," or "le système Gribeauval," named after General Jean-Baptiste Vaquette de Gribeauval, who revolutionized Napoleon's artillery by attempting to make uniform field guns that did not sacrifice range despite their compact size. De Gribeauval commissioned gunsmith Honoré Blanc to manufacture muskets with interchangeable flintlock, and Blanc is said to have achieved this (in a limited way) around 1778. Unfortunately, there was no funding available to manufacture such guns in pre-Revolutionary France, and America's ambassador to France, Thomas Jefferson, could not convince Blanc to immigrate. Without a European expert available, Washington awarded a contract for twelve thousand similar guns to Eli Whitney in 1788.[39] Later, Thayer learned the de Gribeauval system and noticed that the French had since extended the principle from field guns and musket flintlocks to the interior of military personnel's minds. Like the French, Thayer decided to create a corps of civil engineers who were as interchangeable as pieces of field artillery. His motto was "Every man in every subject, every man proficient in everything; every man every day."[40] The Thayer method was "an integrated pedagogical and disciplinary regime that put each candidate under tremendous stress, immersed him in a demanding curriculum, and gave him little time to call his own . . . [it] depended upon a system of quantifiable standards . . . Thayer developed a four-year curriculum that prescribed the courses each cadet would study and master before graduation and commissioning . . . not only did each cadet have to master his subject; he had to prove his competence in daily oral and written recitation. To facilitate this method, West Point pioneered the use of classroom blackboards."[41]

Such a curriculum aimed to create officers who were not only self-sufficient but also immediately replaceable in the exigencies of war. The principle of uniformity (and the standardization it implies) is a modern military necessity that French military strategists imposed on ordinary soldiers with the invention of uniforms in 1660. Eventually they applied it, as de Gribeauval did, to the manufacture of military ordnance, specifying the precise dimensions of field pieces and their conditions of manufacture. Military engineering academies like Metz's Artillery and Engineering School, the École

Polytechnique, and USMA West Point simply extended the principle of uniformity to include the expertise of the officers they produced.

The comparison between men and machines had become common among French intellectuals since René Descartes first described the human body as a "machine made by the hands of god that is incomparably better arranged . . . than is any machine of human invention." The first automata appeared in the seventeenth century. All were imitations of biological forms, and many were actually human. Progressively, the Cartesian notion that man is little more than a biological mechanism gained notoriety in France following its exposition by the atheist-physician Julien Offray de La Mettrie in *L'Homme machine* (1748). So, in a very real sense, the virtue of "interchangeability" that characterizes the ultimate goal of all professions was probably a French notion brought to the United States by Louis de Tousard in 1795 and Sylvanus Thayer in 1817.

No matter what its origin, the modern and secular features of the idea that men have become essentially similar and replaceable demonstrates the shift from premodern, metaphysical concerns about soul, spirit, and honor to a much more utilitarian view of man as a functioning military, economic, or industrial unit. As premodern or traditional society faded, what it is to be human had diminished under pressures from technology and from the application of economic reasoning to every aspect of human life. By 2010, the size of the average American workspace declined from the ninety square feet allotted to workers in 1994 to only seventy-five square feet. Man, too, has shrunk, becoming an atomic unit orbiting, serving, and servicing the machinery of his city—his economy. Today, human longing persists, but it is no longer projected backward toward our divine, parental origins. Instead we project our longing into the technological future where we imagine—again—that we will soon be fulfilled and finally free.

MODERN ALTERNATIVES TO TRUST: STANDARDIZATION

> Because owners of standardized goods are unable to identify goods sold legitimately or stolen, possession tends to be synonymous with legal ownership . . . that is if someone is in possession of a standardized good, he will be presumed to be the legal owner. Today possession and ownership are bundled together. . . . The opposite is true of an artisan good.
>
> —Douglas Allen

Before mass production, manufacturing involved lengthy processes of craftsman "finishing" products. Goods produced in this artisanal way are distinct from each in myriad details. Connoisseurship is little more than the ability to distinguish, and compare such minute detail. But in the nineteenth century, interchangeability, a clumsy word, became a central characteristic of manufacturers" emerging mindset. This was especially true in America. The achievement of real interchangeability among manufactured parts gave the United States its unique technological manufacturing advantage over the rest of the world.[42] The adoption of interchangeability had profound economic significance, but it was much more significant culturally because it facilitated the emergence of mass (or, as it was called at the time, "crowd") consumer culture. Once marketing was invented to create mass desire, everybody could own the same mass-produced thing, and once desire and its objects became standardized, people too—at least for economic purposes—became virtually identical, just as they became identical in legal terms. Legal ownership, after standardization, was simplified to a matter of mere possession since mass-produced, non-artisanal objects could not be distinguished from each other. An owner was an owner if he was in possession of such a mass-produced object, and for this reason each owner was more or less the same, legally and economically, as the product he owned.

For this reason, interchangeability was the first step toward mass culture.

The American System of Manufacture/Production made standardized individual components that could be combined at random into manufactured goods. The immediate advantages of such a system appeared in the areas of production, assembly, and repair. Ignorant of the later terms *assembly line* or *division of labor*, an early contractor nonetheless reported: "By confining a worker to one particular limb of the pistol, until he has made two thousand, I save at least one quarter of his labor."[43] The American System involves semiskilled labor using *machines* and *jigs* to make standardized, identical, interchangeable *parts*, which are then assembled with minimal time, skill, and craftsmen ordinarily required to "fit" the component pieces into a finished product. In all manufacturing areas, the American System provided consistent quality and much lower—completely predictable—production times and costs. It was an essential step to mass production and mass culture.

The full range of advantages provided by the American System may not have been immediately clear to early American manufacturers pursuing interchangeability; nonetheless, it became the holy grail of mechanical-shop culture in the post-colonial United States. In his treatise *American Artillerist's Companion* (1809), Tousard refers to this virtue as "uniformity," and it touches on many military things, from the casting of artillery, to cavalry equipment and the interchangeability of weapon parts to facilitate their repair. In its largest sense, interchangeability was part of the same military mindset that developed "regimentation" and the military "uniforms" that preceded uniformity. In American hands, it came to encompass—as we've seen—the knowledge base of military engineers as well as the personal arms they commissioned from private manufacturers. Eli Whitney is reputed to be the first American mechanical engineer to achieve true "interchangeability" among the manufactured parts of his guns, and this took place around 1801, but the tentative terms on which this claim is based need to be remembered:

> If gun parts were then called "uniform," it must be recollected that the present generation [published in 1882] stands upon a plane of mechanical intelligence so much higher, and with facilities for observations so much more extensive than existed in those times [1801] that the very language of expression has changed. Uniformity in gun work was then, as now, a comparative term; but then it meant within a thirty-second of an inch or more, where it now means within half a thousandth of an inch. Then interchangeability may have signified a great deal of filing and fitting, and an uneven joining when fitted, where now it signifies slipping in a piece, turning a screw-driver and having a close even fit.[44]

Among Tousard's American colleagues in the US Corps of Artillerists and Engineers was a young captain who would later become the army's first chief of ordnance, Col. Decius Wadsworth. From Tousard, Wadsworth so absorbed the need for military uniformity that he adopted it into a personal motto that imitated *Liberté, Égalité, Fraternité*, the call to arms of the French Revolution. Wadsworth characterized his own mission as US ordnance chief with the motto "Uniformity, Simplicity, Solidarity." He was a close friend of Eli Whitney and indulged the inventor when Whitney delivered only five hundred of the twelve thousand guns specified by his army contract.[45] But the quest for uniformity became an ideal demanded by Wadsworth and by George Bomford, his deputy and the man who succeeded him in 1821. An 1813 War Department contract awarded to Connecticut gunsmith Simeon North for twenty thousand pistols stipulated that "component parts of these pistols are to correspond so exactly that any limb or any part . . . may be fitted to any other pistol of the twenty thousand."[46] Although North abandoned his attempt to fulfill this difficult condition after manufacturing only a few hundred pistols, this contractual specification is a watershed, marking the end of handicraft techniques and the beginning of mass production.

Mass production was pursued at the Springfield Armory by its new superintendent, Roswell Lee, after the Ordnance Department gained control of both federal armories in 1815. In the recent war of 1812, "vast numbers of arms had been damaged beyond repair in the field," causing resupply delays requiring great additional expenditure.[47] Knowing the examples of Blanc, Whitney, and North, Wadsworth and Bomford theorized that in future conflicts many damaged weapons might be salvaged and repaired *in the field* if their parts were manufactured to be truly interchangeable. This goal led to increasingly specific demands to army contractors, as well as to a much more precise system of inspections at both the Springfield and Harpers Ferry Armories. John Hall invented a breech-loading gun in 1811 and received a contract for the manufacture of one hundred such guns from the Ordnance Department in 1817.

Around this time, Hall encountered the idea of "uniformity" and set himself the objective of making his gun parts completely interchangeable and therefore more attractive to the War Department. A deeply practical man, he devoted considerable thought to the mechanics of the problems presented by such manufacture, while familiarizing himself with the best current practices. Finally, Hall settled on an elaborate system of gauges and fixtures to set and maintain the quality of production for each manufactured part to a degree that was unlike anything that preceded him.[48] In 1851, the vernier caliper (also called a nonius) initiated a new era of precision toolmaking when it was refined and reinvented by Joseph R. Brown of Brown and Sharpe Ltd. This inexpensive, easy-to-produce tool enabled machinists to detect dimensions as small as one-thousandth of an inch, and it radically raised the standards of mechanical engineering in metal throughout the United States. Already in 1819, John Hall had used an elaborate system of master gauges to detect extremely fine dimensions of difference among his rifle's parts during their manufacture. Improvements in the vernier caliper eventually made Hall's model easier to follow.

The War Department awarded Hall a contract requiring he work in the Harpers Ferry Armory. Undoubtedly, the Ordnance Department wanted his expertise in interchangeability transferred to their site, and he was given a free hand in designing the armory's rifle works. Hall began work on one thousand breechloaders in 1820 and finished them in 1824. He then claimed to have solved the problem of interchangeability and along the way to have invented the idea of economies of scale. In 1828, when the War Department requested he manufacture one thousand rifles, Hall wrote back to Colonel Bomford, telling him that the fixed costs for three thousand rifles would not be greater than for the thousand Bomford had requested.[49] By 1852, the American System—then known as the Armory System—of manufacture was firmly established. Although many manufacturers, like Samuel Colt, for example, could not pass a real test of interchangeability among the parts of their guns, nonetheless, both the Springfield and Harpers Ferry Armories could. An English visitor inspecting the Springfield Armory in 1852 wrote: "This manufactory is reduced to an almost perfect system; a pistol being composed of a certain number of distinct pieces, each piece is produced in appropriate quantity by machinery . . . each operation being performed by a special machine made on purpose, many of these machines requiring hardly any skill from the attendant . . . once the machine is properly set it will produce thousands."[50]

Mass production had begun. By 1873, the difficult English word *interchangeable* had been replaced with a newer, more flexible adjective *standardized*, which could also easily function as a verb. *Standardization*, the abstract process of standardizing something, entered American English a few years later, and soon most human activities, as Veblen observed in 1904, had been affected by the "enforcement of precise mechanical measurements and adjustments and the reduction of all manner of things, purposes, acts, necessities, conveniences and amenities of life to standard units."[51]

Soon (in 1913) Frederick Winslow Taylor would apply such standardization to the best practices of the best workers in order to "scientifically manage" their industrial production. Of course, the economic imposition of such discipline on workers contributed considerably to the psychic shift then transforming the citizens of the United States.

MODERN ALTERNATIVES TO TRUST: RELIABLE MACHINES

> Whether the gods are well or ill-disposed, the car will start, the rifle will fire, the stereo will play. . . . Technology is founded on the implicit belief that machines are not possessed of psychology.
>
> —Norman Mailer, *Of a Fire on the Moon*, 1970

Simultaneously, as intimacy was being transformed by the processes of modernization, reliable methods of manufacture were developed, and among the goods produced were, after all, the first truly reliable machines developed for mass consumption. The phrase "accurate and reliable machine" first appears in the postwar period (around 1874 or so), and it was probably first used to describe sewing machines. The mechanical "reliability" of these devices was an abstract quality, which, like trust, enabled individuals to predict future outcomes based on a previous performance. But a seamstress required less skill to operate a sewing machine than to work a needle and thread. Using a machine, her productivity was incrementally increased and became extremely predictable after a modest amount of training. So, unlike trust, reliability does not presuppose very much about human beings or their relationships. Only a living being such as a friend, a dog, or a horse can be trustworthy. Judging from the evidence of contemporary print advertisements, in the final decades of the nineteenth century, reliability and accuracy became qualities increasingly associated with (and desired from) machines as human trust became increasingly more abstract. Clocks, sewing machines, bicycles, and crop reapers were among these transformative technologies. Increasingly, Americans relied on inventors to deliver such innovations and on a growing professional class of mechanical engineers to manufacture them. As they did so, they relied on each other less, trusted each other less, and accepted the absence of trust as part of the modern condition.

The first truly reliable products of the Armory System were guns. It should be remembered that although the country was in transition, America was still a predominantly rural nation (until the 1920s), and hunting game was a nutritional strategy, not the recreational activity it has become for most North Americans. As a consequence, before professional sport was invented, shooting *was* the national sport, and before the midcentury, most American men owned guns, especially long guns, or rifles. The best gun of its day, John Hall's remarkable breech-loading rifle, was nonetheless potentially dangerous to operate, and, at forty dollars, it was beyond the range of most nineteenth-century Americans. It was refined by Benjamin Henry in the 1850s, and on a good day, his Henry repeating rifle could fire up to twenty-two rounds per minute, a vast improvement over paper cartridge/percussion cap rifles that, even in the best hands, could fire only three rounds per minute. Despite its many advantages, the breech-loading Henry repeating rifle was an unreliable tool that packed only a small punch and frequently jammed or exploded. Often Hall's rifle parts did not fit together precisely, and, in field conditions, grit from the environment or residue from repeated fire would cause the gun to jam. Even so, the Henry repeater was a very popular weapon, and for a few years it represented the cutting-edge of American machine technology of the day.

By 1857, however, a gifted American mechanical engineer named Christopher Miner Spencer used the model of the Henry rifle to develop another long gun that was remarkable for its period in a variety of ways. It debuted one year before the War between the States. Like the Henry, it was a breech-loading weapon. Like the Henry, too, it used copper-jacketed rim-fire cartridges. These were held in a metal tube inside the gun's stock, just as they were with the Henry repeater, but there all comparisons end. The Spencer repeating rifle was a small revolution in mechanical precision. Using his thirteen years' experience in the most commercial machine shops of the era, Spencer had succeeded in mass-producing precise weapon parts that facilitated the speedy, unskilled assembly of a gun that could easily fire twelve rounds per minute, while never exploding or jamming. The rifle could be reloaded very quickly, and it also required little maintenance. It packed a bigger punch than a Henry rifle and could reliably bring down a deer or, as the Civil War would soon demonstrate, an enemy. Spencer charged the War Department $37.50 for each of the 12,471 guns he sold them before the war ended in 1865.

The most remarkable thing about the Spencer repeating rifle was its reliability. It could be trusted to do its job. Eighty-seven years before the debut of the Avtomat Kalashnikova (AK) model in 1947, Spencer anticipated Mikhail Kalashnikov's formula for success in a long gun. He kept it simple. In an age when human trust was becoming obsolete, reliable machines were beginning to appear that obviated the need for trust. These included Singer sewing machines and early McCormick reapers. Similarly, the Spencer repeating rifle and its little brother, the Spencer carbine, were just such reliable machines. Although the gun debuted in 1860, it was not well-known outside of Boston until after the Union victory at Gettysburg in 1863. But in the summer of 1862, an article from the *Boston Post* was reprinted in local papers throughout the Union, including the *New Hampshire Statesman*, which reissued the piece on August 23:

> Among the many extraordinary inventions of the day none, we think, exceed the Spencer Breech-loading rifle. . . . For accuracy and force it is second to no other rifle, and for safety and rapidity of discharge no other gun can be compared to it . . . the . . . range of the gun . . . in the hands of an experienced shot certain to hit an object the size of a man 400 yards off or one-fourth of a mile. Fifty cartridges weigh less than four pounds, so that . . . a man can carry a large amount of ammunition. They are perfectly water proof and can be carried safely anywhere. One great defect of other breech-loading arms is the escape of fire and gas at the breech. Owing to the superior mechanism of this gun it is entirely free from this error. Another trouble . . . has been that from expansion caused by the heat of firing the machinery cannot be worked, but this rifle has been proved by long and continuous fire to be free of this error. It was fired, we think, over five hundred times at the Washington Navy Yard without any trouble. One other trouble is the fouling of breech loading arms. This rifle has been dis-

> charged seven hundred times without cleaning. . . . Under the direction of Major Dyer at Fortress Monro, the working portion of the rifle was filled with sand and soaked in water . . . but under all and every circumstance it was found to be efficient and effective. . . . So great a weapon has only to be known to make its way into public favor.

By October, the Spencer rifle had been successfully used in battle and began attracting considerable attention among Union infantry and cavalry officers to whom Spencer sold the gun and its cartridges at a slight discount.[52] In 1861, the War Department had provided Spencer's company with a contract for ten thousand guns, but in April 1862, the treasurer of the Spencer Repeating Rifle Company wrote to the War Department, reporting that "owing to some unexpected, and to our Company, very expensive delays in perfecting the machinery in our armory, we are unable to make the deliveries called for in the first four months, and, according to the letter of the contract, we lose the right to deliver the number of rifles required in those months . . . we respectfully ask that we may have the right to furnish the whole 10,000 rifles."[53]

By that time, there was a new chief of ordnance. Brigadier General James Wolfe "Old Fogey" Ripley was a man whose military service began at the defense of Sackets Harbor late in the War of 1812. Ripley graduated from West Point in 1814 and thus predated Thayer's redesign of the army's curriculum for officers. A staunch conservative who resented the encroachment of technology and engineering on the US military, Ripley noted the unproven nature of the Spencer rifle and the fact that seventy-three thousand other guns, including older Henry repeating rifles, had already been ordered by the War Department. He wrote that he did "not find any important advantage of these arms over several other breech loaders," and deemed it unadvisable to "entertain or accept . . . the [company's] propositions for furnishing these arms."[54]

Having invested over $135,000 on retooling his armory to accommodate the Union contract, Christopher Spencer was confronted with the loss of a substantial personal fortune if any portion of the contract was canceled. Desperately, he pulled every string he could find, including one attached to Samuel Colt, then the most respected arms manufacturer in the world. In August, Christopher Spencer traveled from Boston to Washington for a personal interview with President Lincoln after dinner on the White House grounds. The president, a devoted marksman and lover of gadgetry, had his first practice session with the new gun and was delighted with it. He invited Spencer to return at the same time next evening to shoot again. John Hay's diary records: "This evening and yesterday evening, an hour was spent by the President . . . shooting with Spencer's new repeating rifle. A wonderful gun, loading with absolutely contemptible simplicity and ease with seven balls . . . firing the whole readily . . . in less than half a minute. The President made some pretty good shots. Spencer, the inventor, [is] a quiet little Yankee who sold himself in relentless slavery to his idea for six weary years before it was perfected [he] did some splendid shooting."[55]

Unfortunately, despite Lincoln's intervention, Ripley continued to drag his feet. Some have speculated that although he was born in Connecticut, he had Southern sympathies, including a close relationship with his nephew, Roswell S. Ripley, who became a Confederate brigadier general the same year that Ripley became chief of ordnance. In any case, the War Department purchased only 12,471 Spencer rifles before 1865, although 94,196 units of the lighter, smaller, and—at $25.50—cheaper Spencer carbine found their way into Union hands before the war's end. By this time, Spencer had so perfected his production techniques that the company was easily able to fill these later, larger orders. Moreover, his gunsmithy probably invented what I call elsewhere *repetitive* consumption since, during the war, they supplied the Union with what Ripley disdained as "special ammunition," 58,238,924 copper-jacketed cartridges priced at 2.5 cents apiece.[56]

By the late summer of 1863, it was well known among Union soldiers that the Spencer rifle was a precision offensive weapon designed to render both the bayonet and the infantry charge obsolete. Even the best-trained soldier equipped with the best Springfield rifle (from Harpers Ferry Rifle Shop) of the day could fire, at the absolute most, four rounds a minute. (The Henry repeater was faster but presented a real danger of overheating and jamming during the continuous fire of combat.) After his appointment as chief of ordnance in 1861, Ripley held off ordering more Springfield rifles, mistakenly claiming that the army's surplus stock of older, smooth-bored muskets could be re-rifled and reused. Nonetheless, during an infantry charge, there was little opportunity to reload even the best standard-issue, single-shot rifles, so foot soldiers of the day were forced to rely on socket-style bayonets that turned their firearm into a lance whose tactics were as old as Thermopylae. Many officers and gun enthusiasts among the volunteer units of the Union recognized a lifesaver in the Spencer's rapid-fire potential as soon as the gun became available, and they equipped their units with as many of these weapons as they could afford. Eager to get them into Union hands, Christopher Spencer knocked 6.6 percent ($2.50) off the price of the weapons he sold to Union volunteers. His guns proved decisive in two battles during the summer of 1863.

During General William Rosencrans's Tullahoma campaign against the confederates of middle Tennessee, John Wilder's "Lightning Brigade" attacked Hoover's Gap, a narrow strip of wilderness trail that served as one of three passes between two that separated the Duck and Stones Rivers. The pass was commanded by Confederate entrenchments on the ridges, but these were manned by a single cavalry regiment. On June 24,

Wilder's volunteers rode through the Confederates in a frontal and flanking attack without pausing to reload. They drove the Confederate cavalry back the entire length of the gap—seven miles—to the main body of Southern troops.[57]

However, another battle that summer turned the Spencer rifle into the stuff of legend. At Gettysburg, ten days after Wilder's success in Tennessee, Captain George Custer's second battle halted an infantry advance by fifteen hundred or more of Gen. Jeb Stuart's "Invincibles," with only 479 Spencer repeating rifles. It was a badly needed victory. The previous day, the rash, green Captain Custer lost nearly half of his soldiers and narrowly escaped with his life when he impetuously decided to lead his men on an un-reconnoitered charge against a Confederate position. But then, on June 3, the last day of battle at Gettysburg, Custer situated his men behind the cover of a fence before

> the Rebels . . . broke into a charge . . . [Custer's] 5th Michigan . . . waited until they were just 120 yards away before [ordering] a volley. Five hundred Yankee rifles crashed and smoke shrouded the 5th's line . . . Confederate officers urged their men forward shouting "now for them before they can reload!" But Stuart's Invincibles did not know they were facing repeaters . . . before they could get closer their ranks were stopped by a second volley, withered by a third, and sent running by a fourth. Several Rebels were pinned down . . . right in front of . . . the Michiganers [who] called on them to surrender. . . . Most of them, stunned by the Spencers' performance, did so. "One tall, lean lank Johnny . . . after he came in asked to see our guns, saying: 'You'uns load in the morning and fire all day.'"[58]

Following this brief victory, Custer immediately ordered another charge that also ended in near disaster. Very early in his career, he had set the pattern that would destroy him:

rash charges against superior forces that relied on dumb luck and the power of the Spencer repeating rifle or, in the case of Little Big Horn, the Spencer carbine. At Gettysburg, Spencer repeating rifles "became synonymous with combat prowess," heralding "a change that would virtually reshape modern warfare."[59] Custer himself recommended the weapon wholeheartedly, saying that "the Spencer Repeating Rifle . . . in the hands of brave determined men . . . is the most effective weapon for our cavalry."[60]

Victory at Gettysburg ended Lee's northern invasion and turned the tide of the war. As stories of the battles were repeated across the nation during the remainder of the summer, the Spencer repeating rifle became an emblem of Northern technological superiority, and its fame swept the nation. It was the first "accurate and reliable" machine to be mass-produced. For this reason, General Ripley was replaced as chief of ordnance on September 15, 1863.[61] The new chief placed large orders for Christopher Spencer's lighter, more compact, and cheaper Spencer carbine.

Like General Ripley, military engineers of the early nineteenth century were drawn from an educated class, and so the military adoption of technology was controlled by organizational hierarchies who were drawn from the most privileged Americans families. The Civil War, however, thinned the sons of privilege among the officer classes of the North and South, replacing them with many less-privileged survivors. Simultaneously, many barriers to the adoption of technology were broken. Engineers, as naval historian William McBride points out, could not be recruited fast enough from the privileged classes. As technological superiority showed itself to be a decisive factor in the naval war, and as class barriers among officers were increasingly broken, so, too, were technological innovations adopted at a breakneck pace.[62] Reliance on technological innovation became decisive in all branches of the

Civil War military, and technological wonders occurred on most days of the war. One of the greatest of these accomplishments has disappeared into the past, but it is worth remembering that the greatest technological wonder of the war was the pontoon bridge, and its greatest practitioner was Major James Chapman Duane, whose years of experience during the war culminated in his achievements during Grant's siege of Petersburg, Virginia. In about eighteen hours, on June 13, 1864, Duane built the longest temporary bridge of the war out of 101 pontoons and three schooners. It was 2,170 feet in length, and it spanned the James River for five days as it was tirelessly crossed by a fifty-mile column of the Army of the Potomac and about three thousand head of cattle.

The war's rapid adoption of successful technologies prompted what historian of technology David Nye calls the emergence of the "technological sublime" in America's vivid, post–Civil War imagination.[63] The technological sublime focuses on scientific and engineering achievements that replace our sense of wonder at the natural world with awe at the power and force of man's own creation. Such "shock and awe" is a major source of America's unique faith in its machines, and it is a direct result of the Civil War during which the destruction of Southern technological infrastructure was accompanied by a wealth of technological innovations that the North deployed to wage its total war. These included military railroads, railroad artillery, submarines, snorkels, periscopes (for trench warfare), entire fields of land mines, military telegraphs, naval torpedoes, aerial reconnaissance, antiaircraft fire, telescopic sights, fixed ammunition, ironclad navies, steel ships, revolving gun turrets, machine guns, and electric ordnance triggers.[64]

Not for the first time in human history, technological superiority brought about a clear and decisive military victory, but this time it was a victory derived from the reliance on reliable machines with interchangeable mass-produced parts. Before the Civil War, the nineteenth century had prepared America to conceive and accept technology in a variety of ways. While ideological assumptions about the universe and human society met challenge after challenge from science, families became smaller, and their members dispersed from rural homesteads into Eastern towns and cities. Simultaneously, increasing wealth reached lower into the social hierarchy. As these changes took hold, old codes and loyalties were challenged, suspended, and discarded. In the urban setting, wealth was the preeminent virtue since it opened most other doors. Technology quickly became an emblem of wealth; electric lights, telephones, fans, phonographs, and automobiles broadcast the affluence and success of their owners. Consequently, Yankee ingenuity was first and foremost the ability to make technology reliable, and then to turn it toward moneymaking ends. The tacit acceptance of technological progress also inevitably recognized that social change must accompany each new technology. Invariably, these changes were interpreted as progress. . . .

Successive waves of immigration had made the North heterogeneous. Its manufacturing economy was a sharp contrast to that of the agrarian South, where slave labor was used to support cotton and tobacco production. The North had ample supplies of iron, copper, and lumber and an extensive rail, road, and canal network by the time the South attacked Fort Sumter in 1861. By the 1850s, technology affected most aspects of Northern life, and it was difficult to find a Northern politician or businessman without close ties to mechanized industry or strong technological opinions. Abraham Lincoln first formed his views about the necessity of establishing a continental railway in the 1850s when he was a lawyer defending the freight rights of Chicago's Rock Island line against the river men whose monopoly was rendered obsolete by railroads. In the antebellum South, however, technology had much less impact. Although the cotton gin was a technological revolution that made Southern cotton an economical crop, nonetheless, the South's industry had not progressed much since its invention in 1794. Technologically, the South was underdeveloped. Raw harvested produce went to Northern factories to be turned into finished goods.

In a vicious cycle, value was added to Southern crops in Northern factories and then stayed in the North where it paid for more and more technological progress. Northern influence (both economic and political) spiraled upward. Southern antagonism toward the North's industrial development and "new money" prosperity rivaled Northern antagonism toward its technologically backward neighbor. In the South, outdated notions of rank, honor, and social class comingled with the practice of African American slavery, which offended many Northerners on religious grounds. Nonetheless, slavery had been an accepted part of Southern culture since a Dutch man-of-war brought twenty African "servants" to Virginia in exchange for tobacco in 1619. Since the 1830s, however, black Americans had increasingly become the coreligionists of many white sects, although very few churches—even in the urban North—practiced integrated services on a regular basis. There was irregular, muted, and reluctant tolerance of freedmen in the North, but there was little real integration.

Nonetheless, the world was changing. Slavery was already banned in a rapidly industrializing Europe, including Great Britain. By the 1850s, abolition—an ideology that did not preclude segregation or racism—was perceived as the most enlightened view on the issue of slavery. Increasingly, Northern white Americans held that African-descended slaves did indeed have souls and were thus entitled to religious freedom, as well as to education, freedom of movement (especially to escape slavery and find work), and financial rewards for their labor. Slavery was increasingly an ugly and outmoded concept in the technological North. A growing number of Northerners believed that at some point in the near future, the most onerous human tasks would be assigned to a new generation of reliable machines—robots—and that as slavery became technologically obsolete, all of humankind would enjoy a new "American" freedom.

It was the most creatively destructive age in human history, described poetically in James Oppenheim's novel *The Olympian* (1912):

> It was Science tearing off the crust of the earth and releasing the power and riches of Nature. Busily the race seized on these, a chaos of rough enterprise—mines, manufactories, laboratories, exchanges. And in the swift trade that followed three mighty gods began to roughly organize the chaos—Steam, Electricity, Steel. The railroad came, the post, the mill and farm machinery, the typewriter, the telegraph, the telephone, the automobile. And all these were like nerves and blood vessels laid out through the chaos till it began to coalesce, the parts aware of each other, the Earth gradually shaping into one body.[65]

NATIONAL CRISIS OF TRUST

> Frauds perpetuated by repeaters; frauds due to conspiracies; frauds in the count; frauds consummated by violence; frauds open and brazen; frauds subtle and silent; frauds in the third [district]; frauds in the tenth; frauds in respectable parts of town and frauds such as one might expect in the Red Light District.
>
> —"The Recent Elections,"
> *Louisville Evening-Post*, November 13, 1905

During the decades that constructed modern America's cherished image of technology as savior, conflicts like "Bleeding Kansas" (1854–1861) made it clear that the metaphysical arguments of the abolitionists had political and economic dimensions. Northern ideologues focused on the expansion of slavery into new states as an emotional issue with clear regional loyalties, but accompanying the passions, contradictions, and lacunae of the abolitionist debate were profound differences in regional economic realities and the central question of which region would hold the greatest economic, political, and ideological power in North America. Southern businessmen hoped that since they continued to control the production of cotton and tobacco they could also hold a large share of the nation's economic power. They also hoped they might be able to break off their partnership with the North at will and market their crops directly to Europe. But they were outnumbered.

In 1846, there were fifteen states permitting slavery and only fourteen "free states." Still, these slave states had already become a minority in the House of Representatives and faced a future as a perpetual and diminishing minority in the Senate and electoral college against the increasingly powerful North. The number of Northern free states expanded from seventeen in 1858 to nineteen by 1861, when the decisive war about the future of slavery began. It was a known political reality that as the West expanded and more territories demanded statehood, the proportion of slave states would diminish while the number of free states would increase. By 1854, Salmon Portland Chase, who would become Lincoln's main rival for the presidential nomination of 1860, had articulated the "slave power conspiracy" thesis, which held that landowners of the Southern states were determined to seize control of the federal government and block the progress of liberty forever.

The question of expanding slavery into the Kansas Territory as it became a state was highly charged for these reasons, and the issue of technological superiority entered the fray when abolitionist preacher Henry Ward Beecher collected funds from Kansas settlers and armed 1,200 New England volunteers with precise long-range Sharps rifles in 1855. For a time, the abolitionists had superior firepower, and for six more years, the nation watched, wondering if Kansas would become a free state supporting the Northern majority and selling its tobacco and cotton to Northern markets, or if it would become a means to perpetuate and expand the slave economy of the South. This tense conflict was filled with many reversals, and most of these centered around the difficulty of conducting free and fair elections in an age before secret ballots and reliably enforced laws protecting citizens' rights to vote unimpeded. In 1992, I witnessed what happens in an established and highly developed society when trust evaporates. The Rodney King riots in Los Angeles were my first glimpse at anarchy. They lasted six days. The confusion in the Kansas Territory, however, lasted six years and literally brought the entire nation to war.

Illinois Democratic senator Stephen Douglas introduced the Kansas–Nebraska Act in 1854 as an attempt to allow new states *themselves* to determine whether or not they would allow slavery. Douglas's idea was called "popular sovereignty." An election in Kansas to determine a delegate to vote on this issue in Washington was co-opted by out-of-state visitors attempting to increase the numbers of "free-staters" or "slave-staters." New Americans recruited by the Emigrant Aid Society of the Northeast arrived, as did neighboring Missourians who resented the interference of abolitionist Northerners. This proslavery Missouri faction used the frameworks of established fraternal organizations to form secret societies like the Blue Lodge and the Sons of the South, which supported their candidate, John Whitfield. On Election Day, large companies of armed men crossed the western border with Missouri and flooded into towns like Douglas. They surrounded the polls, threatening abolitionists with death. Typically, although only thirty-five locals were registered to vote, Whitfield won the Douglas poll, 261 to 26.[66]

These tactics offended some Northern Democrats who

began to trickle away from their party to join a new coalition called the Republicans. A congressional investigation into the election was also initiated. It found the election itself a "crime of great magnitude," prompting a state census and a new election in 1855. But the Missourians' tactics of surrounding polls with armed gunmen and intimidating anyone suspected of abolitionism were repeated. This time, Missouri's proslavery forces were organized by a former senator, David Atchison, who later described how the proslavery forces defeated the abolitionists in this second round: "We had about 7,000 men in the territory on the day of the election. . . . We are playing for a mighty stake and the game must be played boldly."[67] Free-state Kansans, however, refused to recognize the government formed in this corrupt election and instead formed their own government, while the proslavery legislature formed a territorial militia sworn to attack "free-state revolutionaries." This is exactly what they did in 1856, sacking the town of Lawrence and burning the free-state governor's residence to the ground. At this point, John Brown and his sons entered the fray by traveling to the Kansas Territory and murdering several proslavery supporters.[68]

Matters were not helped at the federal level, since the democratic president, James Buchanan, was overwhelmed by his conflicting responsibilities and by the very real prospect of plunging the country into Civil War. Many held that just such a war had already begun. In an 1857 article about the Kansas conflict, one Northern paper wrote: "Heaven knows the end of the civil war thus righteously begun."[69] In Kansas, the fraudulently elected proslavery legislature sponsored a constitutional convention boycotted by abolitionists that upheld the rights of slave owners. Buchanan rubber-stamped this the Lecompton Constitution and effectively sanctioned the extension of slavery into the emerging new state. In so doing, he deepened fissures in his own party and benefited the Republicans, who were quickly becoming identified with abolitionism using the slogan "Free soil. Free labor. Free Men."[70] The term *dough-face* may be related etymologically to the modern terms *doofus* or *simpleton*, but in antebellum America, *doughface* had two contemporary meanings, both of which applied to President Buchanan: he was an indecisive, easily led man dominated by his cabinet; and he was a Northerner with Southern sympathies. Buchanan was challenged over the Lecompton Constitution by Senator Douglas, a fellow Democrat who felt the proslavery Constitution was a "swindle." Eventually, Congress agreed with Douglas and permitted the first federally supervised free and fair election in the Kansas Territory, during which slavery was rejected by a majority of 11,300 to 1,788.[71]

Nonetheless, severe damage had been done to the credibility of America's electoral process and to the claim to legitimacy of any government, local or federal. American democracy, in other words, was a well-known public sham, and elections were more about the outcome of a dogfight than the will of the people. In the face of highly developed and completely unscrupulous local political machines, there was no other way to guarantee fair elections other than by deploying troops to protect the polls. Too often there was insufficient political will to do so. Reluctantly, President Buchanan was compelled to do exactly this by Washington mayor J. B. Magruder in 1857, when Know-Nothing thugs from Baltimore came to Washington to "fix" the city's elections.[72] Abraham Lincoln also did it—much more willingly—by stationing General Butler and six thousand troops outside New York City in 1864 to support a citizen surveillance system created to report the kind of election fraud that had cost Lincoln New York's support in the 1860 election. Completely intimidated by Butler's troops, the Tammany Hall machine refrained from interfering in the presidential election in 1864, which was one of the most orderly in New York's colorful history.[73]

Still, the crisis in trust persisted. Political machines sought to "regulate" elections, and their tactics were especially desperate when the stakes were high. In 1870, the Fifteenth Amendment guaranteed that citizens' rights to vote "shall not be denied or abridged by any State on the account of race, color, nativity, property, creed or previous condition of servitude." So after 1870, the stakes of elections in Southern regions (where there were numerous black voters) were especially high and especially subject to fraud, violence, and deception.

The first attempt to restore trust in America's electoral process involved widespread acceptance of the secret, or "Australian," ballot.

On January 29, 1861, Kansas finally entered the Union as a free state. Following the election of Abraham Lincoln in November 1860, however, it became clear that the South had lost its ability to influence the national politics of the United States, and eleven slave states quickly seceded from the Union. On April 11, 1861, Confederate general P. G. T. Beauregard demanded surrender from the Union forces occupying Fort Sumter, South Carolina. On the following day, US Army major Robert Anderson refused, and the fort was bombarded by Confederate artillery until Anderson surrendered on April 13. The remaining slave states soon joined the confederacy in rebellion, and the Civil War began in earnest.

After the South's secession, a trade boycott reduced Northern cotton manufacturers to between 25 and 50 percent of their prewar production, much as Southern politicians and businessmen had hoped, but this had a disastrous effect. Union generals William Sherman and Henry Halleck developed the controversial policy of "total war" both to win the conflict and to ensure the durability of any peace that might follow. Total war meant that civilian sites were legitimate targets for Northern military action. Essentially, this was an economic strategy that systematically destroyed the technological infrastructure of the South in order to cripple its ability to wage effective war or to present an economic challenge to the North once peace had been achieved. The Northern blockade of Southern ports prevented the South from earning war revenue by exporting cotton and tobacco to Europe. It also prevented the Confederacy from importing food and war matériel as the North ramped up its own war industry, becoming self-sufficient in munitions production by late 1861. In the meantime, eager to gain a supply of Southern cotton, Britain courted the Confederacy by building and providing them with two warships, the CSS *Alabama* and the CSS *Florida*.

The strategy of physically destroying the technological base of the South's economy was preceded by a presidential ultimatum in the fall of 1862. During the first eighteen months of war, the North retooled its industry for war production, awarding contracts for new ordnance to Yankee machine shops throughout New England. Lincoln then demanded the Confederate states return to Union control by New Year's Day, 1863, or suffer the emancipation of their four million slaves. On January 1, the Emancipation Proclamation declared the freedom of all slaves without making them American citizens. The immediate political costs of this maneuver were devastating for Lincoln domestically, but internationally the move recast the Civil War as a principled fight to abolish the remnants of slavery throughout the Americas. For this reason, it cost the Confederacy all further English and European support, and so by eliminating the South's military supplier and its largest potential agricultural market, Lincoln cleverly outmaneuvered the South and guaranteed his Union's victory and the North's economic preeminence over the postwar United States. One year later, Sherman's Savannah campaign destroyed much of the South's manufacturing base, while other Union campaigns targeted economic centers of Confederate production in the West. In this way, after 1861, technology became a principal focus of the war and a source of the Union victory.

After the Civil War, the United States became an increasingly complex economic, industrial, and political power. Its determination to expand in size and complexity is demonstrated by the Alaska Purchase of 1867. Visionaries like Secretary of State William H. Seward showed every intention of expanding American dominion throughout the entire continent and then trading a rich assortment of regional goods to all nations across both of the earth's largest oceans.[74] In 1864, during the last days of the war, Lincoln called for a railroad to span the continent and to unite the nation, allowing commerce and prosperity to flow freely from coast to coast. This herculean feat was accomplished by 1869, the same year that the overland telegraph reached California and rendered the Pony Express obsolete. Such political complexity could be imagined as the result of the revolution in human communications, and the second (and much more durable) transatlantic cable became operational in 1866. By 1872, it was possible for a freight or shipping broker in San Francisco to relay telegraph messages to most Asian ports, although such messages were still routed across the Atlantic Ocean.

Much more abstractly, however, this revolutionary enlargement of the complexity of our human community demanded a total overhaul of the conception and practice of human trust. Premodern trust, as Giddens points out, is personal, local, homogeneous, and traditional to such an extent as to be nearly tangible or tactile. Premodern trust was doomed to failure in the increasingly complex and monetized social orders that, during and after the Civil War, were more frequently called "economies."[75] Technological society, Thorstein Veblen observed in 1904, differs from traditional society in that "its scheme of knowledge and of inference is based on the laws of material causation, not on those of immemorial custom, authenticity or authoritative enactment. Its metaphysical basis is the law of cause and effect."[76]

Moreover, the Civil War had not removed the old white-supremacist order of the South. It had merely entrenched the empowered class and made their tactics so desperate and widespread that they presented an effective and nearly unopposed (opposition) to integration and economic renewal until the 1960s. After 1865, proponents of white Southern privilege and caste fought on—bitterly—to end Reconstruction and to "redeem" the Southern defeat. Nowhere was this more obvious than in Louisville.

Louisville was the border city in a border state during the final years of Reconstruction and the beginning of Jim Crow ascendancy, which was sometimes called "Redemption" by white Southern Democrats. The political scheming that Louisville's central geographic location engendered is reminiscent of the Bleeding Kansas conflict before the war. Elections in Louisville were always hotly contested. In the 1850s, Louisville had a population of about forty-three thousand, but in 1855, the city hosted the Bloody Monday election riots when a Protestant mob of nationalist "American Party" Know-Nothings rampaged through the streets accompanied by a cannon. They attacked German and Irish Catholic neighborhoods, killing over one hundred immigrants and forcing a wave of out-migration ten thousand strong that ended only at the outbreak of the Civil War.

Surrounded by eight states and served by the Ohio River as a transportation and freight hub, Louisville was in an ideal spot to become economically powerful. After the war, its growth resumed: there were 100,000 residents by 1870, 120,000 by 1880, and over 200,000 by 1900. Its new residents were mainly white Irish Democrats moving west or black American Republicans moving north. During this period, conservative white Democrats in Kentucky enacted no Jim Crow laws but instead systematically disenfranchised black voters through flagrant violence, trickery, and election rigging. The threat black enfranchisement represented to white Southern Democrats was very real: "In 1867, black turnout for a constitutional referendum in Georgia reached nearly 70 percent."[77] In Virginia, a similar vote attracted nearly 90 percent of the black population.[78] Quickly, white vigilante groups were organized to prevent new black voters from exercising their franchise through threats, intimidation, mob violence, and murder.

Just south of Kentucky, in Tennessee, white vigilantes, determined to reestablish the antebellum racial hierarchy, organized themselves into the Ku Klux Klan. Throughout the South, the Klan and other emerging groups quickly spread the "don't vote" message to black voters through a campaign of local murder. In Camilla, Georgia, nine victims were killed shortly before one election, and afterward very few black voters were reckless enough to go to the polls. African Americans attempting to vote in Mississippi's constitutional amendment in 1868 were driven from the polls by armed gangs, and the Constitution—which would have prevented former confederates from holding state-elected office—was defeated.[79]

The problem of rigging, fixing, or stealing elections, however, was not confined to the South. Border states, especially prosperous ones with growing populations and rich economic bases, attracted Democratic political machinery. This is what happened in Louisville.

In the mid-1870s, an ambitious young man named John Henry Whallen arrived in Louisville from Cincinnati. He was Irish American, born in New Orleans in 1850, and his political sympathies were formed very early in the white, conservative South. At age twelve, he ran away to join Captain J. J. Schoolfield's Battery in the first year of the war, becoming a powder monkey, then a scout, and finally a courier for Confederate brigadier general John Hunt Morgan. Whallen would have been thirteen when Morgan waged a deeply personal private war on the North, which Southern sympathizers still call the "Great Raid of 1863," a thousand-mile destructive slash-and-grab cavalry campaign into the heartland of Indiana and Ohio. Morgan's raid may or may not have served as a diversion from Lee's preparations for a Northern invasion. Morgan's tactic, which alternated between terror and outright theft, certainly diverted the nation. His Southern cavalrymen stole horses, dry goods, and money, which led the Northern papers to call it the "Calico Raid." Nonetheless, as instruments of terror and as morale boosters for the Confederacy, Morgan's two thousand or so raiders were extremely effective. They took prisoners and then paroled about six thousand Union troops. They destroyed thirty-four bridges and caused general mayhem for two weeks in July until Morgan's capture and subsequent daring escape from a Cincinnati prison. Morgan continued fighting for the South, proving himself such a worthy pest that, following a second capture, Union troops simply murdered him rather than risk a second escape by this extremely effective adversary.

General Morgan's brazenness made a deep impression on Whallen as a thirteen-year-old soldier. A generation later, he opened his first saloon on Green Street in Louisville. When Whallen's application for a liquor license failed to pass the Republican-controlled board, Democratic councilman Barney McAtee intervened on his behalf. Whallen then repaid McAtee by helping him win local elections. During these early sorties into politics, Whallen discovered he had a facility for getting his saloon patrons out to vote "early and often," as the saying goes. Before he turned thirty, Whallen was a successful businessman with extremely solid local political connections in America's eighteenth-largest city. During the 1870s, he grew naturally from volunteer party "organizer" to backroom political boss (the "Buckingham Boss"), raking in a cut from all local prostitution and gambling until he engineered the election of P. Booker Reed as Louisville mayor in 1884, easily circumventing newly enacted voter registration legislation. A grateful Mayor Reed opened the floodgates to Whallen's corruption by appointing him Louisville chief of police.

The difficulty of establishing a fair electoral process was already pronounced in 1884 when Louisville representative Albert Stoll won passage of a bill forcing mandatory registration for Louisville voters. This was the first attempt to control repeat and fraudulent voting in Louisville. Unfortunately, it didn't work. During the next (1887) mayoral race, election fraud became flagrant when a popular Democratic mayoral candidate, Charles Jacob, ran against Whallen's handpicked Democrat, William Holt. Whallen's machine fought the election with every dirty trick it could muster. It was common knowledge, at the time, that the clerks who recorded Louisville's votes had accepted bribes. But more cleverly, Whallen had situated the columns representing candidates' names so close together that his clerks could easily record a vote in the wrong column unnoticed. The publisher of the local *Courier-Journal*, Henry Watterson, one of Whallen's closest friends, lamented that, even for Louisville, the 1887 election was "without parallel . . . for fraud and corruption."[80] Watterson formed a committee called the Commonwealth Club to examine the excesses of the 1887 mayoral race.

A member of this club, Arthur Wallace, was a state representative. Wallace had read a newspaper article about the new practice of "secret ballots" pioneered in Australia. He consulted lawyers and judges and then championed the new practice, successfully seeing it enacted as law for all future Louisville elections. Although enacted at the state level, the Wallace Election Bill could not be applied to the entire state without a referendum, so Wallace simply went ahead, calling in favors and garnering support for his bill. It passed without fanfare, and Louisville became the first city in America to adopt secret ballots, but the new law caught the town's political machinery unprepared, and the municipal elections of 1888 were quiet and fair although the practice of vote buying outside the polls persisted.[81] This election was the fairest that the town had seen since Unionist John Delph was elected mayor following the attack on Fort Sumter twenty-seven years earlier, and the results were closely attended by the press in neighboring states. Between 1888 and 1892, Wisconsin (1889), Ohio (1891), Michigan (1891), Illinois (1891), and Iowa (1892) adopted the practice of the secret ballot and an accompanying system of registering eligible voters in order to prevent repeaters and imposters.[82] By the turn of the century, voting by secret ballot became the norm almost everywhere the United States.[83]

Unfortunately, the secret ballot itself became an object of trickery and deceit. The old practice of tampering with ballots returned: by 1856, in San Francisco, backroom political strategists designed a special ballot box with secret doors that allowed them to replace genuine votes with fixed ones.[84] By the 1890s, tactics had become more sophisticated and complex. Ballots intended to confuse and stymie the barely literate voter were introduced in both the North and the South. (A bit later, legislation to limit this practice also appeared.) Both before and after the adoption of the Australian ballot, increasingly robust literacy laws were enacted that intentionally excluded many foreign-born voters in the North as well as uneducated black voters in the South. The arguments for these stringent literacy laws were sometimes sound, but there was and is to this day no constitutional basis for literacy as a criterion for a democratic franchise in America. Nonetheless, state legislators argued that illiterate men lacked the intelligence and worldly knowledge to vote wisely; that a thorough knowledge of English was necessary to understand American issues as well as values and beliefs; and, finally, that by demanding literacy among its voters, America encouraged the socially useful processes of assimilation and education.[85] As a result of these "reforms," election fraud continued to be a very real threat to American democracy.

Back in Louisville, the results of an entire election were overturned by the state Court of Appeals in 1907, where Whallen remained boss until his death in 1912. The introduction of secret ballots had proved to be little more than a speed bump in Whallen's path. He quickly developed techniques to subvert it by buying votes outside the polling stations, registering dead voters, and employing impersonators to vote in their names. He also closed stations early in Republican neighborhoods and refused to register black voters or simply threatened them physically when they arrived at a polling station to vote. In 1904, electoral practices in Louisville became so outrageous that Whallen's mayor was forced to resign, and an interim mayor was appointed until the courts ruled on the charges of electoral fraud. The courts reversed the results of the election and damned Louisville as a city of slaves: "No people can be said to govern themselves whose elections are controlled by force, fear or fraud . . . people who do not govern themselves are slaves."[86]

The lack of integrity in Louisville's elections, it should be remembered, was only a small part of a truly dire *national* problem. Because of the persistence and scope of electoral fraud in America, there were many attempts to protect the process of exercising one's democratic franchise. Even though the legal profession succeeded in changing American laws so that the secret ballot became a uniform practice throughout the country, the effort to protect the electoral process simply by "changing the law" failed spectacularly and often. Many of these failures focused on the ballots themselves; on their security before, during, and after elections; as well as on their wording, complexity, and format. Laws to standardize ballots and ballot-counting procedures were enacted by many states. But another group of professionals was also attempting to solve the problem. These were the inventors and engineers.

Contemporary America's reliance on voting machines, despite the problems they create, is a subject of curiosity for Europeans and Canadians. To an outsider it sometimes seems that a very simple process is complicated by the addition of machines. But there is nothing simple about the history or procedure of any American election, and, in fact, the earliest experiments with voting machines were European. Nonetheless, it was Americans who turned them into an article of faith. Thomas Edison patented an electric vote counter for use in the legislature soon after the end of the Civil War. The topic remained active for another decade, during which time the inventor of Woodward's Wheel, a famous perpetual-motion device of the era, described a voting machine to the readers of *American Machinist* in 1884. By 1889, there were at least two working models. One was invented by John Rhines of St. Paul, who found himself "disgusted with corrupt counting methods and with the vicious government of machine politicians, he determined to invent a mechanical device which should do something toward effecting an improvement."[87]

That same year, another inventor, Jacob Meyer, developed a much more sophisticated machine, the Meyer Voting Booth, which was soon used experimentally in a municipal election in Lockport, New York, one year after the Louisville election of 1888. Meyer's automatic booth was activated by a manual lever that closed a privacy curtain around the voter, permitting him to vote in secret. A year before New York became the first state to execute a murderer using an electric chair, these "automated booths" began offering a similarly welcome technological solution to the problem of election fraud. This solution and other technological solutions that soon followed became known as "technological fixes": the word *fix*, familiar from phrases like "party fixer," "the big fix," or "the fix is in," was borrowed into engineering from the corrupt practices of contemporary machine politics and organized gambling.

Ironically, local political machinery had provided convenient working models for the emergence of large-scale organized crime. In 1887, the city chancellor of New York described the nature of machine politics in a lengthy article for *Harper's*, writing "So long as the election law remains as it is today, party machinery will be dominant, corruption will be rife."[88] But in the popular press, voting machines were touted as the exact and equal opposite of machine politics: "Between the political machine and the voting machine . . . there is neither affinity, friendship nor sympathy. . . . Each is the implacable foe of the other. It is the aim of the former to facilitate . . . the corruption of the ballot by . . . repeating, intimidating and stuffing."[89]

The technological fix offered by Meyer's machine was really the tacit guarantee that every "vote is counted and recorded with a mechanical precision and certainty which no human mind can emulate."[90] So in a world in which no politician and no political process could be trusted, Americans were willing (or desperate enough) to invest their faith in the inhuman agency of a reliable machine: this is reflected again and again in descriptions of Meyer's device in contemporary newspapers: "The simplicity, ease and celerity [speed] with which the voting is done constitute one of its chief merits, but even greater than that is its absolute and impenetrable security. . . . *The counting is invisible, but it has the certainty of clockwork and is safe from manipulation* [my emphasis]. . . . It [the voting machine] seems to furnish the final solution of the problem of secret voting."[91]

Human trust, in other words, had proved inadequate in the matter of democratic elections, and in its place America fell back on a burgeoning faith in "reliable machines" that delivered results for which "there is no chance of dispute over the validity of nay vote cast or the accuracy of any computation [made]."[92] The unequivocal status of voting-machine results was guaranteed when it became clear that political machines like Tammany Hall in New York City were completely opposed to adopting Meyer's devices or those of his major competitor, the Standard Voting Machine Company.

Despite the fact that many constituencies around the country readily adopted voting machines and the fact that the New York State Constitution was modified twice to accommodate their use, the machines were kept out of New York for over a decade. In the interim, machine politics experienced very unpleasant defeats at the hands of the voting booth, including the one by Bill Thompson, the "Gloucester Boss," who in 1904 "employed counsel to protest the use of voting machines at the polling places of the state . . . Thompson was a candidate for a seat in the Gloucester City Common Council and was overwhelmingly defeated. He attributes the failure of his candidacy to the presence of the machines in the precincts his candidacy covered, and his contest against the machine is really for a writ overturning the poll."[93]

Opposition by machine politicians was the best recommendation Meyer could get. By 1896, his device was standard for all elections in Meyer's native Rochester, New York. By the 1920s, special legislation mandated similar gear-and-lever voting booths in California, Colorado, Connecticut, Illinois, Indiana, Iowa, Kansas, Michigan, Minnesota, Montana, New Jersey, New York, Ohio, Utah, Washington, and Wisconsin.[94] These booths became the norm in every major American city in that decade, so that by the 1930s, paper ballots were largely obsolete in the United States. Meyer's automatic booth and its major competitor, the Standard Voting Machine, facilitated elections because they made the entire electoral process—from soup to nuts—very fast. A citizen could be in and out of the booth in about ten seconds, and votes were tabulated as they occurred.[95] These machines were faster, better, and more reliable than human beings who were sometimes clumsy and inaccurate but who were, more often, completely and utterly untrustworthy. It was also the reliability of these early machines that led to the practice of "branding" consumer products. Early mass-produced machinery like Singer sewing machines and McCormick reapers included metal "brand tags" riveted in an eye-catching position on the device. These prominently displayed the company name, making it a byword for machine reliability.[96]

Soon the branding strategy would be adopted by other consumer products, including food, cigars, and automobiles, but fundamentally, Americans learned to trust brands, machines, and professions because of a bedrock suspicion and distrust of human agency. This distrust forced America to create and to rely on its machines. And this, in turn, is why our machines, again and again, are designed to empower an individual user and to empower him or her by making them independent of other human assistance. Sewing machines, for example, reduced a team of seamstresses to one seamstress; mechanized reapers reduced a team of field workers to one farmer; and power tools like the Spencer repeating rifle reduced a squad of musketeers to one man, while sanders, drills, and electrical saws (which all began to emerge in the early years of the new century) turned individual Americans into tiny one-man construction crews who could assemble a mail-order craftsman home with little or no additional help. The do-it-yourself movement, in other words, depended on reliable machine tools and freed Americans from their dependence on dishonest and costly contractors and their work crews.

As a consequence of America's century-old habituation to using reliable machines, many Americans are predisposed to feel more comfortable with human contact when it is mediated by machinery. In our own era, our willingness to use machine intermediaries has been taken to ridiculous lengths. In the news this morning, a device called the kessenger has been developed to allow long-distance Skype dates to kiss each other using two pairs of artificial lips.

O brave, new world!

THE ARTS AND CRAFTS OF MACHINES

> There are some things which a machine can do as well as a man's hand, plus a tool, can do . . . a few simple contrivances will do it all perfectly well, and leave him free to smoke his pipe and think . . . so let us follow our machine-inventor a step farther . . . in order to gain more leisure . . . he uses a power-loom and foregoes the small advantage of the little extra art in the cloth. But so doing . . . he has made a bargain between art and labor; and got a makeshift as a consequence. . . . Carry the machine . . . a step farther, and he becomes an unreasonable man, if he values art and is free . . . I must say that I am thinking of the modern machine . . . to which the man is auxiliary, and not of the old machine, the improved tool, which is auxiliary to the man.
>
> —William Morris, "The Aims of Art,"
> *Signs of Change: Seven Letters*, 1888

Although the Arts and Crafts movement had considerable impact in England, it did not fare as well in the United States. Gustav Stickley, one of the main American spokesmen of the movement, was a mundane designer and a poor businessman whose various "craftsman" enterprises failed by the end of World War I. Like many of the Americans who wrote for his magazine, the *Craftsman*, Stickley did not have the same antipathy for machines and industrial processes that the writings of John Ruskin inspired in William Morris in another country half a century before. One year after Morris's death in 1896, the Boston Museum hosted a major exhibition of American Arts and Crafts intended to spark a flowering of the handicraft in America. Although this exhibit did influence the fields of pottery, architecture, furniture making, and jewelry, many Americans did not share the elitist culture that informed the gentlemanly pursuits of British handicrafts. The American system of production had developed in order to supply a new continent where costly finished goods were previously available only as imports from Europe. By the time the ideas and ideals of the Arts and Crafts movement reached New England, Americans had developed indigenous and very different ideas about production. Handicrafts that supplied a uniquely beautiful product at a leisurely pace were unsuited to the American appetite for finished goods. Stickley describes the American attitude to production:

> Given the real need for production and the fundamental desire for honest self-expression, the machine can be put to all its legitimate uses as an aid to, and a preparation for, the work of the hand, and the result be quite as vital and satisfying as the best work of the hand alone. The mere question of hand work as opposed to machine work is largely superficial. The prime object of the industrial arts is to produce articles which satisfy some material or mechanical requirement, and any method of working is allowable which really effects that object in the simplest and most straightforward manner.[97]

The pronounced impact of reliable machines on turn-of-the-century America fixed them forever in America's consciousness. By the 1890s, America had undergone a technological conversion, making much of the country a nation of devout tinkerers and fans of tinkerers. In generations to come, great technological enterprises would succeed because they captured the fascination and faith of ordinary Americans confronted with technology. These projects included the transcontinental railroad, the Model T's replacement of the horse, the Panama Canal, Lindbergh's solo flight, the emergence of broadcast radio, the mobilization for war, the D-Day landing, the Manhattan Project, and the Space Race. All these events appealed specifically and uniquely to a nation that revered its machines.

Norman Mailer, a nearly forgotten master of elegant prose, captured America's relationship to its technology in a book about the first moon landing, which I read hungrily in my teens. I found Mailer by accident in my high-school library and felt that he grasped the essence of a nation that had acquired a fascination for me as an eleven-year-old sleeping on a beach in the Keys outside a gleaming Airstream® trailer for two weeks every December. For me, America was limited to Interstate 75, but even the diversity of that slice of the United States included the soul stations of the motor city, the bluegrass music of the Kentucky hills, the unintelligible accents of Tennessee, the segregated roadside washrooms of Georgia, and a side trip to see the launchpad at Cape Canaveral. All these brought me into contact with something much larger and more important than *Hockey Night in Canada*. At the time, I believed my country was not really a country at all; it was only a season—winter—and it could not compare to the land of marvels to which I traveled every year at Christmastime. When school got out, I got into my father's Scout® as though I were passing through a wardrobe into Narnia. The long-haul truckers with cowboy hats and rebel flags, the gleaming white astronauts, even the neoprene-clad scuba divers who brought me conchs live from the ocean floor were very different beings from any Canadian I had ever met. Each of these men worked with alien and wonderful machinery. For me, Mailer captured the essence of this difference in his description of a typical fellow countryman attending the first moon launch: "He has worked with machines all his life, he has tooled cars to the point where he has felt they respond to his care, he has known them and slept beside them as trustingly as if they were hunting dogs, he knows a thousand things about the collaboration between a man and a machine. . . . He has spent his life with machines, they are all he has ever trusted."[98]

This typical American faith in its machines, Mailer notes, is often misplaced in something he describes as "pure American lunacy. Shoddy technology . . . was replacing men with machines which did not do the work as well as the men."[99] Nonetheless, the faith existed and still exists, it is integral to the American consciousness and way of life, and it accounts—first—for the adoption of voting machines and—second—for their persistence for a hundred years despite the frequent frauds, deceptions, and failures that are constantly associated with them. Around the turn of the nineteenth century, an emerging technological optimism was constructing the glowing ideology of technology expressed again and again in the cultural record at the turn of the century. Frank Lloyd Wright puts the case beautifully in his lecture "The Art and Craft of the Machine" (1901):

> Invincible, triumphant, the machine goes on, gathering force and knitting the material necessities of mankind ever closer into a universal automatic fabric; the engine, the motor, and the battle-ship, the works of art of the century! The Machine is Intellect mastering the drudgery of earth that the plastic art may live; that the margin of leisure and strength by which man's life upon the earth can be made beautiful, may immeasurably widen; its function ultimately to emancipate human expression! It is a universal educator, surely raising the level of human intelligence, so carrying within itself the power to destroy, by its own momentum, the greed which in Morris' time and still in our own time turns it to a deadly engine of enslavement.[100]

A less well-known proponent of emergent techno-optimism also elevated America's new faith to poetry in *Voice of the Machines* (1905). Congregationalist clergyman Gerald Stanley Lee was a devoted techno-optimist who returned to the topic in several books, including *Crowds* (1913), in which he rejoiced that "our new machines have turned upon us and are creating new men.

The telephone changes the structure of the brain." Lee wrote, "Men live in wider distances and think in larger figures."[101]

WORLD WITHOUT OXYTOCIN

> This place is cruel, nowhere could be much colder. . . .
> —Stevie Wonder, "Living for the City," 1973

There is an immediate chemical payoff to the activities of trusting and being trusted, but since the Civil War, at least, we have increasingly forestalled our need for such human bonding out of greed, ignorance, fear, or some other, more subtle, cause. When human beings bond—by hugging, kissing, touching, having sex, eating together, giving massages, or even when singing together or speaking reassuring words—oxytocin brings us "in from the cold," warming us—quite literally—as it redirects blood flow into hands, feet, chests, and cheeks. We also become temporarily less "frigid" since, as we enjoy moments of "human warmth," each successful social interaction stimulates our dopamine receptors, encouraging (most of) us to seek more company and to become more trusting.[102]

Most fascinating of all, recent research into the relationship between oxytocin and trust has important insights into the processes connected with the creation of "social capital," as well as for the social consequences of using personal communication devices to shut ourselves off from others in the urban environment. In 2005, a team of researchers adapted a process called the trust game, which economists interested in the dynamics of investment had used to "measure the degree of trust between unacquainted people."[103]

In this exchange, test subjects (S1s) were given money and allowed to forward some or all of it to other test subjects (S2s) with the chance of increasing their initial stakes. Once forwarded, the money initiated a system of rewards based on a scale reflecting the size of each S1's investment (or transfer). Rewards were then presented to the S2s, who could choose to return none or some of the reward money to their unknown S1 partners without any recrimination if they chose the greediest path. The initial action of S1 investors is thought to reflect "trust," while the response of S2 collectors is thought to represent "trustworthiness."

Researchers found that about 85 percent of the S1s sent some money to the S2 strangers, and that 98 percent of the S2s who received money returned some of it to their unknown partners. Neither group, however, could explain "why they were trusting or trustworthy," suggesting, of course, that *human* trust (just as it is in other mammalian species) is a preconscious, nonrational behavior prompted by biochemical activity.[104] Interestingly, the S2s who received a "trust signal" (transferred money) from the S1s reported feeling "trusted," and their blood revealed oxytocin had been released during the successful "social contact with others."[105]

Researchers then took their experiments a step further by administering a nasal dose of synthetic oxytocin to participants during the game. They found overall that oxytocin-treated S1s generally sent 17 percent more money to their partners than S1s in an untreated control group. Moreover, there was a doubling in the number of treated S1s who "exhibited maximum trust" by sending all their money to their partners. This demonstrates that "a rise of oxytocin in the brain reduces our natural . . . anxiety over interacting with a stranger."[106] Researchers concluded, "Oxytocin constitutes a very positive side of interpersonal reactions; it literally feels good when someone seems to trust you, and this recognition motivates you to reciprocate."[107]

This fundamental mechanism of initiating mutual trust seems to be the best candidate to explain the concept of "social capital," the unspoken, mutual trust that binds strangers safely together. During my travels as an academic for hire, I've experienced the power of social capital in odd ways. I am a sandy-haired, blue-eyed Canadian man. I traveled extensively in Saudi Arabia alone in the late 1990s and found I could defuse the hostile glances of a roomful of strangers by saying "Salaam Aleichem," which initiated an introductory ritual exchange with those seated or standing next to me. The more I did this, the more I became convinced of the elegant wisdom of this Muslim ritual that every Gulf Arab uses hundreds of times a day. In the most traditional of all cultures, the responding phrase, "Aleichem Salaam," automatically eases the tensions of xenophobia and racial difference even in the most hostile rooms. My few words of Arabic allowed me to rest among my hosts or to pass freely from them, even though it was quite clear I was not Muslim.

Unfortunately, the urgency and scope of our largest cities has reconfigured human trust in radical ways. Many of us come to them having left our primary relationships in some other, smaller place, so cities can be quite lonely and isolating at the beginning of our new urban lives. But also the city introduces a fundamental problem—volume—into the neurological structure of human trust. We may simply be inadequately equipped "psycho-bio-chemically" to interact successfully with so many people so often.

Whether he is correct or not, anthropologist Robin Dunbar suggests the size of our neocortex actually limits the maximum size of our human social universe to about 150 people, the size of a big Neolithic village.[108] Other, slightly larger, figures have been suggested by other investigators, but the highest of these simply double what has come to be called Dunbar's number.[109] Acclimation may play a role in our ability to deal with increasing numbers of strangers, since many of us remember "growing" a tolerance for large crowds after first migrating to a big city.

Nonetheless, many anthropologists agree that there is probably an upward social ceiling that limits the maximum size of our immediate human community (whatever that number may be).

Among city dwellers, therefore, there is a problem of how to keep so many strangers out. By the 1960s, we had developed silent social behaviors like Erving Goffman's "civil inattention" to quickly and quietly negotiate the double obligation of recognizing others with whom we temporarily share a space while simultaneously convincing them that our interest contains no threat. This use of the gaze is much quicker than "Salaam Aleichem," but even this practice during rush hour, in the megapolis, could initiate hundreds or thousands of exhausting and time-consuming exchanges. Many of us do not have sufficient time, attention, or energy to "give . . . enough visual notice to demonstrate that one appreciates the other . . . while at the next moment withdrawing one's attention . . . so as . . . not [to] constitute a target of special curiosity or design."[110]

Stanley Milgram hypothesized that the largest cities create psychological "overloads" in their residents and that this forces them to act unsociably. I'm fascinated by the fact that Milgram published this opinion around the time Stevie Wonder wrote "Living for the City." Milgram's overload observation appeared in 1977. Only two short years before the introduction of the Walkman®, he wrote, "The observed behavior of the urbanite appears to be determined largely by a variety of adaptations to overload."[111] Ironically, Milgram borrowed the term *overload* from systems science, applying an engineering term to human psychology the same year that *Star Wars* (featuring R2-D2 and C3-PO) premiered. A recent attempt to investigate Milgram's hypothesis by another psychologist, Robert Levine, observed that when they were surveyed for helpfulness, New Yorkers generally

> were willing to offer help only when it could occur with the assurance of no further contact as if to say "I'll meet my social obligation but, make no mistake, this is as far as we go together." How much of this is motivated by fear and how much by simply not wanting to waste time is hard to know . . . in more helpful [smaller] cities, like Rochester and much of the Midwest and South, it often seemed that human contact was the very motive for helping. People were more likely to help with a direct smile and to welcome the "thank you."[112]

This passage neatly expresses the double-bind of modern life in our largest cities: only human bonds are capable of making us feel fulfilled, and yet whenever we find ourselves awash in a "sea" of potential relationships, we increasingly prevent ourselves from making contact in order to avoid becoming "overloaded" or (to use a more human term) overwhelmed. I believe this explanation captures the main reasons we rely on "technologies of distraction" to help us cut an unobstructed path across the urban grid.

In our hominin past, the human problems associated with sociability were different. Some researchers speculate that in earlier times, the altriciality of human children (including their prolonged adolescence) was a sufficient evolutionary factor to select parents "who could bond strongly with others over a long time." An epiphenomenon of this facility for pair bonding might therefore be "that humans have a powerful propensity for attachment and thus also strongly attach to non-kin who become friends, neighbors or spouses. If . . . correct, it is no surprise that humans also bond to pets, places and even their cars."[113]

This characteristic distinguishes us from other primates, even fairly sociable ones like chimpanzees, which have much lower "social tolerance" and also shorter adolescences than humans.[114] Human beings appear to have developed more advanced mechanisms to facilitate what neuroscientists call "approach behavior," the ability to overcome "a natural avoidance of offspring or strangers" while initiating "pro-social, proximity seeking" strategies.[115] Just as our ancestors developed music and speech to facilitate oxytocin release and thereby bond across distances, they also developed other strategies to encourage the physical sensation of trust. Many of them are delightfully human, like "kissing," which is thought to derive from the practice of primate mothers chewing food for their infants and then feeding it directly into the infants' mouths. Philematologists (those who study kissing) have found the custom builds trust by facilitating a cascade of brain and body chemicals, including oxytocin.[116]

In the city, however, we are not trying to win over everyone within our orbit. The most pressing urban survival problem has become how to keep so many strangers away from us. Unfortunately, we have become so good at it that very few people get to penetrate our circles, and then they remain there for prolonged periods of time. Our cell phones and MP3 players may not have been specifically designed to fill the market niche of excluding strangers, but that is certainly one of their main modern uses, and it is too successful. At a moment in our history when more than 80 percent of all North Americans live and work in cities, 25 percent—a rising figure—have no trusted friend or confidant, and 40 percent—also a rising figure—live alone. Jane Jacobs has pointed out that the casual interactions of walking neighborhoods have been factored out of urban lives in many areas. There are few brick-and-mortar sites to meet people face-to-face, and also fewer occasions to do so. Although life itself is risk, we rely on technology to get us to work in physical safety, without any danger of interpersonal risk. We also rely on technology to fill our basic and undeniable human need for sex. We "hook up" on Facebook® for a series of one-time encounters that may be superficially rewarding. Still, these are mediated by machines that cannot deliver the oxytocin release that we need to establish trust, build human relationships, and release dopamine.

Moreover, by learning to live without other human beings, we have taken the premises of scientific management into our deepest thoughts, and perhaps because of this we have allowed our beliefs about the nature of humanity to be reconditioned. For the major portion of our workday, we now think of ourselves as little more than replaceable economic machinery serving whichever corporation or institution houses our daytime offices. Expressions of personal preference, conscience, inhibition, or reservation are discouraged as lacking detachment or being unprofessional. Among our coworkers, many of us are concerned about providing too much personal information or becoming too close. We look for sexual connections and friendships away from the work environment since at work we are often competing for advancement with coworkers. Emotional ties can become very awkward in an ongoing professional environment. In fact, as long as we remain unattached, we are better able to compete professionally by forming the kinds of temporary liaisons and friendships that are most advantageous in our current professional situations.

These strategies have cost us much of what is most worth having in life: acceptance, approval, fulfillment, friendship, and love. Without these things, we are unattached economic atoms, useful only as consumers of manufactured goods. But with attachment, life becomes an incredibly rich gift. Which way was chosen for you, gentle reader?

Which way will you now choose?

CONCLUSION

MACHINES AS FRIENDS

> Whether it is a god, a devil, an animal, a machine ("Old Betsy"), a landmark, or a piece of cast-off sports equipment, the anthropomorphized being becomes a social surrogate, and the same neural systems that are activated when we make judgments about other humans are activated when we assess these parasocial relationships.
>
> —John Cacioppo

Gradually, steam locomotives were assigned personalities and names. Rev. Wilbert Awdry famously exploited this fact when he published *Thomas the Tank Engine* in 1946, when the habit of personifying steam engines had become well established. Early American engines had less anthropomorphized names, beginning in the 1850s with *Madison* (1850), *Eureka* (1851), and the *Pioneer*. After the end of the Civil War, steam locomotives shifted from wood to coal, which had a greater BTU (British thermal units) content. As the range, power, and speed of steam locomotives increased, they lost their image as functional machinery and received the affectionate projections of a grateful nation. The *Antelope* famously made the first 138-mile run across the Sierra Nevadas from Sacramento to Reno in 1868. One year later, America's most famous steam engine, *Jupiter*, joined the continent at Promontory, Utah.

Still, the possibility that a mechanical device might become an independent being (or surrogate friend) had to wait until the technology of transportation permitted personal ownership. This emerged with the Model T. America's favorite machine-friend appeared at the same historic moment that the world was developing a fascination with robots. Ford's obstinate, unreliable, and fussy first car began to feature in songs and stories in 1903, spawning the long line of anthropomorphized vehicles that have been a motif of American culture ever since. We used to name our horses, after all, so it was not a big stretch to attach names to the machines replacing them, even if those machines were finicky and possessed very little that was heartwarming. The progressive changes in our personifications of the automobile reflect a deepening relationship with technology. At first car names were merely incidental, examples of casual, playful humor, like "Tin Lizzie." Then the names acquired personalities with their own narratives, as with, for example, the mostly harmless 1965–66 NBC sitcom *My Mother the Car*. Later there were feature-length films and television shows about machines with far more elaborate personalities and complex tales to tell, including *The Love Bug* (1968), *Christine* (1983), *Knight Rider* (1982–86), and, of course, *Cars* (Pixar, 2006), featuring Lightning McQueen. As the pervasiveness of mobile electromechanical devices increased, Americans increasingly projected personalities onto their cars. This change was picked up in the lyrics of the songs of a new music that Americans were listening to *in their cars* during the postwar era of prosperity. Perhaps it was Willie Dixon who first exploited the car–man metaphor in his 1959 hit "Built for Comfort" (*I ain't built for speed*), but, for my money, the best anthropomorphized car song of all time must be Prince's "Little Red Corvette" (1983): "You must be a limousine . . ."

Before cars were humanized, the names of American locomotives were increasingly anthropomorphized during the period in which diesel replaced steam. The last steam superlocomotive appeared in 1941 and was affectionately named

American Big-Boy. Union Pacific refined the locomotive's design in 1944, producing the class-II *Big Boy*. Interestingly, several months later, when the prototype nuclear bomb, *Thin Man*, failed its tests at the Manhattan Project site in New Mexico, army engineer Leslie Groves chose the name *Little Boy* for the reengineered nuclear device that would soon be exploded over Hiroshima.

Despite visible increases in the American habit of anthropomorphizing technology, the possibility of mobile *miniaturized and electronic* friendship did not develop until long after the exigencies of a world war demanded widespread miniaturization and created a technology capable of producing mobile entertainment devices. The first pocket radio—the Belmont Boulevard—appeared in 1949, using the same miniature vacuum tubes that had been developed for the proximity fuses of antiaircraft shells. Transistors became commercially available a few years earlier, and in 1954, Texas Instruments introduced a four-transistor shirt-pocket radio called the Regency TR-1 for $49.95. Over the next decade, as the price of Zenith, Motorola, and Sony transistor radios came down, their prevalence increased. But despite their portability, transistor radios were fundamentally social devices. Like boom boxes, most pocket-sized transistors offered an external speaker, and many included dual earphone jacks so that rock 'n' roll—the emergent revolutionary music—could be shared with a friend at noon hour, recess, break time. Twenty years later, Akio Morita, who designed Sony's TR-63 transistor radio in 1957, repeated its dual jack/dual sound–control option when his company introduced the Walkman® in 1979. Without an external speaker, the Walkman generation was isolated from unpleasant city sounds by stereophonic supra-aural headphones. Solitary use of personal music devices became normal during the 1980s, when Morita removed the second jack, but few people projected a personality either onto the Walkman or onto the flurry of personal tech devices that followed them: CD players, Game Boys™, MP3 players, or cell phones. Ultimately, social acceptance of our projection of personality and friendship onto an electronic device had to wait another generation, until the turn of the millennia.

It bears repeating that, remarkably, the 2000 census revealed that one in four American households consisted of a person living alone. That same year, the film *Cast Away* depicted an island-bound airplane crash survivor who used a washed-up volleyball to create a companion he named "Wilson." Perhaps the creation of this personal "fetish" marks a turning point in how America has dealt with chronic loneliness ever since; that film validated the practice of projecting humanity onto an inanimate totem, a suggestion that our forbears would have interpreted, no doubt, as outright insanity. The following year saw the debut of Apple's iPod®, a truly totemic device whose sleek, compact design invites anthropomorphic projections. Both the iPod and iPhone® are shiny, playful, mass-produced Wilsons whose friendship we can all afford. After all, the first iPod ad emphasized its practicality as a street companion for the solitary listener. It encouraged its users to "Think Different." America listened. Its children are listening now, too, but to what effect?

Norman Nie, a clever researcher at Stanford University, wanted to resolve the question of whether the technology of the Internet is a socially enabling tool or one that displaces or replaces social interaction with technological ones. In 2002, Nie demonstrated that "for every hour spent on the Internet at home" his subjects spent "an average of almost thirty fewer minutes with their family."[1] In other words, the more time we spend using technology, the less time we spend in real human interaction. Thus have devices once used to relieve loneliness now become, in effect, generators of loneliness. For this reason, UCLA neuroscientist Gary Small believes that "the digital evolution of our brains increases social isolation and diminishes the spontaneity of interpersonal relationships."[2]

This simple fact is especially alarming because, according to an astonishing report by the Kaiser Family Foundation, American children in 2010 spend on average seven hours and thirty-eight minutes online per day.[3] In previous decades, nearly four hours of this time would have been devoted to interacting with family members. But now the intensity of online engagement has a much greater appeal than family life; it is chock-full of sometimes literally addictive games, music, and videos.[4] And for every seven hours a child spends online, he or she actually logs eleven hours of multitasking activities. In the online world, distraction is piled on distraction to deliver an intensity of experience that mere reality cannot hope to match. Case in point: in a clever experiment, so many people were engrossed in cell phone conversations that only 25 percent of them noticed a clown ride past them on a unicycle.[5] For members of the *Avatar* generation, immediate surroundings appear to be less important—much less exotic, interesting, and intense—than whatever happens in cyberspace. And so have we fabricated the means to no longer be psychologically alone, but only at the cost of actually being alone. Solitude in cyberspace is all right in small doses, but studies of e-mail usage indicate that exclusive use of e-mail as a social interface impairs chronic users' abilities to read nonverbal social cues and leaves the extensive social neural networks of their brains underdeveloped.[6] Moreover, as Gary Small observes, "Digital Immigrants note worsening of depression symptoms from too much exposure to technology. Previous studies have shown that social isolation clearly increases the risk for depression and worsens its symptoms. Despite the availability of social networks, email, and instant messaging, these electronic communication modes lack the emotional warmth of direct human contact and worsen a person's feelings of isolation."[7]

Among cyber natives, low self-esteem, depression, and isolation contribute to the testiness responsible for flaming, cyberbullying, and generalized lack of empathy and interpersonal skill. Early in my online career, when strangers made intense attacks against my personality rather than the substance of my blogs, older bloggers told me it was possible to gauge how much time an attacker spent online by the violence of the attack. Such people cannot gauge the real psychological impact of their attacks on others. They have lost the gift of empathy in much the same way that chronically lonely people do, simply because the neural pathways of social connection have not been used enough. They are socially clumsy, awkward, and very poor "mind-readers," who need considerable reentry time to readjust to community life. I believe this disconnection is endemic to cyber life and further disconnects us from one another.

My colleagues at *HuffingtonPost.com* also told me that cyberbullies are loners with low self-esteem. The bully's satisfaction in tearing you down lies in making you feel worse about yourself than they do about themselves. Now there is evidence to support this intuition.[8] But the violence of their attacks (what I call the "chained-dog effect") result from the lack of empathy in a disassociated, textual medium. Cyberbullies have no satisfyingly visible impact on *others*, so they generally choose the most offensive response like a chained dog barking as you pass by on the street: "I'd tear you apart if I could get to you," they seem to say. In all the years I wrote for *HuffPo*, the shrill vituperation of bloggers trying to intimidate never became an insignificant part of the job. These days, whenever the curt, megalomaniacal voice of the isolated cyber native rings out across the web, I find an excuse to discontinue communication politely but as firmly as possible. Cyber-crazies are damned souls that float through the ether of cyberspace. You must learn to identify and avoid them. Like addicts, only they can decide to help themselves.

Nonetheless, there is much more danger in not being present to our surroundings than simply being intimidating and rude. In a brilliant series of articles for the *New York Times*, Matt Richtel has outlined the full extent of the dangers of cell-phone distraction while driving. Unfortunately, this is not a message anyone appears to be heeding. Legislation banning cell-phone use while driving seems impossible to enforce, and both the IT and auto industries are determined to produce a generation of video- and Internet-ready automobiles that will exacerbate the challenges to driving with undivided attention.

Meanwhile, on sidewalks, on public transportation, in cafés, or in our offices, our focus on the tiny devices that fill the void left by social connection has surprising consequences. Even though so-called behavioral addictions are viewed as spurious by many diagnosticians classically trained to view addiction primarily as the abuse of a substance, still there are behaviors like gambling, sexual addiction, addiction to rage, and Internet or video-game addiction that seem to fulfill most if not all addictive criteria. When such people are deprived of their phones, they can become disproportionately anxious and unable to handle their daily routines. Cell phones are often used as instruments of juvenile bullying; as a means of violating others' privacy; and as a way to incur substantial debt through online gambling, online Internet access, and the purchase of downloadable apps, games, songs, and videos.[9] Psychologist Lisa Merlo believes that by the first decade of the twenty-first century, many people had become addicted to their cell phones. People sleep with them and describe them as "crack-berries." Merlo says, "Watching people who get their first smart phone, there's a very quick progression from having a basic phone you don't talk about to people who love their iPhone, name their phone and buy their phone outfits [protective cases] . . . the more bells and whistles the phone has . . . the more likely they are to become attached."[10]

Merlo may be correct in diagnosing this dependence as addictive behavior. But recently, marketing guru Martin Lindstrom claimed that we truly and literally "love" our personal devices. An opinion piece he wrote for the *New York Times* in the fall of 2011 called attention to tests he had commissioned at MindSign Neuromarketing in San Diego. MindSign conducts functional magnetic resonance imaging, or functional MRI (fMRI) scans, testing marketing propositions for ad agencies. Since the early 1990s, fMRI has come to dominate brain-mapping research because it requires no shots, surgery, or radioactive substances. Basically, fMRI procedures measure brain activity by detecting and recording changes in blood flow through the brain. These changes are called the "hemodynamic response." The main type (of fMRI) contrasts blood-oxygen levels to record neural activity in subjects' brains and spinal cords, imaging the change in blood flow, which corresponds closely to the way brain cells acquire and use energy. Lindstrom's claims in the *New York Times* are based on a few passages describing the result of these tests in his most recent book: "I carried out an fMRI experiment to find out whether iPhones were addictive . . . most striking . . . was the flurry of activity in the insular cortex of the brain, which is associated with feelings of love and compassion . . . subjects didn't demonstrate the classic brain-based signs of addiction. Instead they *loved* their iPhones. As we embrace new technology that does everything but kiss us on the mouth, we risk cutting ourselves off from human interaction. For many, the iPhone has become a best friend, partner, lifeline, companion and, yes, even a Valentine."[11]

Here, Lindstrom has captured precise evidence of the biochemistry of anthropomorphism.

Such discoveries are quite timely because we are about to enter a new age of robotics that surpasses the very good but not quite good enough simulation of robots that currently causes most people to react with revulsion to not quite human machines. Roboticists call this juncture the "uncanny valley." On the other side of this valley—very soon—we will encounter a new generation of mechanical beings whose sentience, consciousness, and existence all *appear to* equal or surpass our own. We will enter an age of electronic personal assistants who are quite human and much more engaging than the iPad's® "Siri." Out of sheer familiarity and everyday use, they will become our friends. David Levy believes many of us will come to love and have sex with these robots, while Lisa Merlo and Martin Lindstrom observe that—in many cases—these devices are already acting as substitutes for friendship, love, and connection.

I believe that our progressive reliance on technology for companionship is part of a prolonged and increasing disconnection from nature. A large part of this is the disconnection from our own humanity, which I have described. But my current topic is only a small part of a much larger one. In recasting our machines as friends, we deny a genuine human need for company that is as fundamental to our species as breathing; drinking water; or eating healthy, restorative food. In the absence of other human beings, we anthropomorphize everything in order to make substitutions for missing friendships and family. These cannot really satisfy. And any effort to live like self-sufficient machines or machinelike beings is simply a denial of what is most fundamental to nature and to our natures.

We are radically social animals. I have tried to show how we invented music and speech to serve the interpersonal connections that matter most to us. Machines, even the most sophisticated devices of the near future, are simply *not* the most suitable company for human beings. Using them is an undoubtedly safer activity than interacting with real human beings (who can be quite troublesome), but despite their annoyances, only other human beings provide us with lasting, biochemical bonds. During the prolonged attempt to make ourselves over into machines, we simultaneously isolated ourselves inside our cities and increasingly disconnected ourselves from the natural world. It should not surprise anyone that when we are immersed in nature, we become more pro-social (connected and caring) both to other human beings and to other biota. Social psychologist Richard M. Ryan believes this is because we feel more connected to the world and are therefore more aware of our responsibility to it.[12] More than half of humanity now lives and works in cities, and the number grows every year. We have chosen collectively to serve our urban economic machinery; and our view of nature is now predominantly economic and urban. We see nature simply as a source for exploitable and exhaustible material resources or a place to deposit industrial and consumer waste. Any crisis in nature is a matter of great indifference to us until it interferes with our economies and cities. I do not think it is an exaggeration to claim that the same time we lost the tight human bonds of premodern biochemical trust, we also lost our spiritual connection to nature and to the rest of creation.

The progressive denial of the natural world since the Industrial Revolution encompasses our denial of human nature. One is a subset of the other. When our view of the universe became mechanical, we began to see ourselves as machines. To paraphrase my friend the environmental activist David Suzuki, "The brain is a computer; the heart a pump; the kidneys, filters." Suzuki continues, "As long as we understand these analogies are not meant to be taken literally it's fine, but the mechanical notion of the human body is now deeply accepted."[13] Still, we are not machines. The truth remains that, while technology is a powerful servant, we can never escape our organic forms and become either mechanical *or* immortal. If we do, we will simply cease to be human beings. Consciousness endowed us with our biggest burden: that we will die. So death has become a challenge to be conquered, and, similarly, aging has become a disease. But if we give in to our fear of death and engineer a disconnection from it, we will create the biggest disconnect of all, losing along the path the remainder of our humanity and our connection to nature itself.

For me, humanity is a collective organism, much like a living forest. Individually, we are like leaves. Our great hope is that the forest itself may prove to be immortal, but sadly, (and also wonderfully) as individuals we are quite temporary. We fall away in turn. Senescence and death are essential, since without death there is no selection and adaptation as the world changes. Instead of immortality, we look to our children to perpetuate our life, our species, our special role on the earth as its caretaker and proprietor. As David Suzuki says, "We have lost . . . the sense of identity as part of a bigger world, nature. We no longer know that we emerged from nature, are maintained by nature, and upon death, return to be recycled through nature."[14] We must regain that sense of our connection to the natural world and to each other.

So what is the role of technology in a pro-social, pro-natural world?

In a recent book, Richard Louv, author of *The Last Child in the Woods* (2005), describes how we can begin to build community and comfort into our lives using what he calls "the Nature Principle." Louv writes, "The Nature Principle offers its own design rule: use natural systems to enhance human beings' physical, psychological and spiritual life; preserve and plant nature everywhere; rather than plan for obsolescence plan for long-term organic growth. . . . Whereas technology immersion results in walls that become screens, and machines that enter our bodies, more nature in our lives offers us homes and workplaces and natural communities that produce human energy . . . [and] products and environments that make life more comfortable for people."[15]

I cannot agree with this view too strongly. There is nothing inherently evil about technology. Human culture itself is a technology that helps us cope with our rapidly changing world. We cannot change our reliance on culture-technology without fundamentally changing ourselves. But, as Richard Louv says, although "many people believe that technology is the antithesis of nature," there is "an alternative view: a fishing rod is technology. So is that fancy backpack. Or a compass. Or a tent."[16] We are imprisoned by our technology only when we use it in naïve and uncreative ways. We can use any new technology to support and foster human relationships and our relationship to nature itself.

Mark Katz will soon publish a wonderful book, *Groove Music: The Art and Culture of the Hip-Hop DJ*, about the emergence in the 1970s of a new kind of music that used the potentially isolating nature of recording technology against itself. Basically, an entire generation of music freaks who had spent too much time with their record collections began to use their knowledge of music *socially* as the center of a vibrant DJ culture that supported block parties and turntablist showdowns in the South Bronx.[17] Similarly, in Paris these days, degrowth proponent Serge Latouche tells me in imperfect English and beautiful French that there is a vogue of iPod parties at which people gather together to dance collectively to music they hear individually on their iPods.[18] Never an academic to be "scotched [scotch-taped] to my desk all day," Serge, now in his seventies, has been to more than one of these parties.[19] Like the emergence of DJ culture, this is a compelling example of how technology can be used creatively to establish interpersonal interaction and foster interpersonal trust and friendship.

My favorite development along these lines, however, is the invention of conceptual artists like Liz Sherman. Every summer for Manhattan's "Summer Streets" festival, Liz organizes "Joyride," a weekly event at which strangers gather with their bicycles in Foley Square. Throughout the year, many New Yorkers defy or comply unwillingly with a bylaw banning headphones in traffic. Although it's a good idea not to ride a bike while listening to music in New York, it is a pleasure, and sometimes cyclists pay lip service to the law by using only one earphone. But Joyride is different. After they are given MP3 players loaded with a mix by film-music composer Duncan Bridgeman (*1 Giant Leap*, 2002), the group forms a peloton and rides north on Park Avenue through the sectioned-off streets of Manhattan listening to preprogrammed music. The architecture, the music, the bicycle in motion, and the company of a very well-disposed group of fairly cool and like-minded sybarites make these Saturday morning rides a delight. But there is more.

At Central Park, a sumptuous picnic (last summer there were delicious lobster-salad sandwiches) awaits the cyclists, who've worked up an appetite and who now have a lot to say to each other. "People love the music and the meals," Liz Sherman says, "and they talk naturally outside. They make friends and come back year after year. It's so easy to rent a bike in New York, and it's so hard to make friends . . . worth it though, isn't it?"[20]

Social psychologists tell us that "nature strips away the artifices of society that alienate us from one another."[21] Concrete proof of the pro-social benefits of natural surroundings has existed for more than a decade now. It is widely known that heart-attack patients recover more quickly in rooms exposed to trees and greenery. Moreover, in Chicago around the turn of the millennia, it was discovered that the high instance of mental fatigue among women living in housing projects in urban Chicago directly correlated to the number of incidences of violence against their partners. Significantly, this did not occur among women who lived in identical buildings featuring nearby trees and greenery.[22] Generally, greener neighborhoods with more trees have many fewer incidences of violence. Residents in green surroundings also report lower levels of anxiety and outright fear, and much less public and private incivility, in addition to much less explicitly aggressive and violent behavior. In general, the greener a building's surroundings are, the less crime occurs in and around it. This generalization applies across a wide range of violations from rape and violent assaults to simple property crimes like break-and-enter and bicycle theft.[23] Simply put, we are more sociable when we are connected to nature, and without nature we manifest antisocial behavior more regularly and rely on technological substitutes more and more.

Please contact me with your reactions and experiences at gilesslade.com.

We'll have to leave it there.

ACKNOWLEDGMENTS

How *dull it is to* pause to *make an end.*

This book would not have happened without the support of many people: that thought makes me reflect about what a lucky man I have actually been so far in my life. Without a word of complaint, Sandra puts up with my unaffiliated, lone-wolf writerdom, while I puzzle these things out and tap them slowly into Word®. Before I began writing today, there, on the floor of our walk-in closet, I found my wedding ring, which had been lost for ten days. I was incomplete without it in a way that all women and some men will understand. Thirty-two years and three sons later, I am still, in Sandra's eyes, the stormy young poet she met in Los Angeles in our twenties. There is no greater gift than the personal freedom that flows from her acceptance of me. How wisely my spirit chose her. I have not always been so wise.

In these books, I am trying to work backward to discover what caused the explosions in population, as well as the economic and technological growth that shaped our modern world and caused us to ignore or devalue the most fundamental human satisfactions. I believe that when I consult the record and start over at the beginning, many obscure things become clear. Conversations with Leonard Lopate (WNYC), Donna Seaman (Open Books), and Terry Milewski (CBC) challenged me and made me realize that *Made to Break* had left the job unfinished. I am grateful to have such skilled readers, and I am grateful for the attention that *Made to Break* garnered. This was a direct result of the effort devoted to the book by Michael Fisher, Susan Boehmer, and RoseAnn Miller of Harvard University Press, all of whom I have never met in person or thanked adequately.

Lew Daly (of Demos in Manhattan) introduced me to his agent, Andrew Stuart, who sold this book for me with great patience and great faith. The conversations, exchanges, and ideas I've gleaned from Tom Bentley-Harapnuik, Lester R. Brown, Chris Bucci, Michael Bugeja, Joe Cacioppo, Nicholas Christakis, Cari Copeman-Haynes, Robert Copeman-Haynes, Richard Crawford, Cosima Dannoritzer, Alain de Botton, Ellen Dissanayake, Brian Dolan, Sonni Efron, Dean Falk, Stanley Fish, Adam Garfinkle, Anthony Giddens, Clive Hamilton, Paul Headrick, Christopher Hitchens, Mark Katz, Tsukao "Toby" Kawahigashi, Ned Kock, Elizabeth Kolbert, Serge Latouche, Cameron MacPhee, Bill McKibben, Andrew Nikiforuk, David Nye, Henry Petroski, Murray Phillips, David Pogue, Laura Pappano, Elizabeth Royte, Matt Richtel, Eric Rumble, Liz Sherman (of Joyride!), Mandy Sigurgeirson, Susan Strasser, Gus Speth, David Suzuki, Sherry Turkle, John Vaillant, Fred Weil, and Chris Wood shaped my thoughts or jolted me to react. I deeply regret not being able to speak with Steve Jobs, who died before we could meet. In my mind, he is a figure like Thomas Edison or Henry Ford. I wanted to talk to him as much as I still want to speak with Bill Gates, who I hope will read this and agree before I sit down to write the third book in what I have come to think of as *The Potlatch Trilogy*, a trio of books exploring the emergent consciousness of consumer society. How 'bout it, Bill? At the very least, it would be an interesting chat.

I would also like to thank the people at Prometheus Books for their forbearance. Linda Greenspan Regan acquired this title and began steering it toward completion before retiring. I am in her debt. In her stead, Steven L. Mitchell deserves considerable thanks for patiently and wisely giving me enough time to complete the research into the dozen different fields that contribute to the document you are now reading. Cate Roberts-Abel kept us all on track as we tried to meet the tight deadlines that resulted from protracted drafts. Melissa Shofner demonstrated the patience and graciousness of a true believer as she tracked down permissions and potential reviewers. I should also thank the nameless marketing executive who suggested the book's current title, *The Big Disconnect*; it was a very good call.

There's just a bit more work to do before finishing the entire project, but meanwhile, dear reader, please *enjoy* my book.

NOTES

INTRODUCTION. IMMORTALITY AND FREE WILL

1. Paul Simon, *Lyrics, 1964–2008* (New York: Simon & Schuster, 2008), p. 5.

2. Ibid.

3. See my *Made to Break: Technology and Obsolescence in America* (Cambridge, MA: Harvard University Press, 2006), p. 289, n. 25. This idea (the obsolescence of humankind) would eventually receive its highest expression in Günther Anders's 1956 philosophical treatise *The Obsolescence of Man* (never translated into English). Writing in German twenty years after immigrating to the United States, Anders predicted the complete replacement of humans by machines and the end of human history. He saw the Holocaust as the first attempt at the systematic extermination of a whole people by industrial means. Anders was probably not influenced by (Archibald) MacLeish (see pp. 67–72). It is more likely that he read Norman Cousins's famous essay "Modern Man Is Obsolete," which followed the attacks on Hiroshima and Nagasaki in August 1945 (see chap. 5).

4. Lewis Mumford, *Technics and Civilization* (London: Routledge & Kegan Paul, 1967), p. 51.

5. John Cacioppo and William Patrick, *Loneliness: Human Nature and the Need for Social Connection* (New York: Norton, 2008), p. 8.

CHAPTER 1. BREADCRUMBS

1. See Stephanie Rosenbloom, "Would You Sign My Kindle?" *New York Times*, April 13, 2011, http://www.nytimes.com/2011/04/14/fashion/14NOTICED.html (accessed October 10, 2011).

2. See Alexandra Horowitz, "Will the E-book Kill the Footnote?" *New York*

Times, October 7, 2011, http://www.nytimes.com/2011/10/09/books/review/will-the-e-book-kill-the-footnote.html?pagewanted=all (accessed October 10, 2011).

3. For more on the implications of this interesting observation, see George Basalla's exploration of "artifactual continuity" in *The Evolution of Technology* (Cambridge: Cambridge University Press, 1988), pp. 25, 30, 43, 55, 62, 63, 208. Page 63: "In the earliest, and unsuccessful, mechanical reaper, attempts were made to duplicate the swinging motion of the scythe as it cut through the grain or to imitate the clipping action of scissors or shears. The McCormick reaper, which brought large-scale mechanical reaping to the farms of America, utilized an oscillating serrated (toothed) blade to saw through the grain stalks. McCormick's machine copied the action of the very ancient hand sickle, whose serrated blade was used in a sawing motion to sever the stalks."

4. It is important to note that of the ten most common fears that cause people to seek psychiatric treatment, three concern social anxiety, fear of crowds, fear of meeting new people, and fear of speaking in public.

5. I remember going online to order Salman Rushdie's *Satanic Verses* and Stanley Fish's wonderful book about Milton's *Paradise Lost* during my tenure in Saudi Arabia during the late '90s. Unfortunately, *Satanic Verses* was stopped by an overzealous *mutawa'ah* opening foreign packages in a fetid backroom in Riyadh. Because that book was intercepted, I was *Surprised by Sin* when it arrived in time for Ramadan, enabling me to enjoy my former teacher's acutely Jewish observations about Christianity's Satan during a long, dull month in al-Khobar when all the shops, restaurants, and my favorite pool hall remained closed until sunset so that the faithful could be strengthened for their lifelong struggle against "Iblis" (Despair), the aptly named devil of Islam.

6. John Markoff, "The Passion of Steve Jobs," *New York Times*, January 15, 2008. Full quote: "'It doesn't matter how good or bad the product [Kindle] is, the fact is that people don't read anymore," he [S J] said 'Forty percent of the people in the U.S. read one book or less last year. The whole conception is flawed at the top,'" http://bits.blogs.nytimes.com/2008/01/15/the-passion-of-steve-jobs/?scp=1&sq=steve%20jobs%20people%20don%27t%20read%20any%20 more &st=cse (accessed March 10, 2011).

7. Jane Jacobs, *The Death and Life of Great American Cities* (New York: Vintage, 1992), p. 138.

8. "Aggravating Circumstances: A Status Report on Rudeness in America," Pew Charitable Trusts, 2002, http//www.publicagenda.org/files/pdf/aggravating_circumstances.pdf (accessed March 26, 2011).

9. Jacobs, *Death and Life*, p. 138.

10. Nicholas Epley et al., "On Seeing Human: A Three-Factor Theory of Anthropomorphism," *Psychological Review* 114, no. 4 (2007): 864–65; but see also Nicholas Epley et al., "Creating Social Connection through Inferential Reproduction, Loneliness and Perceived Agency in Gadgets, Gods, and Greyhounds," *Psychological Science* 119, no. 2 (2008): 114–20.

11. Chaeyoon Lim and Robert Putnam, "Religion, Social Networks, and Life Satisfaction," *American Sociological Review* 75, no. 6 (December 2010): 914–33.

12. Excerpted from a personal message (December 28, 2010) from Sherry Turkle. This excerpt is given in greater length in my review "Alone Together, Reviewing Sherry Turkle and Michael Bugeja," January 20, 2011, at http://www.huffingtonpost.com/giles-slade/alone-together-reviewing-_b_803256.html.

13. Ellen Gibson, "Sleep with Your iPhone? You're Not Alone," *Kansas City Star*, July 26, 2011, http://www.kansascity.com/2011/07/26/v-print/3037100/sleep/ (accessed July 26, 2011). Note: At the time of publication, this URL was inactive.

14. Michael Wilson, "Ray's Pizza, the First of Many, Counts Down to Its Last Slice," *New York Times*, September 17, 2011, http://www.nytimes.com/2011/09/18/nyregion/rays-pizza-the-first-of-many-counts-down-to-last-slice.html?pagewanted=all (accessed September 17).

15. Miller McPherson and Lynn Smith-Lovin, "Social Isolation in America: Changes in Core Discussion Networks over Two Decades," *American Sociological Review* 71 (June 2006): 353–75.

16. J. Peen et al., "The Current Status of Urban-Rural Differences in Psychiatric Disorders," *Acta Psychiatrica Scandinavica* 121 (2010): 92.

17. Linda Krabbendam et al., "Schizophrenia and Urbanicity: A Major Environmental Influence," *Schizophrenia Bulletin* 31, no. 4:798.

18. Florian Lederbogen et al., "City Living and Urban Upbringing Affect Neural Social Stress Processing in Humans," *Nature* 474 (June 23, 2011): 498.

19. Philip Slater, *The Pursuit of Loneliness* (Boston: Beacon Press, 1970), p. 26.

20. Sami Yenigun, "Few Consumers Are Cracking the QR Code," NPR, *All Things Considered*, http://www.npr.org/2011/09/26/140805493/few-consumers-are-cracking-the-qr-code (accessed September 27, 2011).

21. Jacobs, *Death and Life*, p. 56.

22. Waldo Walker, "Slot Machines Amass Riches from Pennies," *New York Times*, November 13, 1927.

23. Texts of early American postcards were very short since no messages were allowed on the addressed side until after 1907.

24. Georg Simmel, "The Metropolis and Mental Life" in *The Blackwell City Reader*, edited by Gary Bridge and Sophie Watson (Oxford and Malden, MA: Wiley-Blackwell, 2002), p. 15.

25. A fellow writing instructor, Melissa Febos of Sarah Lawrence College, refers to such devices as "shields" in "Just Don't Connect," Opinionator, *New York Times*, http://opinionator.blogs.nytimes.com/ 2011/04/27/just-dont-connect/ (accessed April 27, 2011).

26. Erving Goffman, *Relations in Public* (New York: Basic Books, 1971), p. 312.

27. Ibid., p. 267.

28. Jacobs, *Death and Life*, p. 56.

29. In general, smartphones have had a greater impact on American and English slang than vending machines, which contributed many useful phrases that focused on the coins themselves. These include *chump change, nickel-and-dime, penny pincher/pinching, spend-a-penny, slug(s), squeeze a nickel, the penny dropped, thin dime*, and *wooden nickel.* Texting has already developed a richer assortment of idioms. Text-messaging programs like SMS or Twitter® require that users limit their communications to 160 or 140 characters, respectively. This encourages short, superficial abbreviations of often quite crude slang expressions. The machines make using swearwords a safe option for young users attracted to the coolness of tough speech. It's easy to see a decline in civility by comparing the idioms of the vending-machine era with those of our own: AAMOF = as a matter of fact; abt = about; AISI = as i see it; ATM = at the moment; BAMF = bad ass motherfucker; bc or b/c = because; BS = bullshit; dubs = W; FFS = for fuck's sake; FUBAR = fucked up beyond all repair; GG = good game; g2g = got to go; HB = hurry back; Hi5 = high five; ILU = i love you; KISS = keep it simple, stupid; NM = not much or never mind (never mind is more commonly NVM); noob or n00b or newb = newbie; OIC = oh, i see!; OMG = oh, my god!; PDQ = pretty darn quick; POV = point of view; SOL = shit out (of) luck; sry = sorry; STFU = shut the fuck up; TC = take care; TL;DR = too long, didn't read (I love this one); TMI = too much information . . .

30. William Young and Nancy Young, eds., *The Great Depression in America: A Cultural Encyclopedia*, vol. 11 (Westport, CT: Greenwood, 2007), p. 195.

31. Selwyn Raab, *Five Families: The Rise, Decline, and Resurgence of America's Most Powerful Mafia Families* (New York: Macmillan, 2006), p. 60.

32. Jean Baudrillard, *America*, trans. Chris Turner (New York: Verso, 1986), p. 15. I thank Professor Baudrillard's friend and colleague Serge LaTouche for bringing this to my attention.

33. With its musical connotations, the word *Orpheum* (derived from *Orpheus*) seems a strange choice for a theater showing silent films, but the other original form of entertainment at this venue was "illustrated songs," an obsolescent kind of performance art that accompanied and promoted the latest musical hits.

34. Norbert Elias, *The Civilizing Process*, trans. E. Jebcott (Oxford, UK: Blackwell, 1994), pp. 135–57.

35. Bertram Wyatt-Brown, *The Shaping of Southern Culture: Honor, Grace, and War, 1760s–1880s* (Chapel Hill: University of North Carolina Press, 2001), p. 91.

36. John F. Kasson, *Rudeness and Civility: Manners in Nineteenth-Century Urban America* (New York: Hill & Wang, 1990), p. 71.

37. Also worth noting is the odd fact that pay toilets were not introduced in America until 1910.

38. Mark Twain, *Travels with Mr. Brown* (1866): I am grateful to John Kasson for his discovery of this passage. His excellent book *Rudeness and Civility* includes several other contemporary descriptions, including the following by an Austrian visitor to America in 1871: "I mix with the crowd, which drags me on with it. I strive to read their physiognomies, and I find everywhere the same expression. Everyone is in a hurry, if only to get home as fast as possible to save the few hours of rest, after having made the most of the long hours of work. Everyone seems to suspect a competitor in his neighbor. The crowd is the embodiment of isolation. The moral atmosphere is not charity but rivalry" (p. 80).

39. Paul Williams, "Sounds of Silence—Simon and Garfunkel," *Crawdaddy!* premier issue, 1966; reprinted in *The Crawdaddy Book, Writings and Images from the Magazine of Rock* (New York: Hal Leonard, 2002), p. 11.

40. Hyacinthe Dubreuil, *Standards* (Paris: Bernard Grasset, 1929); published in English as *Robots or Men? A French Workman's Experience in America*, trans. Frances Merrill and Mason Merrill (New York: Harper & Brothers, 1930), p. 23.

41. Pitirim Sorokin and Clarence Berger, *Time Budgets of Human Behavior* (Cambridge, MA: Harvard University Press, 1939), pp. 150, 153.

42. Slater, *Pursuit of Loneliness*, p. 7.

43. There are precursors to spam from as early as 1978 on the ARPANET, but the turning point was Laurence Canter and Martha Siegel, *How to Make a Fortune on the Information Superhighway, Everyone's Guerrilla Guide to Marketing on the Internet and Other On-Line Services* (New York: HarperCollins, 1995). See Tom Abate, "A Very Unhappy Birthday to Spam, Age 30," *San Francisco Chronicle*, May 3, 2008.

44. G. R. Schreiber, *A Concise History of Vending in the U.S.A.* (Chicago: Vend, 1961), p. 14.

45. "Silent Salesmen? Not at All—Newest Automatics Talk to You," *Automatic Age* 4 (1928): 13; "Robot to Supplement Human Salesmen in Retail Groceries," *Automatic Age* 5 (1929): 43. From 1928 until the beginning of World War II, America's newspapers and business press were full of articles about "Robot Salesmen." Some of the most representative pieces follow. Notice that the final article is dated 1927, before talking vending machines. It does not use the phrase, "robot salesman." "But When Will Robots Eat and Sleep for Us?" *Literary Digest* 102 (September 7, 1929): 53; "Jobs Galore for Robot Salesmen," *BusinessWeek*, April 16, 1930, p. 28; "The Machine as Salesman," *Fortune* 35 (March 1947): 117; Robots to Mimic Actors," *New York Times*, June 17, 1928; "Sales Robot Makes Change, Rejects Slugs," *BusinessWeek*, October 29, 1930; and Walker, "Slot Machines Amass Riches from Pennies."

46. Kerry Segrave, *Vending Machines: An American Social History* (Jefferson, NC: McFarland, 2002), p. 27.

47. The starting place for anyone interested in robots and vending machines is Chris Rasmussen's excellent paper "Jobs Galore for Robots: Robot Salesmen, Robot Entertainers, and the 'National Machine' of Prosperity in the 1920s and 1930s," *Rethinking History* 5, no. 1 (2001): 149–62. Professor Rasmussen tells me he's currently working on a book-length social history of the vending machine to be called *The Automatic Age*.

48. Ibid., p. 149.

49. It's now well-known that the word *robot* first appeared in Karel Čapek's play *R.U.R.* (Rossum's Universal Robots, 1920) and was invented by the playwright's brother, Josef, as a derivative of *robota*, the Czech word for *work* or *labor*. In the play, the word describes what we today call biological clones or replicants, the serfs of speculative fiction, which are produced by technological processes including genetic engineering and artificial incubation. Čapek's robots relieved their human masters of onerous and tedious work. But in real life, robots held the same economic appeal as slavery (abolished in 1865, only fifty-five years earlier). Like slaves, robots provide cheap labor. Mechanical men preexisted Čapek's play by several centuries. Undoubtedly it was René Descartes who first got people thinking about man as a machine when he described the human body as a "machine made by the hands of god that is incomparably better arranged . . . than is any machine of human invention." Oddly, the first robot, Jacques de Vaucanson's clockwork, Flute Player (1737), appeared exactly one hundred years after Descartes

formulated his cogito, ergo sum. Many other anthropomorphic automata followed during the eighteenth century, including those by Pierre Jacquet-Droz. Unlike *karakuri*, such robots were only expensive novelties that did not perform commercial tasks. Meanwhile, the Cartesian idea that man is little more than a biological mechanism gained notoriety following its adoption by the atheist-physician Julien Offray de La Mettrie in *L'Homme machine* (1748). Mary Shelley's *Frankenstein* (1818) is an articulation of a metaphor that became accepted medical wisdom after Mettrie. According to this view, man is "a machine of exquisite mechanical structure." A machine, of course, is easy to fix and manipulate since its processes are known and finite. In the century that followed, self-propelled devices became increasingly sophisticated and gained universal acceptance. By the turn of the next century, many began to wonder if art and science would ever combine to create a human-like being. It wasn't long before this speculation began to affect our most fundamental ideas about humanity and to challenge Descartes's assertion that "we may know the difference between men and brutes (or between men and automata) by the application of two simple tests, does it speak intelligently; and does it reason?"

50. Sherry Turkle, *Alone Together* (New York: Basic Books, 2010), p. xix.

51. Epley et al., "Creating Social Connection," pp. 114–20; Peter F. O'Shea, "Can Selling Be Done by Machinery?" *Magazine of Business*, November 28, 1928, p. 589.

52. Raymond Williams, *Television: Technology and Cultural Form* (London: William Collins & Sons, 1974), p. 22.

53. Shane Mountjoy and Tim McNeese, *Technology and the Civil War* (New York: Infobase, 2009), p. 93.

54. Brian Sutton-Smith, *Toys as Culture* (New York: Gardner, 1986).

55. Katherine Grier, *Pets in America* (Orlando, FL: Harcourt, 2007), p. 21.

56. Olive Thorne Miller, *Our Home Pets* (Whitefish, MT: Kessinger; reprint of rare original edition of 1894, 2010), pp. 195–96.

57. In Herman Melville's 1855 story "The Bell Tower," a creature is constructed out of metal parts and is an artificial being, but Melville glosses over the details of Haman's physical being.

58. Frank Baum, *Ozma of Oz* (Skokie, IL: Rand McNally, 1907).

59. An incomplete list of robot one-reelers follows. These are only the films known to me. I am sure there must be others. Some are available on YouTube: "The Fairylogue and Radio-Plays" (1908); "An Animated Doll" (1908); "The Rubber Man" (1909); "Dr Smith's Automaton" (1910, France); "The Automatic Motorist" (1911, United Kingdom); D. W. Griffith's

"The Inventor's Secret" (1911); "The Electric Leg" (1912, United Kingdom); "Sammy's Automaton" (1914, France); "Tales of Hoffman" (1915, Germany); "Homunculus" (1916, Germany); "The Dancing Mechanical Man" (1919, Germany); and "L'Uomo meccanico" (1921, Italy).

60. R. W. Witkin, *Adorno on Music* (London: Routledge, 1998), p. 20.

61. See, especially, "Word a Day," *Christian Science Monitor*, November 23, 1928, p. 21.

62. David O. Woodbury, "Dramatizing the Robot," letter to the editor, *New York Times*, November 6, 1927.

63. The perplexing challenges that robotic beings posed to man's notion of his own humanity was part of the lifework of Sir Alfred Jules Ayer, professor of logic at Oxford University. In 1936, Ayer developed a protocol to distinguish a conscious from an unconscious machine. Alan Turing, a young member of Ayer's "Ratio Club," was profoundly influenced by these ideas and used them to formulate the landmark "Turing Test" in the 1950s. But as the intellectual basis of the new science of Artificial Intelligence slowly evolved, World War II suddenly intervened. Calculation "engines" became vitally important in England's war effort. These machines had to be capable of complicated mathematical calculations to predict ballistic trajectories or to decode enemy messages. England, America, and Australia set their best minds to the task of creating thinking machines, and by the end of the decade, the following prototypes had been developed: Harvard Mark I computer (United States, 1943); Colossus 1-10 computers (United Kingdom, 1943–1945); ENIAC (United States, 1945); ACE (United Kingdom, 1946); EDVAC (United States, 1947); CSIRAC (Australia, 1949).

64. Simmel, "Metropolis and Mental Life," p. 13.

65. Dubreuil, *Standards*, p. 183.

66. There is a lot of dispute about the date of this original robot toy, but the website of Alphadrome, "the Tin Toy collectors," lists a prototype of this robot toy dated from 1937. (The date usually given in print sources is 1939.) This information can be found at http://www.danefield.com/data/display-image-1-2578.html (accessed November 11, 2011).

67. I am indebted to Alphadrome, the tin toy collectors website for all this information, available online at http://danefield.com/alpha/forums/topic/5911-atomic-robot-man/ (accessed November 11, 2011).

68. Shuzaburo Hironaga, *Bunraku: Japan's Unique Puppet Theatre* (Tokyo: Tokyo News Service, 1964), p. xxi. Also known as "ningyo joruri," Bunraku was the preferred theatrical form of Japan's best-known dramatist, Chikamatsu Monzaemon. There are no robots in Monzaemon's plays, but through his anthro-

pomorphic puppet characters, Japanese audiences experience the deepest and most complex of human emotions. For this reason, Monzaemon is often called Japan's Shakespeare. In 1926, fire destroyed the leading Bunraku theaters in Osaka, burning a repository of irreplaceable and historic carved puppet heads. It was a national tragedy. Deprived of its traditional venues, Bunraku began to travel. In Tokyo, the form found a large, enthusiastic audience who funded a new, "national" theater, which opened in 1929. Then, in 1933, the Diet acted to preserve the endangered Bunraku form with the first Japanese legislation devoting modest financial support to a traditional performing art. For the fascinating history of this puppet theater, see Benito Ortolani's wonderfully written study *The Japanese Theatre: From Shamanistic Ritual to Contemporary Pluralism* (Princeton, NJ: Princeton University Press, 1995), p. 227.

69. See Jane Marie Law, *Puppets of Nostalgia: The Life, Death, and Rebirth of the Japanese Awaji Ningyo Tradition* (Princeton, NJ: Princeton University Press, 1997).

70. T. N. Hornyak, *Loving the Machine: The Art and Science of Japanese Robots* (Tokyo: Kodansha International, 2006), pp. 32–37.

71. Milton Wright, "Robots for Salesman," *Scientific American* 140, January 1929, p. 24.

72. *International Musician* 25, no. 1 (June 1929).

73. H. L. Mencken, *American Mercury* 19 (June 1930): ii.

74. *Outlook and Independent* 158 (1931): 439.

75. In 1929, three short days before the stock-market crash, *Editor and Publisher* magazine wrote: "The talkie has thrown 5,000 members of the American Federation of Musicians out of work and threatens thousands more. The public cannot be said to be sensitive to such economic injustice. Few of us care about the other fellow's job." See "The Musician Fights," *Editor and Publisher*, October 26, 1929, p. 54. Concerning technological unemployment during the Depression, see Giles Slade, *Made to Break: Technology and Obsolescence in America* (Cambridge, MA: Harvard University Press, 2006), pp. 65–67, and Amy Sue Bix, *Inventing Ourselves out of Jobs: America's Debate over Technological Unemployment, 1929–1981* (Baltimore: Johns Hopkins University Press, 2000), pp. 96–99.

76. Vern Countryman, "The Organized Musicians: II," *University of Chicago Law Review* 16, no. 2 (1949): 244.

77. Ibid., p. 245.

78. H. L. Mencken, ed., *American Mercury* 22 (1931): xxix.

79. Marvin Kitman, "Don't Make Me Laugh," *Channels of Communication*, August/September 1981.

80. Alene F. Parry, "Censorship during the Depression: The Banning of You and Machines," *OAH Magazine of History* 16, no. 1, Fall 2001, p. 77.

81. Issue 10 of *New Adventure Comics* features the Federal Men in a story called "The Mechanical Isle." I was not able to find an original copy since few libraries collect such disposable literature, but I did find small illustrations of some panels depicting the robot in Paul Levitz, *75 Years of DC Comics: The Art of Modern Mythmaking* (Cologne, Germany: Taschen, 2011). Levitz gives the year of publication of issue 10 as 1935.

82. Video-game cartridges were the invention of Gerald (Jerry) A. Lawson, who worked as a consultant on the Atari 2600 system. See Dennis McClellan, "Gerald Lawson Dies at 70: Engineer Brought Cartridge-Based Video Game Consoles to Life," *Los Angeles Times*, April 23, http://www.latimes.com/news/obituaries/la-me-gerald-lawson-20110423,0,4057605 (story published on April 26, 2011).

83. Sherry Turkle, *The Second Self: Computers and the Human Spirit* (New York: Simon & Schuster, 1984), pp. 64–92.

84. William Sims Bainbridge, *Berkshire Encyclopedia of Human-Computer Interactions*, vol. 2 (Great Barrington, MA: Berkshire, 2004), p. 469.

85. For anecdotal accounts of the widespread children's belief during the 1930s that "real little people lived in the radio," see Ray Barfield, *Listening to Radio, 1920–1950* (Westport, CT: Praeger, 1996), pp. 17, 19.

86. Lewis Mumford, *Technics and Civilization*, 9th ed. (London: Routledge & Kegan Paul, 1967), p. 51.

87. See Nobuhito Kishi, *Robots Will Rescue Japan!* (Tokyo: Bungei, 2011).

88. See Jennifer Robertson, "Robots of the Rising Sun," *American Interest* 6, no. 1 (September/October 2010): 60–72.

89. Masahiro Mori, "Bukimi no Tani Genshō/The Uncanny Valley," trans. K. F. MacDorman and T. Minato, *Energy* 7, no. 4 (1970): 33–35.

90. David Levy, *Love and Sex with Robots*, Kindle ed., 2007. It was while reading this book that I became aware of the inadequate provisions Kindle now makes for endnotes. However, notice that a bibliographic citation for an eBook doesn't require a page number, since the pages are unnumbered and the whole book is conveniently searchable.

91. James J. Flink, *America Adopts the Automobile, 1895–1910* (Cambridge, MA: MIT Press, 1970), p. 101.

92. Charles Buryea, "How to Select An Automobile," *Independent* 66 (June 1909): 1213.

93. Jacobs, *Death and Life*, p. 65.

94. Emily Badger, "Slugging: The People's Transit," *Miller-McClune*,

March 7, 2011, https://www.miller-mccune.com/culture-society/slugging-the-peoples-transit-28068/ (accessed January 4, 2012).

95. See the second "rule" of slugging at http://www.slug-lines.com/Slugging/Etiquette.asp.

96. Vivian Carter, "Anglo-American Contrasts," *Rotarian* 34, no. 4 (April 1929): 21–22.

97. Sinclair Lewis, *Babbitt* (London: Jonathan Cape, 1932), pp. 143–44.

98. Strangely, even as the popular word for autos became *cars*, car radios continued to be called *auto-radios*. However, by the late '30s, auto-radios and car radios were synonymous terms, and eventually *auto-radio* disappeared after the war. This linguistic change probably reflects the generational change among speakers of American English.

99. David Gartman, *Auto Opium: A Social History of American Automobile Design* (New York: Routledge, 1994), p. 45. Gartman's book is a great read.

100. *Automotive Industries*, April 1927, p. 56 (Radnor, PA: Chilton), p. 229. The useful chart on this page includes comparative figures for the years 1919–1926.

101. Ibid., p. 228.

102. "Widely Separated Inventors Develop Systems to Open Garage Doors with Radio Impulses," *Popular Science*, February 1931, p. 32.

103. Gartman, *Auto Opium*, pp. 27, 45; but see also P. Wilson's useful but hard to obtain *Chrome Dreams, Automobile Styling since 1893* (Radnor, PA: Chilton, 1976), pp. 90–103.

104. *Automotive Industries*, November 1906, pp. 15, 614.

105. Octavus Roy Cohen, *Midnight* (Rockville, MD: Munseys, 2008; original ed., 1921), p. 5.

106. Harold F. Blanchard, "Durability, Silence, Comfort, Roominess Required," *Automotive Manufacturer*, June 1926, pp. 49, 68.

107. Emily Thompson, *The Soundscape of Modernity: Architectural Acoustics and the Culture of Listening in America, 1900–1933* (Cambridge, MA: MIT Press, 2003) is a brilliant compendium of the available research on sound changes in the modern world. See also R. Murray Schafer's *The Tuning of the World* (New York: Random House, 1977).

108. Evan Eisenberg, *The Recording Angel: Explorations in Phonography* (New York: McGraw-Hill, 1987), p. 44.

109. J. B. Smith, "A Radio Set for Your Car," *Popular Mechanics*, August 1926, pp. 301–303.

110. Eric P. Wenaas, *Radiola: The Golden Age of RCA, 1919–1929* (Chandler, AZ: Sonoran, 2007), p. 307.

111. Harry M. Petrakis, *The Founder's Touch: The Life of Paul Galvin of Motorola* (Chicago: Motorola University Press, 1991), p. 92.

112. Susan J. Douglas, *Listening In: Radio and the American Imagination* (Minneapolis: University of Minnesota Press, 2004), p. 226.

113. Jacobs, *Death and Life*, pp. 350–51.

114. Ibid., p. 7.

115. Ibid.

116. Susan J. Douglas, *Listening In: Radio and the American Imagination* (New York: Random House, 1999), p. 226; see also "More Listen to Radio in Cars Than at Home, Study Shows," *Advertising Age*, July 8, 1963, p. 28.

117. Susan J. Douglas, *Inventing American Broadcasting, 1899–1922* (Baltimore: Johns Hopkins University Press, 1987), p. 293.

118. Ibid., p. 295; see also Georgette Carneal, *A Conqueror of Space: An Authorized Biography of the Life and Work of Lee DeForest* (New York: Horace Liveright, 1930).

119. Richard Butsch, *The Making of American Audiences: From Stage to Television, 1750–1990* (Cambridge: Cambridge University Press, 2000), p. 174.

120. Ibid., p. 175.

121. Raymond F. Yates, "What Will Happen to Broadcasting?" *Outlook* 13 (April 9, 1924): 604.

122. J. Fred MacDonald, *Don't Touch That Dial: Radio Programming in American Life from 1920 to 1960* (Chicago: Nelson-Hall, 1979), pp. 10–11.

123. McPherson was raised attending revival meetings throughout New England and small-town Canada. She was Pentecostal by birth, but the tent meetings she attended as a child followed the older Methodist tradition of camp meetings. They aimed at making new converts through striking demonstrations of the power of faith that relied—for followers of the Assembly of God—on the occurrence of miracles like glossolalia (speaking in tongues) and faith healing. Most of all, these meetings were overtly musical events involving group hymn singing with strongly improvisational elements. This is exactly the kind of group-singing activities that we now know synchronize group emotions and produce heightened levels of oxytocin while simultaneously reducing cortisol (stress) levels. In McPherson's hands, these feel-good musical events became structured and extremely profitable musical theater. McPherson was famous for using new and unorthodox techniques to reach the widest audience. In an age of media experiments, she was a devoutly experimental showperson. If she was genuinely interested in saving souls, she was equally interested making money. She regularly accepted cash contributions from the local Ku Klux Klan, who represented her audience members

in places like Denver and Southern California. Eventually, McPherson left the Pentecostal fold in order to appeal to a wider, more general and generous Protestant base. As early as 1917, she played an organ on a flatbed truck winding through the streets of St. Petersburg to drum up interest in a revival meeting. In 1918, she undertook her first transcontinental tour, crisscrossing the United States while holding huge tent shows that showcased her healing abilities, her talent for speaking in tongues, and her abilities as a hymn and gospel singer. Middle America was clearly hungry for what she had to offer. At the height of her career, she could raise as much as $70,000 at a single large revival such as the one in Denver, Colorado. Initially, the press was skeptical, but an apparently successful act of faith healing in Corona, New York, attracted the attention of large national newspapers including the *Baltimore Sun*, the *New York Times*, and the *Los Angeles Times*. By 1921, McPherson had become a nationally recognized figure with a finely honed sense of stardom and of the need for recurrent publicity to sustain her fame. She began raising funds to establish her own station. This effort became quite successful after a revival meeting in Wichita, Kansas, one month later solidified her national fame. When rain threatened to wash out her tent meeting, McPherson prayed in front of the congregation for the rain to end. Whether she ended her prayer when the rain ended or whether her prayer actually ended the rain depends on your point of view. Nonetheless, the *Wichita Eagle*'s headline "Evangelist's Prayers Hold Back Big Rain" was repeated across America. After that, McPherson's call for donations received a flood of national responses. By 1923, McPherson had enough money to build the Angelus Temple, a large revival church in Echo Park, California. The temple sported a fourteen-piece orchestra (complete with a harp and brass band) and a hundred-member choir. It seated 5,300 people. McPherson advertised her services in the theater section of the *Los Angeles Times*, and her "temple" was filled to capacity three times a day, seven days a week. For their "donation," McPherson's white, lower-middle-class, rural-born audience attended an uplifting professional show complete with costumes and sets rented from Hollywood suppliers. The "sermons" were orchestrated by a vaudeville-trained stage manager, Thomas Eade. At the beginning of some sermons, McPherson appeared dressed as Little Bo Peep carrying a milk bucket. As she and a few other Bo Peeps passed through the crowd, people filled their buckets with coins until she cried, "All this clinking is hurting my ears," at which point paper-money donations topped out the milk cans. On other occasions, McPherson would dress as a milk maid and pour milk from her milk can into the audience's cups before passing the empty can so it could be filled with contributions. When, characteristically, she asked the audience if anyone had grown up on a farm, the entire assembly would come to its feet.

124. Tona J. Hangen, *Redeeming the Dial: Radio, Religion & Popular Culture in America* (Chapel Hill: University of North Carolina Press, 2002), p. 66.

125. Ibid., p. 74.

126. Ibid.

127. S. Parkes Cadman, who was not a faith healer, pioneered radio network evangelism in 1928 over NBC's Blue Network. He began his regular religious broadcasts in 1923, one year before McPherson.

128. Anthony Rudel, *Hello, Everybody! The Dawn of American Radio* (New York: Harcourt, 2008), pp. 86–92.

129. MacDonald, *Don't Touch That Dial*, p. 24.

130. "Broadcasting in the United States," *New York Times*, September 14, 1926.

131. Susan Smulyan, *Selling Radio: The Commercialization of American Broadcasting, 1920–1934* (Washington, DC: Smithsonian Institution Press, 1994), pp. 89–90.

132. Alexander Russo, *Points on the Dial: Golden Age Radio beyond the Networks* (Durham, NC: Duke University Press, 2010), pp. 175, 177.

133. Michele Hilmes, *Radio Voices: American Broadcasting, 1922–1952* (Minneapolis: University of Minnesota Press, 1997), p. 155.

134. Robert Allen, *Speaking of Soap Operas* (Chapel Hill: University of North Carolina Press, 1985), p. 18.

135. Hilmes, *Radio Voices*, p. 155.

136. David Morton, *Off the Record: The Technology and Culture of Sound Recording in America* (New Brunswick, NJ: Rutgers University Press, 2000), pp. 51–53.

137. Slade, *Made to Break*, p. 107; see also my friend Michael Schiffer's fascinating book *The Portable Radio in American Life* (Tucson: University of Arizona Press, 1991), pp. 161–62.

138. See "The 1927–1928 Trends in Cabinet Circuit Designs," *Radio Retailing*, February 1927, p. 37, cited in Butsch, *Making American Audiences*, p. 206.

139. Butsch, *Making American Audiences*, p. 207.

140. W. L. Davidson, "What About 1932 Sales?" *Printer's Ink* 157 (October 8, 1931): 79.

141. E. Klinenberg, *Going Solo* (New York: Penguin, 2012), p. 10; a similar claim appears on p. 216.

142. Ted Gioia, *Work Songs* (Durham, NC: Duke University Press, 2006), p. 105.

143. Lincoln Barnett, "Bing Inc.," *Life*, June 18, 1945, p. 87.

144. Finn Jorgensen, "Chapter 10: Early Fixed-Head Video Recorders," in *Magnetic Recording: The First 100 Years*, ed. Eric C. Daniel et al. (Piscataway, NJ: IEEE Press, 1999), p. 138.

145. "Exclusive Hooper—Billboard Survey Charts Bing's Audience," *Billboard*, October 26, 1946, p. 9.

146. *American Heritage: Invention and Technology* 10, September 1994, p. 61.

147. Ibid., p. 137.

148. M. A. Doherty, *Organisation of Nazi Wireless Propaganda: Nazi Wireless Propaganda, Lord Haw-Haw and British Public Opinion in the Second World War* (Edinburgh: Edinburgh University Press, 2000).

149. Eventually this perspective became the basis of French philosopher Jean Baudrillard's theory of hyper-reality in *Simulacra and Simulation* (1981) and *Simulation* (1983).

150. Williams, *Television: Technology and Cultural Form*, p. 20.

151. Ibid., p. 24.

152. "TV in 10 Years Transforms America," *Sales Management*, November 20, 1955, p. 20, cited in Butsch, *Making American Audiences*, p. 206.

153. Butsch, *Making American Audiences*, p. 236.

154. Barbara Arneil, *Diverse Communities: The Problem with Social Capital* (Cambridge: Cambridge University Press, 2006), p. 112.

155. Elaine May, *Homeward Bound* (New York: Basic Books, 1988), pp. 12–15.

156. Kenneth Jackson, *Crabgrass Frontier: The Suburbanization of the United States* (New York: Oxford University Press, 1987), p. 240.

157. Ibid., p. 279.

158. Lynn Spigel, *Make Room for TV: Television and the Family Ideal in Postwar America* (Chicago: University of Chicago Press, 1992), p. 69.

159. Butsch, *Making of American Audiences*, p. 250.

160. Spigel, *Make Room for TV*, p. 37.

161. Tannis MacBeth Williams, ed., *The Impact of Television: A Natural Experiment in Three Communities* (New York: Academic, 1986).

162. John Cacioppo and William Patrick, *Loneliness: Human Nature and the Need for Social Connection* (New York: Norton, 2008), p. 256.

163. Ibid., p. 258.

164. Vance Packard, *A Nation of Strangers* (New York: David McKay, 1972), p. 189.

165. Gerald D. McDonald, "Origins of the Star System: Out of Man's Need for Myths Came the Stars in the Movie Firmament," *Films in Review* 49 (1953): 451.

166. Paul McDonald, *The Star System, Hollywood's Production of Popular Identities* (New York: Wallflower Press, 2000), p. 28.

CHAPTER 2. WIRED FOR SOUND

* Many of the ideas in this section first appeared in my article "Electric Company: Machines as Social Prostheses," *American Interest* 6, no. 1 (September 2010): 73–82.

1. Jacqueline Trescott, "The Boogie Box," *Washington Post*, August 21, 1980.

2. Raymond A. Joseph, "Hey Man! New Cassette Player Outclasses Street People's Box," *Wall Street Journal*, June 23, 1980.

3. Ibid.

4. I am indebted for this point to Mark Katz, author of *Capturing Sound: How Technology Has Changed Music* (Berkeley: University of California Press, 2010).

5. Evan Eisenberg, *The Recording Angel: The Experience of Music from Aristotle to Zappa* (New York: Penguin, 1988), p. 44.

6. George F. Will, "Noise and Other Nuisances," *Washington Post*, June 28, 1981.

7. Theodore Adorno, *Introduction to the Sociology of Music*, trans. E. B. Ashton (New York: Seabury, 1976), p. 46.

8. Iegor Reznikoff and Michel Dauvois "La dimension sonore des grottes ornées," *Bulletin de la Société Préhistorique Française* 85, no. 8 (1988): 238–46, http://www.persee.fr/web/revues/home/prescript/article/bspf_0249-7638_1988_num_85_8_9349 (accessed August 8, 2011). I cannot recommend this fascinating paper highly enough.

9. Aniruddh D. Patel, *Music, Language, and the Brain* (Cambridge, MA: MIT Press, 2000), p. 401.

10. Randy V. Bellomo, "A Methodological Approach for Identifying Archaeological Evidence of Fire Resulting from Human Activities," *Journal of Archaeological Science* 20, (1993): 525–55; Randy V. Bellomo, "Methods of Determining Early Hominid Behavioral Activities Associated with the Controlled Use of Fire at FxJj 20 Main, Koobi Fora, Kenva," *Journal of Human Evolution* 27 (1994): 173–95.

11. Peter Wheeler, "Stand Tall and Stay Cool," *New Scientist* 12, 1988, pp. 60–65.

12. Leslie Aiello, "Terrestriality, Bipedalism, and the Origin of Language," in *Evolution of Social Behavior Patterns in Primates and Man*, edited by W. C. Runciman et al. (Oxford: Oxford University Press, 1996), pp. 269–94.

13. Ibid.

14. Thomas Geissmann, "Gibbon Songs and Human Music from an Evolutionary Perspective," in *The Origins of Music*, edited by N. Wallin et al. (Cambridge, MA: MIT Press, 2000), p. 118.

15. Reznikoff and Dauvois, "La dimension sonore des grottes ornées," p. 238.

16. Charles Darwin, *The Descent of Man* (New York: D. Appleton, 1871), p. 54.

17. Richard Cohen, "The Walkman," *Washington Post*, July 15, 1982.

18. Dean Falk, *Finding Our Tongues: Mothers, Infants and the Origins of Language* (New York: Perseus, 2009), p. 122.

19. Anne Fernald, "Intonation and Communication: Intent in Mother's Speech to Infants. Is the Melody the Message?" *Child Development* 60, no. 6 (December 1989): 1497–1510.

20. Inge Cordes, "Melodic Contours as a Connecting Link between Primate Communication and Human Singing," presented at the Fifth ESCOM Conference, September 8–13, 2003, Hanover University of Music and Drama, in *Music Therapy Today* 4 (cited in Falk, *Finding Our Tongues*, pp. 129, 204).

21. Patel, *Music, Language and the Brain*, p. 370.

22. Ibid., 125.

23. Leslie Seltzer et al., "Social Vocalizations Can Release Oxytocin in Humans," *Proceedings of the Royal Society B*, no. 277 (2010): 2661–66. This study confirms earlier speculation of the association between female speech and OT release in women by neuropsychiatrist Louann Brizendine in *The Female Brain* (Cambridge, MA: Harvard University Press, 2006), p. 36.

24. Kerstin Uvnas Möberg, *The Oxytocin Factor* (Cambridge, MA: Da Capo, 2003), p. 54.

25. Leslie Seltzer et al., "Instant Messages vs. Speech: Hormones and Why We Still Need to Hear Each Other," *Evolution & Human Behavior*, http://www.ehbonline.org/article/S1090-5138%2811%2900047-X/, August 1, 2011. Abstract:

> Human speech evidently conveys an adaptive advantage, given its apparently rapid dissemination through the ancient world and global use today. As such,

speech must be capable of altering human biology in a positive way, possibly through those neuroendocrine mechanisms responsible for strengthening the social bonds between individuals. Indeed, speech between trusted individuals is capable of reducing levels of salivary cortisol, often considered a biomarker of stress, and increasing levels of urinary, a hormone involved in the formation and maintenance of positive relationships. It is not clear, however, whether it is the uniquely human grammar, syntax, content and/or choice of words that causes these physiological changes, or whether the prosodic elements of speech, which are present in the vocal cues of many other species, are responsible. In order to tease apart these elements of human communication, we examined the hormonal responses of female children who instant messaged their mothers after undergoing a stressor. We discovered that unlike children interacting with their mothers in person or over the phone, girls who instant messaged did not release oxytocin; instead, these participants showed levels of salivary cortisol as high as control subjects who did not interact with their parents at all. We conclude that the comforting sound of a familiar voice is responsible for the hormonal differences observed and, hence, that similar differences may be seen in other species using vocal cues to communicate.

26. David Jingjun Xu, Ronald T. Cenfetelli, and Karl Aquino, "The Influence of Media Cue Multiplicity on Deceivers and Those Who Are Deceived," *Journal of Business Ethics*, http://www.springerlink.com/content/c425271447125976/fulltext.pdf, August 31, 2011 (accessed December 21, 2011).

27. J. Short et al., *The Social Psychology of Telecommunications* (London: Wiley, 1976).

28. R. Daft and R. Lengel, "Organizational Information Requirements, Media Richness and Structural Design," *Management Science* 32, no. 5 (1986): 554–71.

29. Nereu (Ned) Florencio Kock, "The Psychobiological Model: Towards a New Theory of Computer-Mediated Communication Based on Darwinian Evolution," *Organization Science* 15, no. 3 (2004): 327–48; Ned Kock, "Media Richness or Media Naturalness? The Evolution of Our Biological Communication Apparatus and Its Influence on Our Behavior toward E-Communication Tools," *IEEE Transactions on Professional Communication* 48, no. 2 (2005): 117–29.

30. Kock, "Media Richness or Media Naturalness?" p. 119.

31. Alladi Venkatesh, "The Tech-Enabled Networked Home: An Analysis of Current Trends and Future Promise," in *Transforming Enterprise: Economic and Social Implications of Information Technology*, ed. William Dutton et al. (Cambridge, MA: MIT Press, 2005), pp. 413–35.

32. A. Street et al., "Mother's Attitudes to Singing to Their Infants," in R. Kopies et al., eds., *Proceedings of the Fifth Triennial ESCOM Conference* (2003): 628; Hanover, Hanover University of Music and Drama, cited in Steven Mithen, *The Singing Neanderthals* (Cambridge, MA: Harvard University Press, 2006), p. 81. I thank Alison Street for generously sending me a digitized copy of this hard-to-find paper.

33. All the following sources are cited in Street et al., "Mother's Attitudes to Singing to Their Infants": R. Moore and J. M. Standley, "Therapeutic Effects of Music and Mother's Voice on Premature Infants," *Pediatric Nursing* 21 (1996): 509–14; J. M. Standley, "The Effect of Music and Multimodal Stimulation on Physiological and Developmental Responses of Premature Infants in Neonatal Intensive Care," *Pediatric Nursing* 24, no. 6 (1998): 532–38; J. M. Standley, "The Effect of Contingent Music to Increase Non-Nutritive Sucking of Premature Infants," *Pediatric Nursing* 26, no. 5 (2000): 493.

34. Dissanayake explains the differences between her theories and those of Dean Falk in a personal e-mail (August 14, 2011), and I am indebted to her for her willingness to correspond with me about the theory in considerable detail:

> My hypothesis about the origin of music, although it comes from mother-infant interaction, tells a different story from Dean's. Apart from the fact that she heard my hypothesis in 1997, and started thinking about the origin of language (and music and language no doubt have a common or intertwined origin so she branched off into music), her version is very different from mine—I don't say that mothers put babies down; rather, they were in the most intimate face-to-face contact and they created "music"—or better, "musicality"—together. And I don't use the term "motherese" but rather "baby talk," always pointing out that it includes facial expressions and head and body movements as well as peculiar vocalizations. If the baby were put down, it would not see the face and body . . . I should say that I think that your book promises to be very good. It is on an important theme. All that red ink is because I felt that what you said about my ideas was misleading and there were a few details that were inaccurate too. Good luck with the book. Let me know when it is coming out. (Thank you, Ellen.)

35. From Dissanayake's comments on an early draft of this chapter attached to an e-mail message of August 14, 2011. Her comment follows: "I do not think that motherese is the origin of music nor that putting the baby down is the origin of music. I think that the entire package of behaviors—vocal, visual, and kinetic—(not just talk or singing) was the origin of music which was itself simultaneously music/dance."

36. See, for example, Philip Ball's excellent book *The Music Instinct* (New York: Oxford University Press, 2010), p. 28. Ball finds Ellen Dissanayake's suggestion that musical sensitivities and competencies developed in the mother-infant interaction "something of a leap of faith and surely invites the question of why often (although by no means universally) it is men who have traditionally engaged in the production of music." Personally, I don't know of any figures that survey the production of music by gender, although perhaps Ball is referring to professional musicians.

37. Falk, *Finding Our Tongues*, p. 99.

38. T. Nakata and S. Trehub, "Infants' Responsiveness to Maternal Speech and Singing," *Infant Behavior & Development* 27 (2004): 455–64.

39. T. Shenfield, S. Trehub, and T. Nakata, "Maternal Singing Modulates Infants Arousal," *Psychology of Music* 31:365–75.

40. I am indebted to Töres Theorell, Professor Emeritus of Psychosocial Environmental Medicine, at the Karolinska Institutet, Stockholm, for these observations about the difficulties of studying oxytocin release. Professor Theorell is the child of a concert pianist and lifelong amateur violinist. He is also the author of *Noter om Musik och Hälsa* (Notes on Music and Health) (Karolinska Institute Press, 2009), which has not yet been translated into English. The full text of Dr. Theorell's message follows:

> Interesting hypothesis indeed I have written a book in Swedish in which I formulate a hypothesis about the prominent role that music may have had for group survival when group cohesion must have been strengthened by dance, music, pictures and rituals Of course oxytocin could have been a chemical bridge but I am sure it is not the only one. Oxytocin is fairly difficult to study because it is excreted in pulses and the blood concentration is very unstable. In addition it is a relatively big molecule so it disintegrates rapidly if the blood samples are not handled very rapidly I know of one group in Arizona who tried to study oxytocin changes during singing a couple of years ago but I am not sure if they found anything.

In a message on the following day, Professor Theorell observes, "The molecule could start disintegrating within half an hour if one does not take care of the blood sample—so rapid handling is really important. The actual assessment is also tricky (once you have the samples safely) since there are several unreliable commercial kits."

41. Christina Grape et al., "Does Singing Promote Well-Being? An Empirical Study of Professional and Amateur Singers during a Singing

Lesson," *Integrative Psychological and Behavioral Science* 38, no. 1 (January–March 2003): 65–74; and Ulrica Nilsson, "Soothing Music Can Increase Oxytocin Levels during Bed Rest after Open-Heart Surgery," *Journal of Clinical Nursing* no. 18 (2009): 2153–61.

42. Adam Gabbatt, "Mexican Teacher Calmed Primary Students with Song during Drug Shooting," *Guardian*, May 31, 2011, http://www.guardian.co.uk/world/2011/may/31/teacher-sang-to-children-during-shooting?INTCMP=SRCH. Cell-phone video of incident available at http://latimesblogs.latimes.com/laplaza/2011/05/mexico-video-kindergarten-shootout-teacher-drug-war html. Note: At the time of publication, this URL was inactive.

43. Robert W. Shumaker et al., *Animal Tool Behavior: The Use and Manufacture of Tools by Animals* (Baltimore: Johns Hopkins University Press, rev. ed., 2011), pp. 16, 129, 137, 147.

44. Harriet Martineau, *Society in America* (Gagliani, 1837; reissued, Cambridge: Cambridge University Press, 2009), p. 116.

45. Richard Crawford, *America's Musical Life* (New York: Norton, 2001), p. 56.

46. Ibid., p. 221.

47. Ibid., p. 226.

48. Andrew Law, *The Art of Singing, Part 1: The Musical Primer* (Cheshire, CT, 1794), p. 8.

49. Richard Crawford, *The American Musical Landscape* (Berkeley: University of California Press, 1993), pp. 129–31.

50. Ibid.

51. Ibid.

52. Sam Cooke, "A Change Is Gonna Come," complete lyrics cited in Bruce Sinclair, *Technology and the African-American Experience* (Cambridge, MA: MIT Press, 2004), pp. 188–89.

53. Samuel S. Hill, *On Jordan's Stormy Banks: Religion in the South* (Macon, GA: Mercer University Press, 1983), p. 65.

54. William Brooks, "Music in America, An Overview," in *The Cambridge History of American Music*, ed. David Nicholls (New York: Cambridge University Press, 1998), pp. 30–48.

55. Crawford, *American Musical Landscape*, p. 231.

56. Ibid., pp. 235–36.

57. John F. Kasson, *Rudeness and Civility: Manners in Nineteenth-Century Urban America* (New York: Hill & Wang, 1990), p. 170.

58. Dale Cockerell, "Nineteenth-Century Popular Music," in Nicholls, *Cambridge History of American Music*, p. 158.

59. Russell Sanjek, *American Popular Music and Its Business: The First Four Hundred Years, Volume II: From 1790–1909* (New York: Oxford University Press, 1998), p. 103.

60. Crawford, *American Musical Landscape*, p. 232.

61. Darcy Kuronen, "James A. Bazin and the Development of Free-Reed Instruments in America," *Journal of the American Musical Instrument Society* 31 (2005): 142.

62. Ibid., pp. 147, 149.

63. Kim Field, *Harmonicas, Harps, and Heavy Breathers* (New York: Simon & Schuster, 1993), p. 34.

64. Steven Cornelius, *Music of the Civil War Era* (Westport, CT: Greenwood, 2004), p. 17; but see also Richard Barksdale Harwell, *Confederate Music* (Chapel Hill: University of North Carolina Press, 1950), pp. 10–11.

65. Richard Symanski, *The Immoral Landscape: Female Prostitution in Western Societies* (Toronto, ON: Butterworths, 1981), pp. 57, 65; see also Mitchell Tepper et al., *Sexual Health: Moral and Cultural Foundations* (New York: Praeger, 2007), p. 112.

66. See Eric Partridge, *Concise New Partridge Dictionary of Slang and Unconventional English* (New York: Routledge, 2007), p. 269, and John Wright, *Language of the Civil War* (Westport, CT: Oryx, 2001), p. 120.

67. John Shepherd, *Continuum Encyclopedia of the Popular Music of the World*, vol. 2 (New York: Continuum International, 2003), p. 483.

68. Henry Clay Whitney, *Life on the Circuit with Lincoln* (New York: Caxton, 1940), p. 54.

69. "Music in Newsboys' Souls," *Folio* 26, no. 5, November 1884, p. 173.

70. There is exciting new research about the banjo's origins by Gambian musicologist Daniel Laemouahuma Jatta.

71. "Excels in Whistlers, Washington Is Very Notable for Their Presence," *Washington Post*, July 12, 1896.

72. Bruce Jackson, *Wake Up Dead Man: Hard Labor and the Southern Blues* (Athens: University of Georgia Press, 1999), p. 26; see also N. K. Bromell, *By the Sweat of the Brow: Literature and Labor in Antebellum America* (Chicago: University of Chicago Press, 1993), pp. 188–89.

73. Ted Gioia, *Work Songs* (Durham, NC: Duke University Press, 2006), p. 245.

74. William L. Alden, "Sailor Songs," *Harper's New Monthly Magazine* 65, no. 386, July 1882, p. 281; cited in Gioia, *Work Songs*.

75. Jacquelyn D. Hall et al., *Like a Family: The Making of a Southern Cotton Mill World* (Chapel Hill: University of North Carolina Press, 1987), p. 88; also cited in Gioia, *Work Songs*.

76. "To My Old Master," *Letters of Note*, http://www.lettersofnote.com/2012/01/to-my-old-master.html (accessed January 31, 2010). The full text follows:

Dayton, Ohio,
August 7, 1865

To My Old Master, Colonel P. H. Anderson, Big Spring, Tennessee: Sir, I got your letter, and was glad to find that you had not forgotten Jourdon, and that you wanted me to come back and live with you again, promising to do better for me than anybody else can. I have often felt uneasy about you. I thought the Yankees would have hung you long before this, for harboring Rebs they found at your house. I suppose they never heard about your going to Colonel Martin's to kill the Union soldier that was left by his company in their stable. Although you shot at me twice before I left you, I did not want to hear of your being hurt, and am glad you are still living. It would do me good to go back to the dear old home again, and see Miss Mary and Miss Martha and Allen, Esther, Green, and Lee. Give my love to them all, and tell them I hope we will meet in the better world, if not in this. I would have gone back to see you all when I was working in the Nashville Hospital, but one of the neighbors told me that Henry intended to shoot me if he ever got a chance. I want to know particularly what the good chance is you propose to give me. I am doing tolerably well here. I get twenty-five dollars a month, with victuals and clothing; have a comfortable home for Mandy,—the folks call her Mrs. Anderson,—and the children—Milly, Jane, and Grundy—go to school and are learning well. The teacher says Grundy has a head for a preacher. They go to Sunday school, and Mandy and me attend church regularly. We are kindly treated. Sometimes we overhear others saying, "Them colored people were slaves" down in Tennessee. The children feel hurt when they hear such remarks; but I tell them it was no disgrace in Tennessee to belong to Colonel Anderson. Many darkeys would have been proud, as I used to be, to call you master. Now if you will write and say what wages you will give me, I will be better able to decide whether it would be to my advantage to move back again.

As to my freedom, which you say I can have, there is nothing to be gained on that score, as I got my free papers in 1864 from the Provost-Marshal-General of the Department of Nashville. Mandy says she would be afraid to go back without some proof that you were disposed to treat us justly and kindly; and we have concluded to test your sincerity by asking you to send us our wages for the time we served you. This will make us forget and forgive old scores, and rely on your justice and friendship in the future. I served you faithfully for thirty-two years, and Mandy twenty years. At twenty-five dollars a month for me, and two dollars a week for Mandy, our earnings would amount to eleven thousand six hundred and eighty dollars. Add to this the interest for the time our wages have been kept back, and deduct what you paid for our clothing, and three doctor's visits to me, and pulling a tooth for Mandy, and the balance will show what we are in justice entitled to. Please send the money by Adams's Express, in care of V. Winters, Esq., Dayton, Ohio. If you fail to pay us for faithful labors in the past, we can have little faith in your promises in the future. We trust the good Maker has opened your eyes to the wrongs which you and your fathers have done to me and my fathers, in making us toil for you for generations without recompense. Here I draw my wages every Saturday night; but in Tennessee there was never any pay-day for the negroes any more than for the horses and cows. Surely there will be a day of reckoning for those who defraud the laborer of his hire.

In answering this letter, please state if there would be any safety for my Milly and Jane, who are now grown up, and both good-looking girls. You know how it was with poor Matilda and Catherine. I would rather stay here and starve—and die, if it come to that—than have my girls brought to shame by the violence and wickedness of their young masters. You will also please state if there has been any schools opened for the colored children in your neighborhood. The great desire of my life now is to give my children an education, and have them form virtuous habits.

Say howdy to George Carter, and thank him for taking the pistol from you when you were shooting at me.

From your old servant,
Jourdon Anderson.

77. Black minstrelsy began around 1830 with performances by Thomas "Jim Crow" Rice and lasted well into the early decades of the twentieth century. Artificial mechanical beings began to appear regularly around 1901.

78. P. Berger et al., *The Homeless Mind: Modernization and Consciousness* (New York: Random House, 1973), p. 29.

79. Evelyn Alloy, *Working Women's Music: The Songs and Struggles of Women in the Cotton Mills, Textile Plants and Needle Trades, Complete with Music for Singing and Playing* (Somerville, MA: New England Free Press, 1976), p. 13.

80. Berger et al., *Homeless Mind*, p. 35.

81. Gioia, *Work Songs*, p. 96.

82. Annie Payson Call, *Power through Repose* (New York: Little, Brown, 1900), pp. 13, 68, 97.

83. William S. Sadler, *Worry and Nervousness, or The Science of Self-Mastery* (Chicago: A. C. McClurg, 1914), p. 107.

84. Philip Cushman, *Constructing the Self, Constructing America* (New York: Perseus, 1995), p. 65.

85. Ibid.

86. Philip Rieff, *The Triumph of the Therapeutic: Uses of Faith after Freud* (Chicago: University of Chicago Press, 1966), p. 261; cited in Cushman, *Constructing the Self*, p. 157.

87. Cushman, *Constructing the Self*, p. 63.

88. David Suisman, *Selling Sounds: The Commercial Revolution in American Music* (Cambridge, MA: Harvard University Press, 2009), p. 125.

89. Timothy Day, *A Century of Recorded Music: Listening to Musical History* (New Haven, CT: Yale University Press, 2000), p. 103.

90. Ibid., p. 4; see also W. R. Moran, "The Recorded Legacy of Enrico Caruso," in *My Father and My Family*, by Enrico Caruso Jr. (Portland: University of Oregon Press, 1990), pp. 608–609.

91. Suisman, *Selling Sounds*, p. 102.

92. I am indebted for these statements to Timothy Day, *A Century of Recorded Music*, p. 10. Day lists the sources for these statements as Mark Hambourg, *From Piano to Forte; A Thousand and One Notes* (London: Cassell, 1931), pp. 288–89, and Sergei Rachmaninoff, "The Artist and the Gramophone," *Gramophone* 8, no. 95 (April 1931): 525.

93. Frederick W. Gaisberg, "Notes from My Diary," *Gramophone* 117 (January 1944).

94. "Reproduced," *Voice of Victor* 2, May 1907, p. 8.

95. These are contemporary quotations concerning Caruso reproduced in Day, *Century of Recorded Music*, p. 216; the original source is listed as H. Wiley Hitchcock, ed., *The Phonograph and Our Musical Life: Proceedings of a Centennial Conference, 7–10 December, 1977* (New York: Institute for Studies in American Music, 1980), pp. 68–69.

96. *Voice of Victor* 5, March–April 1910, p. 4.

97. Theodor Adorno, *Introduction to the Sociology of Music* (New York: Seabury, 1976), p. 45.

98. Ibid., p. 46.

99. *Catalogue*, Library of Wente-Mignon Music Records (New York, 1927), p. 5; cited in Day, *Century of Recorded Music*, p. 13.

100. Brian Dolan, *Inventing Entertainment: The Player Piano and the Origins of an American Musical Industry* (New York: Rowman & Littlefield, 2009), pp. xi–xii.

101. Day, *Century of Recorded Music*, p. 13.

102. Ibid., pp. 16–18.

103. Dennis Hevesi, "Edgar M. Villchur, a Hi-Fi Innovator, Is Dead at 94," *New York Times*, October 17, 2011.

104. Eric Clarke, "The Impact of Recording on Listening," *Twentieth-Century Music* (March 2007): 45.

105. Katz, *Capturing Sound*, p. 189.

106. George Prochnik, *In Pursuit of Silence* (New York: Knopf/Doubleday, 2010).

107. David Kirby, "Celebrities R Us," *American Interest* (Spring 2006); see also Donald Horton and R. Richard Wohl, "Mass Communication and Para-Social Interaction: Observations on Intimacy at a Distance," in *Inter/Media: Interpersonal Communication in a Media World*, ed. Gary Gumpert et al. (New York: Oxford University Press, 1979), pp. 32–55.

108. Clarke, "Impact of Recording on Listening," p. 45.

109. Orlo Williams, "Times and Seasons," *Gramophone* (April 1923): 38–39.

110. Katz, *Capturing Sound*, p. 67.

111. H. Wiley Hitchcock, ed., *The Phonograph and Our Musical Life* (Brooklyn, NY: I.S.A.M. Monographs no. 14, 1977), p. 71.

112. *Disques* 2 (January 1930): 17.

113. Frances Newbery, ed., *Records in Review* (Great Barrington, MA: Wyeth, 1959), http://books.google.com/books?id=XGDgAAAAMAAJ&q=%22shadow+conducting%22&dq=%22shadow+conducting%22&hl=en&ei=yH-sTo6REanXiQLZ5MSgBQ&sa=X&oi=book_result&ct=result&resnum=7&ved=0CEQQ6AEwBjgK (accessed October 29, 2011).

114. This information comes from two private e-mail messages from Richard Crawford on October 29, 2011. The full text of both follows:

> Thanks for your message. It felt good to see that you had come upon the story of my dad's conducting of phonograph recordings, included in The Phonograph and Our Musical Life, edited by H Wiley Hitchcock in 1980. I can't recall seeing a citation of this story, told at Professor Hitchcock's Centennial Conference, held at Brooklyn College in 1977 to mark the anniversary of the phonograph's 100th birthday. But now that you've reminded me of it, I can pass it on to my own siblings and offspring, who can decide whether or not it'll become part of their family lore.
>
> In answer to your question, I'd place my first experience of it in the early 1940s, during World War II I was born in Detroit, Michigan, in 1935. My family lived in rented quarters of various descriptions until the first week of December 1941, when we moved into a brand new house, designed in part by my mother and an architect. Pearl Harbor Day, December, 1941, was our first Sunday in the new house.

The past to which I can attach my dad's conducting "career" is rooted in his personal history. His parents were both born in Glasgow, Scotland, and they emigrated to the U S early in the 20th century. By the time my father was born, in 1909—he was the fourth child in a family of five—they had settled in Detroit, where my grandfather established a grey-iron foundry. (I think he had a partner but am not sure of details)

The family had a Sunday routine in the years ca 1918–28, probably starting with church (they were Presbyterians), continuing to the Statler Hotel in downtown Detroit for Sunday dinner, and then to the Michigan Theater, also downtown, where a typical sabbath routine included a live show and a movie. The show included an orchestra that, as well as accompanying the movie (silent, of course, till the late 1920s), played selections—my anecdote mentions "Poet and Peasant Overture," the William Tell overture, and Light Cavalry overture—from what came to be known as a pops orchestra menu. (I think that one of the highlights of dad's later life as a listener came when my high school band played an arrangement of Tchaikovsky's 1812 overture in 1950. As a ninth-grade tenor sax player, I was only one of many in the middle of the texture, but that I was part of such a musical experience was a big deal for him emotionally, to say the least)

Dad got to know this repertoire as a spectator, and one of his heroes was the Michigan Theater's orchestra conductor, whom he always referred to as "Ed Werner." I think that Ed Werner (whom I just Googled for the first time ever—see Eduard Werner + conductor + Detroit) was Dad's model, the source of the moves he developed when he led his mythical orchestra.

Dad was a highly musical person who, as far as I know, never received any formal musical training. He graduated from Western High School in Detroit, attended Alma College in Alma, Michigan, where he played football, basketball, and met my mom.

Immediately after graduation, he went to work at the family-owned Atlas Foundry Company in Detroit, working for his dad, and then his brothers, until the early 1970s. I wouldn't describe him as much of a concertgoer at all.

I don't know anything of the history of his conducting dreams. It was never discussed. But I'm pretty sure that, when he went into "the library," turned on the phonograph, and conducted records of music he knew by ear and loved, he was in earnest, in a kind of musical choreography that gave him pleasure. Did he throw cues to the "players?" Who knows? Nor did it ever occur to me to ask if the opaque glass that substituted for the library wall had been put in so that he could have his esthetic moment in privacy. Private it was, though. As far as I know none of us kids asked for an explanation.

Best wishes to you and your project.

Richard Crawford./new message./P.S. Now that I'm thinking about this, I can't seem to let go of it. So here is a bit more that may or may not be germane to your project.

> My dad was a highly emotional individual for whom passion and intuition outweighed rational reflection.
>
> I think that for him, the conducting was a self-driven, private activity that allowed him a way to narrow the gap between him and music, which he loved but had no skill in the making of.

115. Ibid.

116. *Disques* 2 (August 1931): 240; I'm indebted to Mark Katz for drawing my attention to this quotation and to the previous one by Orlo Williams.

117. Richard Lichtenstein et al., "Headphone Use and Pedestrian Injury and Death in the United States, 2004–2011," forthcoming in *Injury Prevention.*

118. Erving Goffman, *Behavior in Public Places* (New York: Free Press, 1963), p. 85.

119. Ibid., p. 84, but see also Michael Argyle et al., "Eye Contact, Distance and Affiliation," *Sociometry* 28, no. 3 (September 1965): 289–304.

CHAPTER 3. TRUSTING MACHINES

1. Ferdinand Tönnies, *Community and Society*, ed. Jose Harris (Cambridge: Cambridge University Press, 2001), p. 243.

2. Ibid., p. 18.

3. Ibid.

4. Ibid., p. 19.

5. Ibid., p. 31.

6. Niklas Luhmann, *Trust and Power: Two Works by Niklas Luhmann* (New York: John Wiley, 1979), pp. 49, 66–69, 93. To confess a weakness, I find Luhmann a very tough read, fortunately, an excellent, patient, and comprehensive overview of his theory of social trust is provided in Barbara Misztal, *Trust in Modern Societies* (Cambridge, MA: Polity, 1996), 73–77.

7. Victor Tausk, "On the Origin of the 'Influencing Machine' in Schizophrenia," *Psychoanalytic Quarterly* 2 (1933): 519–56. Originally published in 1919 in *Internationale Zeitschrift für Psychoanalyse.*

8. Paraphrased from Richard Nisbett and Dov Cohen, *Culture of Honor: The Psychology of Violence in the South* (Boulder, CO: Westview, 1995), p. 7.

9. Grady McWhiney, *Cracker Culture: Celtic Ways in the Old South* (Tuscaloosa: University of Alabama Press, 1988), pp. xxxvii, xli.

10. Nisbett and Cohen, *Culture of Honor*, p. 4.

11. Altina Waller, *Feud: Hatfields, McCoys, and Social Change in*

Appalachia, 1860–1900 (Chapel Hill: University of North Carolina Press, 1998).

12. Ibid.

13. Anthony Giddens, *The Consequences of Modernity* (Palo Alto, CA: Stanford University Press, 1990), p. 101.

14. Ibid., p. 103.

15. Ibid., p. 101.

16. Ibid., p. 105.

17. Ibid., p. 103.

18. Ibid.

19. Ibid., p. 104.

20. Bertram Wyatt-Brown, *The Shaping of Southern Culture, Honor, Grace and War, 1760s–1880s* (Chapel Hill: University of North Carolina Press, 2001), pp. 192–93.

21. R. B. Flowers and H. L. Flowers, *Murders in the United States: Crimes, Killers and Victims of the Twentieth Century* (Jefferson, NC: McFarland, 2004), p. 4.

22. Eric H. Monkkonen, *Police in Urban America, 1860–1920* (Cambridge: Cambridge University Press, 2004), p. 2.

23. Charles R. Morris, *The Tycoons: How Andrew Carnegie, John D. Rockefeller, Jay Gould and J. P. Morgan Invented the American Supereconomy* (New York: Macmillan, 2006), p. 193.

24. Anthony Giddens, *The Transformation of Intimacy: Sexuality, Love, and Eroticism in Modern Societies* (New York: Polity, 1992), p. 96.

25. Giddens, *Consequences of Modernity*, p. 114.

26. Ibid.

27. Ibid., pp. 112–13.

28. Morton J. Horwitz, *The Transformation of American Law, 1870–1960: The Crisis of Legal Orthodoxy* (New York: Oxford University Press, 1994), p. 145.

29. Monte A. Calvert, *The Mechanical Engineer in America, 1830–1910* (Baltimore: Johns Hopkins University Press, 1967), p. 11.

30. Giles Oakley, *The Devil's Music: A History of the Blues* (London: Ariel Books, 1983), p. 35. There used to be a two-LP album of traditional standards that accompanied this tremendous book that introduced me to the blues as an adolescent. Sadly, it's no longer available, and my copy has long since disappeared into the strange limbo that houses most favorite possessions.

31. Frederick Law Olmsted, *The Slave States before the Civil War* (New York: Capricorn, 1959), pp. 114–15. Since material about "hollerin'" is hard to find, let me include another (very difficult to find) source: Willis James, "The Romance of the Negro Folk Cry in America," *Phylon* 1 (1955): 16.

32. Erving Goffman, *Behavior in Public Places: Notes on the Social Organization of Gatherings* (New York: Free Press, 1963), p. 83.

33. William M. Evan, "The Engineering Profession: A Cross-Cultural Analysis," in *The Engineers and the Social System*, ed. Robert Perucci and Joel Gerstl (New York: John Wiley, 1969), p. 100. It is very strange to me that although the engineering profession impacts daily life directly and controls a segment of the economy several times larger than that of the legal and medical professions combined, there is so little material available about the history of engineering. It seems to me that programs in the history of consciousness or in technology and society or the history of technology might begin by investigating what engineers have been up to (good and bad) for the past two hundred years.

34. Matthew Moten, *The Delafield Commission and the American Military Profession* (College Station: Texas A&M University Press, 2000), p. 49.

35. Ibid., p. 50.

36. Ibid., p. 51.

37. Ibid., p. 50.

38. Ibid., p. 51, attributed to Capt. John Tidball.

39. James Burke, *Connections* (New York: Little, Brown, 1978), p. 150.

40. Ibid., p. 32.

41. Ibid.

42. Throughout this entire section, I am deeply indebted to David A. Hounshell's brilliantly comprehensive, descriptive, and detailed study *From the American System to Mass Production, 1800–1932* (Baltimore: Johns Hopkins University Press, 1984), pp. 15–65.

43. S. N. D. North and Ralph H. North, *Simeon North: First Official Pistol Maker of the United States* (Concord, NH: Rumford, 1913), p. 64.

44. Charles H. Fitch, *Report on the Manufacture of Firearms and Ammunition* (Washington, DC: US Government Printing Office, 1882), p. 4.

45. Hounshell, *From the American System*, p. 27.

46. North and North, *Simeon North*, p. 81.

47. Hounshell, *From the American System*, p. 33.

48. Ibid., pp. 39–41.

49. Merritt Roe Smith, *Harpers Ferry Armory and the New Technology: The Challenge of Change* (Ithaca, NY: Cornell University Press, 1977), pp. 208–11.

50. Nathan Rosenberg, ed., *The American System of Manufactures, Report on the Committee of the Machinery of the United States 1855; and the Special Reports of George Wallis and John Whitworth 1854* (Edinburgh: Edinburgh University Press, 1969), pp. 21–22.

51. Thorstein Veblen, *The Theory of Business Enterprise* (New York: Cosimo, 2005), p. 146.

52. The gun, a borrowed weapon owned by a fellow volunteer was first used in action by Sgt. Francis O. Lombard, himself a gunsmith, in a skirmish near Cumberland, Maryland, on October 16, 1862. There is not much in the written record about Sergeant Lombard, but the gun's popularity increased incrementally after this date.

53. *Executive Documents of the Senate of the United States, 1861–1862* (Washington, DC: US Government Printing Office, 1862), p. 425.

54. Ibid., p. 426.

55. John Hay and Tyler Dennett, *Lincoln and the Civil War in the Diaries and Letters of John Hay* (Cambridge, MA: Da Capo, 1988), p. 82.

56. David Westwood, *Rifles: An Illustrated History of Their Impact* (Santa Barbara, CA: ABC-CLIO, 2005), p. 73.

57. Frances H. Kennedy, ed., *The Civil War Battlefield Guide/The Conservation Fund*, 2nd ed. (New York: Houghton Mifflin, 1998), pp. 225–26.

58. Gregory J. W. Urwin, *Custer Victorious: The Civil War Battles of General George Armstrong Custer* (Lincoln: University of Nebraska Press, 1983), p. 76.

59. Wiley Sword, *Southern Invincibility: A History of the Confederate Heart* (New York: Macmillan, 2000), p. 209.

60. Ibid.

61. John H. Eicher et al., *Civil War High Commands* (Stanford, CA: Stanford University Press, 2001), p. 454.

62. William McBride, *Technological Change and the United States Navy, 1865–1945* (Baltimore: Johns Hopkins University Press), especially chap. 1, "The Post-Bellum Naval Project."

63. David Nye, *American Technological Sublime* (Cambridge, MA: MIT Press, 1994). David is an underappreciated American resource who currently teaches the history of technology in Denmark.

64. Shane Mountjoy, *Technology and the Civil War*, consulting ed. Tim McNeese (New York: Infobase, 2009), p. 119.

65. Ibid., p. 197. Original passage in James Oppenheim, *The Olympian* (New York: Harper, 1912), pp. 416–17.

66. Tracy Campbell, *Deliver the Vote: A History of Election Fraud, An American Political Tradition, 1742–2004* (New York: Carroll and Graf, 2005), p. 34. This book is an eye-opener and should be taught in every civics class in every high school in America.

67. Ibid., pp. 35–36.

68. Ibid., p. 37.

69. Ibid., p. 40.

70. Ibid., p. 38.

71. Ibid., p. 42.

72. Ibid., p. 47.

73. Ibid., p. 56.

74. Richard E. Welch Jr., "American Public Opinion and the Purchase of Canadian America," *American Slavic and East European Review* 17, no. 4 (1958): 481–94.

75. See, for example, Andrew W. Miller, *National Economy: A History of the American Protective System, and Its Effects upon the Several Branches of Domestic Industry* (New York: N. C. Miller, 1864).

76. Veblen, *Theory of Business Enterprise*, p. 148.

77. Campbell, *Deliver the Vote*, p. 58.

78. Ibid.

79. Ibid., pp. 59–61.

80. Ibid., p. 115: Henry Watterson.

81. Ibid.

82. Richard J. Jensen, *The Winning of the Midwest: Social and Political Conflict, 1888–1896*, vol. 2 (Chicago: University of Chicago Press, 1971), p. 9.

83. I'm deeply indebted to Tracy Campbell's book, *Deliver the Vote*, which describes the speed of America's adoption of the secret ballot on p. 97.

84. This wonderful example was originally reported in the *New York Evening Post* on August 20, 1856, and appears in Campbell, *Deliver the Vote*, p. 45.

85. Alexander Keyssar, *The Right to Vote: The Contested History of Democracy in the United States* (New York: Perseus, 2000), p. 113. I am indebted to Professor Keyssar for his helpful suggestions and for his valuable section on literacy tests, pp. 112–18.

86. Ibid., p. 113.

87. John Henry Wigmore, *The Australian Ballot System as Embodied in the Legislation of Various Countries* (Boston: Boston Book Company, 1889), p. 201.

88. William Ivins, "Machine Politics and Money in Elections in New York City," *Harper's Handy Series*, April 15, 1887, p. 30.

89. "Two Machines," *Washington Post*, January 24, 1906.

90. "Advantages of the Voting Machine," *New York Times*, January 22, 1900.

91. "The Voting Machine," *New York Times*, May 3, 1895.

92. "Advantages of the Voting Machine," *New York Times*.

93. "Attack on Voting Machines," *New York Times*, November 14, 1904.

94. Richard Scher, *The Politics of Disenfranchisement: Why Is It So Hard to Vote in America?* (Armonk, NY: M. E. Sharpe, 2011), p. 118.

95. "Voting by Machinery, *Chautauquan* 20 (1895): 19.

96. Susan Strasser, *Satisfaction Guaranteed: The Making of the American Mass Market* (New York: Pantheon Books, 1989), p. 57; Giles Slade, *Made to Break: Technology and Obsolescence in America* (Cambridge, MA: Harvard University Press, 2006), p. 11.

97. Gustav Stickley, "The Use and Abuse of Machinery, and Its Relation to the Arts and Crafts," *Craftsman* 11, no. 2, November 1906, p. 204.

98. Norman Mailer, *Of a Fire on the Moon* (New York: Little, Brown, 1970), p. 62.

99. Ibid., p. 92.

100. Frank Lloyd Wright, "The Art and Craft of the Machine," 1901, Columbia University Visual Media Center, http://www.learn.columbia.edu/courses/arch20/pdf/art_hum_reading_50.pdf (accessed February 4, 2012).

101. Gerald Stanley Lee, *Crowds: A Moving Picture of Democracy* (New York: Doubleday, 1913), p. 17.

102. John Cacioppo and William Patrick, *Loneliness: Human Nature and the Need for Social Connection* (New York: Norton, 2008), p. 142. Professor Cacioppo's generosity and patience during the early days of this project put me greatly in his debt.

103. Paul J. Zak, "The Neurobiology of Trust," *Scientific American*, June 2008, p. 90.

104. Ibid., p. 91.

105. Ibid.

106. Ibid., p. 92

107. Ibid.

108. Robin I. M. Dunbar, "Neocortex Size as a Constraint on Group Size in Primates," *Journal of Human Evolution* 22, no. 6 (June 1992): 469–93; R. I. M. Dunbar, "Co-evolution of Neocortical Size, Group Size and Language in Humans," *Behavioral and Brain Sciences* 16, no. 4 (1993): 681–73; Robin Dunbar, *Grooming, Gossip, and the Evolution of Language* (Cambridge, MA: Harvard University Press, 1996).

109. C. McCarty et al., "Comparing Two Methods for Estimating Network Size," *Human Organization* 60 (2000): 28–39; Russell H. Bernard, Gene Ann Shelley, and Peter Killworth, "How Much of a Network Does the GSS and RSW Dredge Up?" *Social Networks* 9 (1987): 49–63.

110. Goffman, *Behavior in Public Places*, p. 84, but see also Michael Argyle et al., "Eye Contact, Distance and Affiliation," *Sociometry* 28, no. 3 (September 1965): 289–304.

111. Stanley Milgram, *The Individual in a Social World: Essays and Experiments*, 3rd expanded ed. (London: Pinter & Martin, 2010), p. 12.

112. Robert A. Levine, *A Geography of Time: The Temporal Misadventures of a Social Psychologist, or How Every Culture Keeps Time Just a Little Bit Differently* (New York: Basic Books, 1997), p. 166; in addition to the excellent quality of Levine's research, this book is a really interesting, fun read.

113. Zak, "Neurobiology of Trust," p. 91.

114. J. Silk, "Who Are More Helpful, Humans or Chimpanzees?" *Science* 311 (2006): 1248–49.

115. Thomas Insel and Larry Young, "The Neurobiology of Attachment," *Nature* (February 2001): 134.

116. Chip Walter, "Affairs of the Lips: Why We Kiss," *Scientific American Mind*, February/March 2008, pp. 24–29; like many other articles, this essay refers to a conference paper given at the annual convention of the Society for Neuroscience in November 2007. Psychologist Wendy Hill and her student Carey Wilson examined kissing and oxytocin release among fifteen couples at Lafayette College. Unfortunately, their paper is still unpublished and unavailable except through secondhand accounts. Dean Hill did not respond when I tried to contact her.

CONCLUSION. MACHINES AS FRIENDS

1. Norman H. Nie and D. Sunshine Hillygus, "The Impact of Internet Use on Sociability: Time-Diary Findings," *IT & Society* (Summer 2002): 237–43.

2. Gary Small and Gigi Vorgan, *iBrain: Surviving the Technological Isolation of the Modern Brain* (New York: HarperCollins, 2009), p. 21.

3. "Generation M2, Media in the Lives of 8- to 18-Year-Olds," Kaiser Family Foundation, January 2010.

4. On the addictive nature of electronic games, see Harvey Milkman and Stanley Sunderwirth, *Craving for Ecstasy and Natural Highs: A Positive Approach to Mood Alteration*, sect. 4 (Thousand Oaks, CA: Sage, 2010).

5. Ira E. Hyman Jr. et al., "Did You See the Unicycling Clown? Inattentional Blindness while Walking and Talking on a Cell Phone," *Applied Cognitive Psychology* 24, no. 5 (2010): 597–607.

6. Adam Joinson, "Self-Esteem, Impersonal Risk, and Preference for Email to Face-to-Face Communication," *Cyberpsychology and Behavior* 7 (2004): 427–28.

7. Small and Vorgan, *iBrain*, p. 77.

8. Joinson, "Self-Esteem."

9. A. Bianchi and J. G. Phillips, "Psychological Predictors of Problem Mobile Phone Use," *CyberPsychology & Behavior* 8, no. 1 (2005): 39–51.

10. Ellen Gibson, "Sleep with Your iPhone? You're Not Alone," *Kansas City Star*, July 26, 2011, http://www.kansascity.com/2011/07/26/v-print/3037100/sleep/ (accessed July 26, 2011). Note: At the time of publication, this URL was inactive.

11. Martin Lindstrom, *Brandwashed: Tricks Companies Use to Manipulate Our Minds and Persuade Us to Buy* (New York: Crown Business, 2011), quotation from unpaginated Kindle® edition.

12. Netta Weinstein, Andrew K. Przybylski, and Richard M. Ryan, "Can Nature Make Us More Caring? Effects of Immerson in Nature on Intrinsic Aspirations and Generosity," *Personality and Social Psychology Bulletin* 35, no. 10 (October 2009): 1315–29.

13. The material in this paragraph results from an e-mail exchange with David Suzuki on May 5, 2012.

14. Ibid.

15. Richard Louv, *The Nature Principle* (Chapel Hill, NC: Algonquin Books, 2011), p. 188.

16. Ibid.

17. Mark Katz, *Groove Music: The Art and Culture of the Hip-Hop DJ* (New York: Oxford University Press, forthcoming 2012). Mark is a personal friend of GrandMaster Flash. ;-)

18. Serge Latouche, *Farewell to Growth* (New York: Polity, 2010).

19. E-mail message from Serge Latouche, April 18, 2011.

20. Telephone conversation with Elizabeth Sherman, July 31, 2011.

21. Weinstein, Przybylski, and Ryan, "Can Nature Make Us More Caring?"

22. I am indebted to Richard Louv for the argument about the relevance of greenery to urban crime: see F. E. Kuo and W. C. Sullivan, "Aggression and Violence in the Inner City: Impacts of Environment vs. Mental Fatigue," *Environment and Behavior* 33 no. 4 (2001): 543–71.

23. F. E. Kuo and W. C. Sullivan, "Environment and Crime in the Inner City: Does Vegetation Reduce Crime?" *Environment and Behavior* 33 (2001): 343–67.

INDEX